PROMISE OF E

THE STUDENTS' UNION
BOOKSTORE
(STICK IN BOOK)

Subj **HIST**
Price **15**

DOUG OWRAM

Promise of Eden:
The Canadian Expansionist
Movement and the Idea of
the West, 1856-1900

UNIVERSITY OF TORONTO PRESS
Toronto Buffalo London

© University of Toronto Press Incorporated 1980, 1992
Toronto Buffalo London
Printed in Canada
Reprinted 1981, 1984
Reprinted with new preface 1992
ISBN 0-8020-7390-5

Printed on acid-free paper

Canadian Cataloguing in Publication Data

Owram, Douglas, 1947-
   Promise of Eden
   Includes index.
   ISBN 0-8020-5483-8 bd.   ISBN 0-8020-6385-3 pa.
   1. Northwest, Canadian – History. I. Title.
   FC3217.097   971.2'01   C80-094202-7
   F1060.9.097

TO DEBORAH

Contents

Acknowledgements ix

Preface to the 1992 edition xi

Introduction 3
1 A far and distant corner of the Empire: the image of Rupert's Land before 1850 7
2 New worlds to conquer: the opening of the expansionist campaign, 1856-57 38
3 A means to empire: Canada's reassessment of the West, 1857-69 59
4 Conspiracy and rebellion: the Red River resistance, 1869-70 79
5 The geography of empire: the quest for settlers in the 1870s 101
6 The character of empire: the Britain of the West 125
7 John Macoun's Eden: the final stage of expansionism, 1878-83 149
8 Disillusionment: regional discontent in the 1880s 168
9 The West as past: the foundations of western history 192
Conclusion 217

Notes 225
A note on sources 255
Index 257

Acknowledgements

The research, writing, and publication of a work such as this inevitably leads to the accumulation of a number of debts. Now that the time has come to acknowledge those who have aided me in various ways I realize that it is impossible to mention everyone, and, for those who are here, mere mention is poor and inadequate repayment for the assistance and support that has been given. There is a certain comfort in knowing, however, that I am not the first author to have this feeling, nor will I be the last.

Numerous archivists and librarians went out of their way to assist me in the search for scattered and obscure materials. My colleagues at the University of Alberta, Rod Macleod and John Foster, were kind enough to read portions of the manuscript and to give their advice. Olive Baird, Rhennie Casement, and Dorothy Robinson had the unenviable task of typing and retyping the manuscript as it went through successive revisions; their patience and good humour made the process much easier than otherwise would have been the case. Jean Houston of the University of Toronto Press has been most helpful and patient in guiding me through the labyrinth that leads from the submission of the manuscript to publication. Gerald Hallowell's excellent copy-editing helped bring whatever consistency there is to the footnotes and removed many awkward or redundant sentences from the text. Much of the original research on this topic was made possible through a Canada Council Doctoral Award. The book has been published with the help of a grant from the Social Science Federation of Canada, using funds provided by the Social Sciences and Humanities Research Council of Canada, and a grant to the University of Toronto Press from the Andrew W. Mellon Foundation. An abbreviated version of Chapter 4 was published in *Prairie Forum*, III, 2 (1978).

x Acknowledgements

Finally, a special debt is owed to Carl Berger who has had a long involvement with this project; first as the supervisor of my doctoral thesis for the University of Toronto and subsequently in his encouragement to pursue the subject, he has been an enormous help.

D.R.O.

Preface to the 1992 edition

The reprinting of *Promise of Eden* twelve years after it first appeared is, of course, a matter of satisfaction. No author likes to see their work fade away. At the same time, the reprinting gives me a sense of trepidation. What should be said in a short preface that can somehow eradicate all the omissions and slips and, most of all, reply to all those reviews with their frequently insightful criticisms? Paul Fussell's warning that no author should ever reply to criticism (for it only highlights the flaw) makes the preface even more problematic.

Naturally, *Promise of Eden* owes much to the tradition of historical research and thought in which I was trained. The imprints of two people in particular are present in this work. The first is Carl Berger, for whom the study was initially done as a thesis. It reflects Berger's emphasis on the impact of ideas on broad political movements and his faith that ideas make a practical difference in the 'real world.' The second person who shaped the work was J.M.S. Careless. I took a course with Careless as a graduate student, but even if I had not, his writings on both metropolitanism and limited identities would have influenced the work. His insights have been of immense importance to Canadian historians.

In a broader sense, this book reflects two tendencies popular in the 1960s and 1970s. The first involves Careless's recognition that the happy nationalism of the centennial era was not a realistic reflection of Canadian historical reality. Nation-building had to be seen as a process that often involved regional sensibilities, rivalries, and peculiarities. The second (and seemingly paradoxical) theme is an ongoing emphasis on Canadian nationalism. *Promise of Eden* focuses on the development of a region and a regional consciousness but does so within a nationalist framework. It recognizes regional stresses and follies but also emphasizes the peculiarly Canadian nature of expansionism. Practically all my graduate instructors emphasized the distinctiveness of the Canadian experience. In this sense the historiography of limited identities, at least as viewed from the 1970s, was a modification rather than a repudiation of the earlier nationalist themes of Laurentianism. This book thus views the Canadian western experience as meaningfully different from that south of the border. That, after all, followed naturally from metropolitanism. At the same time I hope I conveyed the sense that much of the anti-American rhetoric of age was hyperbole.

This book also owes much to the particular traditions of Canadian intellectual history. From S.F. Wise onward the predominant emphasis in this sub-discipline has been not so much on the evolution of great ideas as on the relationship between ideas and popular attitudes and movements, at least implicitly. The expansionists were an elite but the ideas themselves were not elitist ones. Indeed, the assumption of this school of intellectual history is that in many instances elite-originated ideas can be profoundly popular. This is a theme present in Canadian intellectual history from S.F. Wise and R.C. Brown's study of anti-Americanism, *Canada Views the United States* (1967), through Berger's *Sense of Power* (1970), to *Promise of Eden* (1980). The rise of more institutionally based intellectual history and the continuing development of the history of ideas in recent years has modified this emphasis somewhat, but it remains a powerful force in Canadian historiography.

After *Promise of Eden* was published, several reviewers raised the point that although an intellectual history, it seemed also to place considerable stress on economic circumstances. At the time there was a real sense of division between the 'materialist' concept of history as driven by economics and the intellectual belief that ideas made a difference. There seemed some confusion on the part of the author (me) as to whether I believed that ideas were determined by economic forces or social developments by ideas. At the time I had not really thought the matter through, but perhaps that is for the best. Much of this debate now seems dated. The notion that ideas always drive economics or economic circumstances always drive ideas strikes me as artificial. Of course ideas are influenced by economic and social circumstances. Of course ideas influence the response of people to their circumstances. Subsequent works of mine, such as *The Government Generation* (1986), have continued to see economic and social circumstances as closely interconnected to ideas without denying the autonomy of either as a force in history. Fortunately this seems a less controversial proposition now than it used to be.

The historiographic premise implicit in *Promise of Eden* has thus survived. I also like to think that in general the basic argument has held up reasonably well. Historians continue to see that expansionism was a concerted nationalist-imperialist drive, that in the process the image of the West was turned on its head, and that, finally, utopianism helped breed disillusionment. This doesn't mean that interpretations have remained static. Broad and imaginative overviews on the nature of the West like Ronald Rees's *New and Naked Land: Making the Prairie Home* or detailed analyses like Paul Voisey's *Vulcan: The Making of a Prairie Community*, as well as many in between, have added a richness and sophistication to our understanding of the West that was not available when I first did research for this work in the 1970s. Overall, however, I would change neither the basic approach nor the fundamental argument put forward in the original edition.

There are, however, specific aspects of the argument that have been challenged. In some instances I cling, perhaps stubbornly, to my original position. In others I would modify my approach were I writing this work now. In his synthesis of Western history, *The Canadian Prairies*, Gerald Friesen has questioned whether the pre-expansionist image of the West was as negative as I portrayed it. He is able to cite Arthur Dobbs's 1749 challenge to the Hudson's Bay Company and the generally optimistic assessment of the territory then made. Friesen is right about Dobbs, but this little flurry of interest does not really challenge the main theme of the first part of the book. Dobbs and the 1749 investigation were an isolated incident. Even if there were wider ripples, the fact remains that by the nineteenth century the image of the North West was negative and the reversal that took place after 1840 is the significant one.

In other instances the questions are more open-ended. There was a strain of criticism that, although never couched in these terms, led me to wonder whether this was too 'eastern' a book. It was, after all, written by a born-and-raised Ontarian whose sole involvement with the West up to the time I was appointed to the University of Alberta had been research trips and one visit to the West Coast. Was I attributing too much western regionalism to this eastern movement and its subsequent disillusionment? Had I underestimated the diversity of western interests and attitudes, even in the 1870s and 1880s? Would a look at the ranching community, or at the urban booster community, have led to different conclusions than did my emphasis on former expansionists and western historians? Perhaps, but I do not think the differences would have been all that great. Work that has been done since 1980 has looked at several of these communities and, while the specifics vary, none have argued that the themes of disillusionment developed here need significant change. The utopianism of western expansion was apparently sufficiently pervasive by the 1880s that all parts of the frontier community were affected by the subsequent disillusionment.

Another set of intriguing questions has been presented by the rise of women's history in the years since research on this book was undertaken. A theme, not so much of the reviews but of subsequent writing, has been the place of women in the aspirations for the new West. *Promise of Eden* contains the views of too few women. This doesn't affect the first part of the study very much (the expansionist movement was a male movement), but it certainly does affect the second, more general part where I try to assess the imagery of the West among the first generation of settlers. Since I have written, there have been various monographs and theses written on women in the West. Gordon Moyles and I have also partly rectified my earlier omission in a chapter on British women and the West in our *Imperial Dreams and Colonial Realities* (1988).

Still, the material on women raises some interesting questions that are yet to be answered fully. Some work has suggested that the isolation of homesteading had a more direct and punishing impact on women than on men. For women homesteading on the frontier, the argument goes, the combination of isolation, child-rearing, and housekeeping was especially gruelling. If this is so it would not really change the basic thesis of the book but it might indicate that disillusionment with the circumstances of the frontier had less to do with grand politics of CPR routes or taxation than with the reality of life in a small cabin on the edge of settlement.

A second gender issue has involved a frontierist interpretation. For women, this theme goes, the frontier was a liberating experience. It released them from the constraints and conventions of older society. This new freedom has been emphasized most directly with middle-class British women. The fact that it seems to contradict the sense of isolation mentioned above only shows how complex reactions to a new society can be.

A third argument is particularly interesting and also difficult to prove. It involves the idea that women, or many women, may actually have perceived the land itself differently. Less directly connected to the work of commercial farming, the argument goes, women were less likely to be fully absorbed by the developmental enthusiasm inherent in the expansionist myth. In its place a more romantic and perhaps even preservationist approach to the land may have reigned. On the other hand, work to date has not indicated that the relationship to the idea of the West was fundamentally different. Nor is it likely to. After all, women sensed the developmental side as their futures and those of their children were tied into it. In turn, men sensed the aesthetic and romantic side of openness and freedom. Nevertheless, the differences of nuance and perspective that existed would help explain certain aspects of prairie development.

Other changes could be suggested, but I fear I will encourage the reader to think of the book that might have been rather than the one that is. Suffice it to say that both intellectual history and western history are fields that I have found enjoyable and challenging. I am pleased to see *Promise of Eden* back in print and hope that it will do its small part in assisting historians to develop their own interest in these fields.

DOUG OWRAM
University of Alberta
June 1992

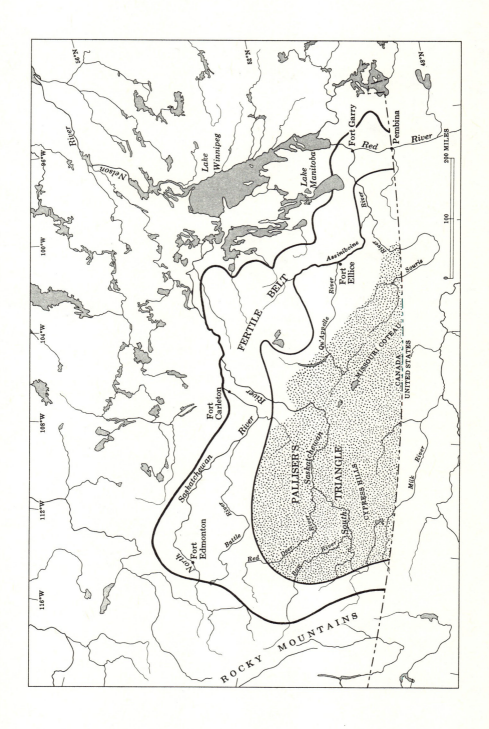

PROMISE OF EDEN

Introduction

In the middle of the nineteenth century a number of Canadians became convinced that the possession and development of the Hudson's Bay territories were essential to the future of Canada. This conviction fostered the growth of a powerful movement that developed very definite ideas as to the potential of the region and of its future role within Canada and the British Empire. Those ideas, in turn, helped to shape the policy of the government, the attitudes of Canadians, and the history of Canada itself as the nation faced the task of opening and settling the West.

The initial task of the 'expansionist movement' was to convince other Canadians that the vast regions to the west should be transferred to Canada and settled. This involved a reassessment of the nature of the soil and climate of the land under the control of the Hudson's Bay Company. Between 1856 and 1869 the image of the West was transformed in Canadian writings from a semi-arctic wilderness to a fertile garden well adapted to agricultural pursuits; subsidiary to this was a new interest in the possibilities of mining, trade, and transportation. This newly discovered potential allowed the West to be seen as the means by which Canada could be lifted from colony to nation, and, eventually, to an empire in its own right.

The terms 'expansionism' and 'expansionist' are, in a sense, artificial. The men who comprised the movement did not coin any single name for themselves, preferring, when they referred to themselves at all, to use the rhetoric of patriotism; they were the 'true Canadians' or the 'far-sighted patriots' who, they argued, understood the destiny of Canada in a way that others did not. Neither did they create any single institution for the development of their ideals, working instead through various organizations, from the Crown Lands Department to the Reform party. Nevertheless, the individuals involved were dedicated to a common and well-defined goal; they were aware of each other's efforts and were often personally linked through friendship, business, or politics. The careers and reputations of the men involved varied a great deal: some, like George Brown and William McDougall, were famous politicians; others, like like George Munro Grant and Sandford Fleming, were almost as well known, though they never held elected office. Still others were men who, had it not been for their interest in the North West, would most likely have led lives outside of the public eye. What brought them together in the 1850s and what made them expansionists was their belief that the North West was essential to Canada. This conviction, and their insistence on immediate development, set them apart from other Canadians, thus justifying their identification as a distinct group.

The members of this group did not feel their task was complete with the transfer of the territories to Canada in 1870. Their belief in the material possibilities of the West had always been tied to a concern for the nature of the society that Canada would develop there. Belief in the importance of British traditions, rule by law, and an independent but conservative agricultural order meant that in many ways the transfer was a beginning rather than a conclusion. It is therefore necessary to follow the course of events through the early settlement period until the ideas of expansionism begin to disintegrate in the face of an emerging regional identity towards the end of the century.

The year 1870 did, however, mark the beginning of a new phase of expansionism. Success had altered its nature and by the time of the transfer it was not so much a specific movement as a widely held set of beliefs within the Canadian community. The West was now a part of Canada and hopes for the future of the region had become inevitably intertwined with the more general national aspirations of the young Dominion. As a result many Canadians who had previously been only casually interested in the North West adopted the goals and rhetoric of expansionism. Most political leaders felt obliged to praise the potential of the West and to urge its rapid development. Groups with other causes, such as the Canada First party, also saw expansionism as related to their own goals. The ideas of the movement had become diffused through English-Canadian society and while the original expansionists remained active they were no longer clearly identifiable as a distinct group. The broadening of the expansionist movement requires a parallel widening of focus for the latter part of this study; the term 'expansionist spirit,' for all its difficulties, becomes more useful than the term 'movement.'

The transfer of the North West to Canada marks a transition in another way as well. Once the North West became a part of Canada new pressures were felt to convert its potential into reality. Having accepted the argument that the development of the region was essential to the development of Canada, many Canadians concluded that it was equally important that it be settled as rapidly as possible. Such an outlook invited even more enthusiastic assessments of the agricultural possibilities of the West in order to encourage the necessary immigrants. It was not long before this new and extremely enthusiastic image of the West was in danger of becoming as unrealistic as the more cynical view of the first half of the century. Excessive pessimism had prevented the West from being seriously considered for large-scale settlement by an earlier generation; excessive optimism was to have a serious impact on the generation that was faced with the enormous task of settling the region after the transfer.

In spite of the diffusion that took place after 1870, one characteristic of expansionist support remained constant: it was primarily an English-Canadian phenomenon. Expansionism originated in English-speaking circles in Canada West and even after 1870 its strength derived from this particular linguistic-cultural group. In essence, these English-speaking, largely Protestant, enthusiasts sought to shape the West according to their own cultural values and economic aspirations. Their successes and failures in doing so have, for better or worse, done much to affect the present nature of Canada.

Of course, this brand of expansionism was not without opponents. Most notably, many in French Canada had an alternate view of the West and resisted the efforts of English Protestants to obtain hegemony over the region. The French Catholic sense of mission has been excellently discussed elsewhere.[1] Nevertheless, this alternate view of the West presented a continual challenge to the English-Canadian brand of expansionism and the often acrimonious clashes between the two visions of the West are inevitably a theme in any study of either English Protestant or French Catholic expansionism. Ultimately, however, the English-Canadian vision of the West predominated and expansionism thus remained a movement reflective of the ideals and goals of one particular element of the Canadian population.

The initial weakness in French Canada's involvement in the West was the hesitation with which it embraced the idea of expansion. It was not until Confederation, a decade after the development of expansionism in Canada West, that French Canadians seriously began to show an interest in the lands that were soon to be transferred to Canada. The apathy of years could not be transformed overnight, and when the land was opened to agricultural settlement after 1870 the majority of people who went west were English Canadians.

Compounding the tardiness of French Canada's entry into the business of 'booming' the West was a persistent ambivalence towards emigration from Quebec. On the one hand, immigration to the West was thought necessary to prevent it from becoming a purely English Protestant region; on the other hand, every French Canadian who left his native province seemed to many to weaken the real centre of French culture and religion in North America. The dilemma was summed up by *La Minerve* on 8 April 1876, when it commented that it was not possible 'encourager aucune émigration régulière de Québec à Manitoba, parce que ce serait travailler à diminuer la force de notre nationalité ici, sous la prétexte de l'augmenter là-bas.'

With this ambivalent attitude, French Quebec could not hope to compete with its English Protestant rivals. The Manitoba Act, it was true, seemed to give some hope that the West would evolve along lines that accommodated the goals and ideals of both major cultural groups. Thereafter, however, English Canada repeatedly rejected French and Catholic input into the region and thereby reinforced the cultural bias present in expansionism from the beginning.

What follows is not a study of the economics of settlement or the problems of transportation. If an initial methodological inspiration can be claimed it is Henry Nash Smith's masterful *Virgin Land: The American West as Symbol and Myth*, published in New York in 1950. But the nature of Canadian expansionism and the particular evolution of the Canadian image of the West have long since altered the organization and content of this study. One basic parallel remains, however, in that, as in Smith's work, this book is primarily concerned with ideas. Man reacts to his perceptions of reality as well as to reality itself. The North West – with its acres of prairie and parkland – remained a constant through the history of the expansionist movement, but the perceptions men had of it grew and changed. Social values, economic opportunities, and the fears and aspirations of Canadians shaped the image of the West and their hopes for its future. Realistic or delusory, noble or selfish, these perceptions determined the evolution of the expansionist movement and of Western Canada as surely as did the harsh economic realities faced by the would-be farmer or merchant on the new frontier.

1

A far and distant corner of the Empire: the image of Rupert's Land before 1850

There is a tract of land in the interior of North America 'consisting of some millions of acres, and, in point of soil and climate, inferior to none of equal extent in British America.'[1] With these words, Thomas Douglas, the 5th Earl of Selkirk, set out to provide relief to the overcrowded population of Scotland by means of emigration. Basing his opinions on the writings of such fur traders as Alexander Mackenzie, Selkirk in 1811 initiated the first settlement in the vast region known as Rupert's Land. It was a bold experiment that ignored the traditional areas of settlement for a site on the banks of the Red River in the middle of the continent.

Selkirk's scheme created considerable controversy. Canadian and British public figures challenged not only Selkirk's judgement but the sincerity of the plan. In 1816 John Strachan, the Anglican clergyman of York (Toronto) and a political force in his own right, published his contribution to the debate. Claiming that Selkirk's colonization scheme was 'one of the most gross impositions that was ever perpetrated on the British public,' Strachan condemned both the Earl and his plan. Strachan felt that the unfortunate colonists had been duped by Selkirk; the land they were purchasing was both unsuitable for settlement and worthless, situated as it was thousands of miles from the nearest settlement. Moreover, it would remain worthless, for the colony would never merge with Upper Canada's line of settlement. 'Trading stations there may be,' he concluded, 'but Upper Canada, the nearest colony, can never extend farther than to the north bank of Lake Huron or to the extremity of its South East bank.' It was a safe guess, in Strachan's estimation, 'that no British colony will ever approach nearer than twelve or thirteen hundred miles' to Red River.[2]

Why, Strachan continued, would any emigrant settle in such an isolated spot when there were still better quality lands available in a better climate in

Canada? In this question there was more at stake than the prosperity of a few colonists. Strachan saw emigration as an imperial as well as a personal matter. The Red River, the geographical position of which determined that a southern route 'must be the outlet of the colony,' had no better future than annexation to the United States. Emigration to Red River, besides being personally costly to the settlers, would ultimately mean the loss of these individuals to the Empire and its natural representative in North America. The climate of the region, its geographical isolation, and the interests of Britain and Canada, all dictated that the North West should remain unsettled: 'Were the same number of families with the same means transported to the Canadas, where there is ample room and a fertile soil, by the time they would be all murdered at Red River, they would nearly have doubled their numbers in Canada.'[3] Strachan's reaction to Selkirk's plan was not unusual. Many who wrote of it expressed opposition to the scheme, which they thought to be at best misguided and at worst a heartless fraud.[4] The North West was thought to be unsuitable for settlement and Canada the natural destination for the British emigrant.

It was not the absence of any connection between Canada and the North West that prompted the scepticism towards Selkirk's colony. From the time La Vérendrye had founded Fort Maurepas near Lake Winnipeg in 1734, the region beyond the Great Lakes had been a hinterland for Canadian fur traders. First under the French regime, and then under the Scottish merchants, Montreal had been the base of operations for a trade that, by the time of Strachan's pamphlet, had reached the Pacific.[5] In fact, at the time Strachan wrote, the most powerful combination in the history of these Montreal companies, the North West Company, was engaged in a bitter and often violent dispute with the Hudson's Bay Company for control of the trade of the North West. This dispute, and the Canadian ties to the North West Company, helped dictate the nature of the Canadian response to the Selkirk colony. Many, Strachan included, saw the Earl's attempt to plant a colony of the Red River as a plot to block the main supply route of the North West Company and thereby end Canadian involvement in the western fur trade. The Selkirk settlement was not only an affront to the logic of settlement but a danger to an important Canadian commercial interest.

Thus, while Canada saw the North West as a fur trade hinterland, it did not see it as a settlement frontier. Strachan, as he made apparent, felt the latter to be impossible for Canada. The creation of a settlement and the destruction of the wilderness on which the fur trade depended would only hurt Canadian interests and, ultimately, the interests of the Empire. Canada had a stake in the area, but it rested on the assumption that the region west of the lakes

9 A far and distant corner of the Empire

would remain for the indefinite future a wilderness suited only for the fur trade.

While harsh, such an attitude was not surprising, given the contemporary state of the Hudson's Bay territories. After all, the terms 'fur trading empire' and 'wilderness' suited the area in that the fur trade was its dominant economic activity and the land remained largely untransformed by agriculture or settlement. Man was, in fact, a relatively small presence in this vast area and it is unlikely that there were ever more than sixty thousand people living between the Rocky Mountains and the head of Lake Superior at any time in the first half of the nineteenth century.[6] Moreover, the great bulk of this population was comprised of nomadic or semi-nomadic peoples whose place of residence changed with the season and with the necessities of the hunt, war, or trade.

There were some permanent establishments. The years after the founding of Selkirk's colony would see the setting up of several church missions and the development of such posts as the Reverend James Evans's Methodist church at Norway House.[7] Around these stations small groups of Christian Indians did adopt a more settled manner of living and provided points of stability in an otherwise fluid population. In addition, there were the fur trading posts that provided the lifeline and gathering system for the trade of the giant companies. While these posts were central to the economy of the region, however, their existence was unlikely to alter an outsider's view of the region. The largest of the inland posts, Fort Edmonton, never had a population of more than 150 individuals and often a good many less. Most other posts were much smaller and the term 'fort,' commonly used in the trade, was a rather grandiose description for what was often a wretched cabin occupied by one or two individuals.

Of course the very existence of a fur trade empire had had an impact on the region. Technologies changed with the introduction of European goods and weapons, tribal balances of power shifted depending on access to these new technologies, and the basic economic patterns of the North West were permanently altered by the introduction of the trade.[8] To the nineteenth-century observer, however, none of these facts gave sufficient reason to see the area as anything but a wilderness. For more important than the presence of trade goods was the absence of other characteristics of European society. Nowhere in the system had there evolved, until the Selkirk colony, a large body of people dependent on agriculture for their survival. The Christian religion was present in the territories but it could hardly be said to be either the dominant religion or the foundation for any pervasive social or moral code.

Finally, the state of government served to accentuate rather than diminish the image of the area as a wilderness. In theory the North West was under the ultimate sovereignty of Great Britain and after 1803 British laws were to be administered through the extension of Canadian jurisdiction. The fact was much less impressive than the theory. Indeed, by the time Strachan wrote, the legal system had become little more than an additional tool in the rivalry between the two fur companies.[9] With the end of the struggle things would improve somewhat. Even then, however, the government presence was weak and law was, at best, loosely enforced by the Hudson's Bay Company, which had a realistic understanding of the fact that it did not have the power to impose British structures or laws on the population. The fur trade was in many ways very well organized, with a highly efficient transportation system and pricing structure, but it was not, in the eyes of the outside world, a 'civilization.' Thus it was Selkirk, rather than his many critics, who was challenging established facts in his attempt to create an agricultural settlement in the midst of the territory. His critics, Strachan included, were convinced he would fail, for to them it was inconceivable that the North West could be anything more than it was.

The rivalry between the two great companies came to an end shortly after Strachan wrote. Exhausted by the struggle, the North West Company and the Hudson's Bay Company agreed to come to terms. The agreement was formally a merger, but in fact it represented the geographical advantages of Hudson Bay over the St Lawrence Valley and resulted in the absorption of the Montreal company. In the reorganization of the newly monopolistic Hudson's Bay Company these geographical advantages were noted. Fort William, the great depot of the North West Company, was abandoned and the route on which it was located fell into disuse. Henceforth only the occasional trip marked the old commercial route from Montreal to the North West. From 1821 on, the fur trade looked to England rather than to Canada; Canada, in its turn, paid little attention to the North West. Nevertheless, over the next quarter-century many people travelled to, lived in, or worked in the Hudson's Bay territories and wrote of their experiences. An examination of this body of literature reveals much about attitudes to that region, before it again became the coveted object of Canada's attention in a way that Strachan had not foreseen.
seen.

In 1849 Major John Griffiths wrote to the Colonial Secretary to give his opinion on the question of settlement of the Hudson's Bay territories. He was able to sum up his position tersely: 'How a country, where there is eight months winter, and snow on the ground for the whole period, is to be opened up, is to

11 A far and distant corner of the Empire

me a riddle.'[10] The similarity between Griffith's incredulity that anyone should think of opening up the region and Strachan's scepticism of Selkirk's decision to plant a colony there, says a great deal about the constancy of views in the intervening period.

In explaining this lack of change and in noting the reaction of other writers in these years, it becomes apparent that there existed a strong preconception as to the nature of the Hudson's Bay territories. This preconception affected not only men who had never been there but those, like Major Griffiths, who had observed the area at first hand and recorded what they saw. Observations of land and climate are not as much a matter of objective fact as might be thought; man's reaction to a geographical setting is determined not only by what he sees but by what he expects and wants to find.[11] The period between 1816, when Strachan wrote, and 1849, when Griffiths gave his report, mark an era. It was an age when the West was viewed through the eyes of the fur trader, arctic explorer, and missionary, but not those of the developer or settler. And in all the observations that were made, one ultimate presupposition stands out: whatever else it might be, to the observer it was a fur trading empire and enduring wilderness.

The interpretations that emerged in this era were simply a hardening of long-standing attitudes towards the Hudson's Bay territories. By the time of Selkirk's colony there were several written commentaries on the region and their general tendency was towards the conclusion that the climate of the North West was, for the most part, unsuited for agricultural settlement. There were, it was true, works with an opposite point of view. As early as 1749 Arthur Dobbs, an Irish member of Parliament and Hudson's Bay Company critic, argued that agricultural settlements would have been established long ago had it not been for the 'avarice' of the company.[12] Forty years later Edward Umfreville had praised the potential of at least part of the region.[13] Even in the eighteenth century, however, such optimistic assessments were the exception rather than the rule. More typical was the comment of the famous explorer and fur trader, Alexander Mackenzie, who concluded that 'its climate is not in general sufficiently genial to bring the fruits of the earth to maturity,' or that in the then unpublished journal of David Thompson stating that the North West territories 'appear to have been given by Providence to the Red Men for ever.'[14] In the first years of the nineteenth century such conclusions became even more common; the exceptions practically ceased to exist.

There were various reasons for the persistence and hardening of this image of the North West. First, once the connection to the fur trade had ended, Canada, the closest colony, had no reason to take an interest in the region; the province had its hands full with internal development. Its empty lands, if not quite so abundant as when Strachan had written, were still, in the 1840s, ample for immediate future considerations. Commercial development focused on a frontier and potential market much closer to home than the North West: the expanding American states of Ohio, Indiana, and Illinois. The expensive canal developments of the 1840s and the commercial strategy of the St Lawrence merchants were aimed southwest rather than northwest. It was enough of a battle to compete for the American carrying trade without thinking of other frontiers.[15] As long as there was some hope of capturing an American hinterland, and as long as good free land existed in Canada, there was no reason for Canadians to think of the West differently than they had in Strachan's time. After surveying the Sault Ste Marie rapids in 1846 an official of the Canadian Board of Works rejected plans for construction of a canal there as having no immediate purpose.[16]

The nature of society and the economy in the Hudson's Bay territory further worked against any development of interest in the region as a field for settlement. The fur trade remained the dominant activity throughout the territory. This basic economic fact gave a particular orientation to the region, one which pointed men to the Mackenzie and Athabasca districts, to the subarctic. In pursuing the fur trade the early traders and explorers followed very different routes and applied very different standards in assessing the lands through which they passed than would men who were interested in settlement. The typical fur trade brigade route ran from York Factory, up the Nelson River to Norway House and Cumberland House, and thence north to the Churchill River, traversing very little of what is now considered agricultural land. A much harsher and more northerly impression was thus given of the climate of the Hudson's Bay territory.

The impact of the fur trade in shaping knowledge of the region was well reflected in early cartography. As late as 1791 John Hodgson's 'An Accurate Map of the Territories of the Hudson's Bay Company in North America' indicated an advanced knowledge of the northern river systems of the Nelson and Churchill but was inaccurate in its representation of Lake Winnipeg; the Red River was not marked on it at all.[17] Hodgson's map was soon to be replaced by the masterful works of British cartographer, Aaron Arrowsmith, which reflected the recent explorations of men like David Thompson. Even the Arrowsmith maps, though they correctly marked the major river systems including the Red and the Saskatchewan, were more detailed for the subarctic than they were for the prairie region.

Nor did knowledge of the territory south of the North Saskatchewan increase much in the first half of the nineteenth century. The Hudson's Bay

13 A far and distant corner of the Empire

Company, though it depended on the buffalo country for provisions, found it an unprofitable region for furs. In addition, the proud, independent tribes of Blackfoot and Plains Cree inhabiting the area discouraged both trader and explorer. In 1822 the company did investigate the fur trade potential of the Bow River area, but as testimony to their respect for the region, sent out a party of a hundred men; when they found there was no great abundance of furs they withdrew.[18]

This northern orientation was further emphasized by the British fascination in the early nineteenth century with the search for the North West Passage. A good proportion of the books written about Rupert's Land dealt with neither the prairie nor even the parkland but with the true Arctic. Popular works such as Sir John Franklin's *Narrative of a Journey to the Shores of the Polar Sea*, published in 1823, naturally tended to draw the public's attention to the far north.[19] In addition, this work and others, especially during the search for Franklin, rather casually lumped the rest of the territory with the Arctic and thus reinforced the image of the land as an arctic or semi-arctic region. When, for instance, British scientist and explorer, Sir John Richardson, recounted his experiences in the far north he attempted to describe not only the territory he had seen but the land as a whole. He had, however, been only on the northern fringes of the region that would eventually be settled, travelling from Sault Ste Marie to Cumberland House and north and returning via York Factory.[20] The result was a work that purported to describe the whole territory but which depended on secondary sources for the south and which had a strong northern bias.

Richardson, more methodical than many explorers, attempted scientific observations of the regions through which he passed. 'Thermometrical readings' were taken and included in his book. The stations he chose for the observations, however, simply reflected the northern thrust of his expedition and probably confirmed in the mind of the reader the semi-arctic nature of the North West. Given that the posts chosen for the readings were York Factory, Rupert House, Oxford House, and Cumberland House, it is perhaps not surprising that the results revealed that 'the three summer months seldom pass without night frosts. These destroy tender plants, and in untoward seasons injure the growth of *cerelia*.'[21] The preoccupation with the Arctic thus reinforced the image of the Hudson's Bay territories as a northerly land.

The few writings that do exist indicate that even had more attention been paid to the southern half of the territory the resultant view of climate and resources would not have been all that different. Travellers in the first half of the century were generally unenthusiastic about the geographical phenomenon of the prairie. In sharp contrast to later generations, these men described the prairies in terms of aridity or sterility.[22] Arctic explorer Thomas Simpson's description of 'barren hills and hollows tossed together in wild wave-like form' was a typical, if picturesque, reaction.[23] What seemed to condition these observers was the almost complete absence of trees. They found it difficult to imagine that a land that could not grow a tree could support agricultural settlement. In the United States a similar belief had encouraged American writers of the early nineteenth century to form the concept of the 'Great American Desert' for their vast plains region.[24] Canadian and British observers saw no need to disagree or to differentiate. In fact, the development of the idea of the 'Great American Desert' may have reinforced the biases of critics of the Hudson's Bay territories. Richardson actually resorted to a description of the Missouri and its tributaries to portray the Canadian prairie landscape. His supposed description of the southern part of Rupert's Land thus completely accepted the current American prejudice against the plains: 'In the interior of the prairie, however, water is scarce, and there is such a total want of wood, that for days together the traveller can find no other fuel than the dung of the buffalo. Near the mountains the soil is coarsely sandy, strewn with boulders, and sterile; further eastward the sand is finer, and the boulders disappear, but they recur in numbers on the lower border of the prairie.'[25] For a Toronto magazine the absence of trees implied a hostile environment whatever the soil, because 'no friendly expanse of forest will shelter them from the full sweep of the famine borne wind, and no useful timber trees afford them their winter's firing.'[26]

The North West was thus doubly damned. The arctic and sub-arctic orientation of trade and travel reinforced the image of a northerly waste, and the notion of the American desert condemned it as an arid and inhospitable land. In both cases the result was a picture of a land that, as Henry Warre, a British military officer, phrased it, had 'little to attract the eye, or tempt the industry, of even the most industrious husbandman.'[27]

For the most part, it should be emphasized, the North West was simply not seen in terms of agricultural possibilities. So deep was the preconception of those who visited the land that they did not consider the availability of such resources. The interests of the men who lived or travelled there were in other things – the fur trade, arctic exploration, or pure adventure. When the occasional comment was made, however, it tended to reinforce the belief that the North West had a soil and climate that was a barrier to the civilization of the region. David Anderson, the first Anglican bishop of Red River, was more concerned than most with the climate as he and his missionaries wanted to convert the Indian to an agricultural economy. Having observed the climate he could only conclude that it 'stands in the way of many social improvements, the period of possible labour being so short; and when the country is bound up for so many months, there is little disposition to indulge in much labour for the sake of mere appearance.' Anderson felt that this affected the Indian, but, more significantly, he feared that 'something of this effect creeps over European minds after a long sojourn here.'[28]

For numerous reasons, therefore, the Hudson's Bay territory was not seen as a promising area for the development of a 'civilized' society. Rather, the largely unchallenged assumption of most writers was that it would remain a wilderness. The occasional community of Christian Indians or retired fur traders might be developed over time, but it seemed that the economy of the region would continue to be based on furs and the way of life of its inhabitants would reflect that fact. The European presence would remain small and European man an isolated individual in the midst of primitive surroundings 'untenanted by aught save a few roving hordes of Indians and myriads of wild animals.'[29]

For reasons of their own writers often tended to emphasize this image of the country as a wild and savage region. The author who could tell of an heroic struggle against nature or fellow man was naturally thought to be more interesting than those who did not. P.F. Tytler prefaced his work on the arctic expeditions by informing the reader that 'the manifold dangers they encountered among the lakes and foaming cataracts ... form a large portion of the following pages.'[30] Canadian artist, Paul Kane, described in great detail the difficulties he and his party faced in descending the eastern slope of the Rocky Mountains.[31] Both Kane and Sir George Simpson, the governor of the Hudson's Bay Company, described violent clashes with or between Indians. Fur trader, Alexander Ross, spent a great deal of time telling of various hazardous encounters with native tribes.[32] The cumulative message was clear: to survive in the North West demanded resourcefulness and alertness. It was a harsh, exacting, and often dangerous place. Its climate, peoples, and the way of life it created did nothing to recommend it for the raising of families or the pursuit of a peaceful agricultural existence.

There was one exception to this image. It was that colony which, in spite of many obstacles, had survived and grown on the banks of the Red River. Most who travelled to or lived in the West visited this straggling settlement. In two ways they saw Red River as an exception to the general rule of life and land typical of the North West. First, it was the one place that people felt was able to support an agricultural population. There was, after all, proof before their eyes that the colony had survived and that it regularly produced crops. Various residents and travellers wrote of the fertility of the land and suitability of climate for agriculture.[33] Even George Simpson, in a passage that was later to come back to haunt him, referred enthusiastically to 'twenty successive years of cultivation, without the relief of manure.'[34] In the period before 1850 Red River was the only area of the North West viewed in terms of its agricultural possibilities and the only area that consistently received positive comments on its climate and resources. Secondly, Red River was the only sizeable established community in the Hudson's Bay territories and thus the only place where social patterns and style of living even approximated the more settled portions of North America. As English missionary historian, Sarah Tucker, put it, it was 'an isolated settlement in the midst of an immense region of barbarism.'[35]

The survival of the Selkirk settlement, however, did not challenge the general image of the North West. The exceptional climatological assessment of Red River and its uniqueness as the only settlement in the territory created an image of it as an 'oasis in the wilderness,' both in social and resource terms. The two were often blended together so that the settlement was portrayed as 'a sort of haven of rest ... free from the cares of residence among wild beasts and wild men.'[36] It was, said Thomas Simpson, 'a comfortable retreat ... for such of the retired officers and servants as prefer spending the evening of their life, with their native families in this oasis in the desert.'[37] The isolated existence of the Red River settlement, in the terms it was portrayed by the majority of writers in these years, tended to reinforce the image of the West as a wilderness rather than dispel it.

The North West was a wilderness and as such had to be approached on its own terms, but there were those for whom such a fact simply enhanced its attractiveness. It had long been a tradition in European writing to depict the wilderness as a place of romance and adventure. It would seem that many people saw the primitive life of the fur trader as a part of this tradition and accordingly found it to possess a certain fascination. This sort of romantic primitivism was by no means comprehensive, but it was present. It is unknown how many youths joined the fur trade with images of James Fenimore Cooper's Leatherstocking tales in mind, or, for that matter, how long it took them to become disabused, but there were those for whom the wilderness implied freedom and adventure.

For those with such ideas the Indian was a natural representative of wilderness life. His nomadic existence and warlike appearance made him a natural symbol of the freedom inherent in a primitive way of life, though, interestingly, he was rarely depicted as having the extreme morality that surrounded the concept of the noble savage in some writings. Those Indians most often cited as examples of the romance of the wilderness were, under-

17 A far and distant corner of the Empire

standably, those least in contact with European civilization. The Blackfoot and the Plains Cree, both because they had retained a relative independence of the fur trade and because the buffalo hunt was a dramatic means of subsistence, often struck the imagination of those who visited them. Henry Warre recounted: 'I can imagine nothing more picturesque and more perfectly graceful than a Blackfoot Indian in his war costume, decorated with paint and feathers.'[38] Paul Kane went west in search of the romantic figure of the Indian that, like George Catlin in the United States, he would capture on canvas. And in his portraits of Indians, particularly in 'The Man that Always Rides' and 'Big Snake, a Blackfoot Chief, recounting his War Exploits,' he depicted the Indian as a more romantic figure than James Fenimore Cooper ever had.[39]

In the second quarter of the nineteenth century it was not the Indian, however, but the fur trade that received the single most romantic treatment at the hands of a writer. Moreover, the man who undertook the work was himself a retired fur trader, first apprenticed to the Hudson's Bay Company at the age of sixteen. R.M. Ballantyne had found his life in the fur trade disappointing and had resigned after one too many clashes with the autocratic Sir George Simpson. His disillusionment with the fur trade, however, did not extend to the wilderness. In a popular children's book Ballantyne compensated for his own bitter experiences by recording a much more idealistic version of the fur trade life than he had kown. In his story the wilderness was not only venturesome but also a morally positive environment where the individual was freed for development and adventure without any loss of civilized attributes.[40]

The Young Fur Trader, first published in 1856, centres around the fictional Kennedy family of Red River. Frank Kennedy, the father, had been in the service of the Hudson's Bay Company but resigned after being posted 'as near, in fact, to the North Pole as it was possible for mortal man to live.' The disillusionment of the father had not rubbed off on the son, however, and young Charley Kennedy's dream was to be posted to some distant and wilderness station. In these two characters Ballantyne set out his own dual image of wilderness life. Frank Kennedy, in his disappointments, closely approximates Ballantyne's own experience, but the son's sense of adventure represents what Ballantyne had hoped to find in the fur trade.

The plot follows a standard line. Charley obtains his wilderness posting on the Saskatchewan and, after a suitable number of adventures, coincidences, and some romantic interest, the story comes to a happy conclusion. The significance of the work lies in the fact that it is the son, Charley, who finds his expectations justified. His search for adventure and his development of self-reliance and character in the wilderness were, unlike Ballantyne's, successful. As Charley made clear in a letter to his friend, Harry Somerville, the wilderness proved all it was supposed to be: 'Roughing it I certainly have been, inasmuch as I have been living on rough fare, associating with rough men, and sleeping on rough beds under the starry sky; but I assure you, that all this is not so rough upon the constitution as what they call leading an easy life; which is simply a life that makes a poor fellow stagnate, body and spirit, till the one becomes unable to digest its food, and the other incompetent to jump at so much as half an idea.' Charley never had reason to regret the time he 'first dashed joyously into almost untrodden wilderness.'[41]

Ballantyne wrote of a life and land he had left behind and his writing was extremely selective, taking the adventurous facets of the fur trader's life while ignoring the dreary. He was thus able to avoid the very important ethical and intellectual problems that life in the wild implied to others. Ballantyne's characters were able to live in the wilderness without losing their civilized character. The wilderness was thus an experience that would heighten mental and physical faculties without any corresponding loss of moral or religious standards. *The Young Fur Trader* was romantic fiction and as such never had to ask whether a primitive life meant an eventual rejection of morals and the other attributes of civilized life that kept men from barbarism.

A more serious and personal attempt to come to terms with the wilderness and man's place in it was made by another fur trader. Alexander Ross had been born in Scotland, but in 1810, while in Canada, he accepted employment with John Jacob Astor's Pacific Fur Company. From then until his death in Red River in 1856 Ross lived in the Hudson's Bay territories. In his own life and in his concerns for his family and his society Ross had to attempt to comprehend the implications of an existence outside civilized society. For Ross, this search for understanding about man's relation to the wilderness involved a complex reaction to the environment and an attempt to reconcile its effects on the individual with a belief in social order, education, and religion.

Ross had a great sympathy for wilderness life. As he made clear, it was a sympathy that resulted not from a pastoral fiction but from an understanding and realistic appraisal by a man who had spent many years in unsettled country. He realized that the wilderness forced men to adapt to a new set of rules for survival and happiness. It also stripped man of his façade, the Indian being the prime example of this natural man. 'In an Indian camp,' he wrote, 'you see life without disguise; the feelings, the passions, the propensities, as they ebb and flow in the savage breast.'[42]

The nature of the wilderness was so different from civilized societies that European man, on entering it, had to learn again how to conduct himself. Ross's criticism of the handling of the fur trade in Oregon by the North West Company after it took over from John Jacob Astor reflected the scorn of a man for those who had not learned the local situation. Similarly, his description of the march inland of the newly arrived Selkirk settlers was a symbolic portrayal of the helplessness of the supposedly advanced European in this totally new situation. 'The journey to Pembina exhibited a strange perversion of things: the savage in aristocratic independence, was completely equipped and mounted on a fine horse, while the child of civilization, degraded and humbled, was compelled to walk after him on foot.'[43]

Such things were the result of inexperience and could be changed. Once adapted to the wilderness, European man could survive and, in fact, find rewards in his continual contact with the natural and primitive. The person who did adapt became, in the natural course of things, an almost heroic figure. 'Whatever the extent of the undertaking,' Ross wrote, 'there is no great preparation made beforehand.' This was understandable for the hardy breed that represented the best of the fur traders realized that 'the ordinary routine of every day duty is as full of adventure and hardship as it would be on a voyage of discovery, even were it to the North Pole.' Such a life, Ross believed, brought out, or rather forced out, the 'ingenuity' in man. The end result was that a person adapted to wilderness life was capable of feats that would have been impossible for the ordinary person: 'An experienced person in the Indian countries, with one or two men, their guns, and a few loads of ammunition, would think no more of crossing the desert from the Atlantic to the Pacific, in the most wild and unfrequented parts, than any other man in ordinary life would of crossing a parish from one side to the other; and they seldom fail with means the most slender.'[44]

Life in the wilderness had a very real attraction for Ross. He was tempted by its charm and by the effects it had on man's character. It could also be a pleasant life in spite of the separation from civilization. He recounted that many retired fur traders preferred 'the difficulties and dangers of their former precarious but independent habits to all the boasted luxuries and restraints of polished society.' Ross even felt that the simplicity and freedom of wilderness life had moral benefits and on occasion he came very close to arguing for the natural goodness of the primitive life as opposed to the temptations of civilization. In a primitive setting, he wrote, 'you can enjoy the pleasures of religion to better advantage, serve your God to more perfection, and be a better Christian, than were your lot cast in the midst of the temptations of the busy world.' There was, however, one significant qualification that prevented Ross from completely accepting the doctrine of primitive moral superiority. Ross believed that the wilderness would allow the morally inclined man time and freedom to do things he might not do in civilization. He did not feel that it was the wilderness that initiated that morality. Rather, that was the product of education and religion taught to man before he left society. Ross was too much of a conservative to believe that man could discover true morality without instruction.

This qualification created a dilemma for Ross. If the wilderness was a positive force in that it freed the moral man, it was also a positive force only in a passive sense. It could not in itself provide a moral code for man. The problem was, thus, the cost that the wilderness might impose in removing man from those forces of morality and religion that were so essential. Ross feared that over time the wilderness could claim man for its own; he noted, for instance, the often repeated case of the fur trader who had spent his life in the wilderness and who on retirement found that civilized society had 'no charms for him, and he begins to pine and sigh for days gone by, never to return.' The wilderness might bring out certain resourceful qualities and allow the contemplation of others, but it could also make a man unfit for the civilized world.

The problem was large enough for the individual who decided to spend his life in the fur trade, but it became greater for the man who contemplated raising a family. This was a very personal problem for Ross. He married, *à la façon du nord*, an Indian woman and had two children. Unlike many, Ross was not willing to treat this as temporary, but rather felt it his duty to assume responsibility for the proper upbringing of his offspring. It was a difficult responsibility for Ross had little faith that a generation raised in the wilderness would be virtuous. He condemned without hesitation the 'young men of vicious and indolent habits' who had been brought up in a primitive setting. They seemed to exhibit the worst traits of European and native societies and became 'more depraved, more designing, and more subtle than the worst of all the Indians.'[45]

The impact of the wilderness could thus be negative as well as positive, and, in the end, Ross decided that although it had much to offer it was also a dangerous temptation. This conclusion was hastened by the fact that, while he felt it possible for civilized man to learn the ways of the wilderness in a few months or years, it was a much more difficult process for the purely natural man to understand and work within civilized society.[46] He could not take the responsibility for what a continued life in isolated fur trading posts might do to his children. In spite of a personal appeal by Sir George Simpson, Ross left the fur trade. The reason he gave was 'the necessity of retiring to a place where I could have the means of giving my children a Christian education, the best portion I could leave them.'[47]

Significantly, he did not return to Scotland or even Canada, but decided to take up residence in Red River. Ross was one of those who saw the colony as a natural metropolis for the fur trader and had earlier described it as 'a resting place for retiring fur traders clogged with Indian families.'[48] Since he fit this description, it is perhaps not surprising that he made the choice he did. It may also have been that Ross found an attraction in the West and in the open land, which he hated to leave altogether. Whatever his reason, Ross had made his choice to attempt to raise his family on the edge of the wilderness.

Ross had a very strong sympathy for the Red River settlement. He hoped that the colony might be the means of reconciling the wilderness with civilization while retaining the benefits of both. His perspective allowed him to see the colony not in terms of imperial or Canadian interests but in relation to the vast country that surrounded it. It was a 'link added to the growing chain of civilization,' and a means of bringing to a land that had often been an object of exploitation the more noble attributes of the civilized world. Unfortunately, Ross found that this attempt to bring civilization to the wilderness was not working out as it should. Rather than the Red River settlement acting as a beacon to the region around it, the wilderness dominated the colony. The seductive attractions of the wilderness were keeping the colony and its residents on 'a middle course between refined civilization on the one hand and a gross darkness on the other.'

The essential problem was that the wilderness was all-pervasive, and thus it distorted the normal economic and social patterns of the community. Ross saw this as graphically illustrated by the farm of a retired fur trader. Here was a man who had supposedly settled down to lead a sedentary agricultural life but who found that the primitive still had its effect on him. The farm, Ross noted in disgust, was in deplorable shape, with 'buffalo hides, mouldy, motheaten and rotten, Bull's heads, old parchment, dog's sleds, snow shoes,' and other items scattered about the yard. The stable entrance was so 'choked up with dung' that another had to be cut. The corn yard was a scene 'of sufficient interest for Hogarth's pencil.'[49]

The causes of such disarray were threefold and in all instances related to the presence of the wilderness. First, the farmer was a retired fur trader with independent means who thus had no real reason to make anything of the farm. Second, the younger generation in the family had not escaped the pull of the wilderness; the attractions of the hunt were fatal to the energy and initiative of the farmer's sons. Third, the economic market was distorted by the Hudson's Bay Company which would purchase inferior goods from the man. This and other cases made Ross pessimistic about Red River's ability to maintain a high level of enterprise and civilization in the face of the pull of the fur trade and the buffalo hunt. The normal forces which operated in a community to encourage those 'civilized' attributes of hard work, forethought, and care were not present in Red River.

Ross himself personified this struggle between the forces of civilization and wilderness. He felt that the Métis, or French half-breeds, had already succumbed to the attractions of the primitive life and had become 'no better than vagrant savages.' This did not mean that Ross saw them as an evil people; the wilderness was, after all, not an evil force, only a dangerous one. The half-breeds were 'by no means a bad people' but they were nevertheless the representatives of barbarism in a contest where Ross had opted for civilization. The French half-breeds were thus a danger to the colony. At the opposite end of the scale were the original Selkirk settlers and their descendants; they were the founders of this island of civilization and they had a right to the land, it having been 'crimsoned with their blood.' In their steady habits and agricultural pursuits they represented civilization in the same way that the French half-breeds represented the wilderness. The result of this clash between the 'European or agricultural party, and the native or aboriginal party,' was an economic and social distortion of the settlement that created 'a singular assemblage of wealth and want, of abundance and wretchedness.'[50]

Ross realized that circumstances were bringing the clash between the two groups and the two ways of life to a head. Changes were being forced on the small colony and in the resolution of these changes would lie the success or failure of Red River as a unique experiment in the reconciliation of the primitive and the civilized. The first force acting on the colony was internal to it. Ross felt there was a dynamic which favoured the primitive. It was most obviously apparent in the demographic trends of the past few years. 'The first ten years of their sojourn in the colony, the Scotch emigrants were almost the only settlers,' but that had changed with the continual drift of fur traders to the Red. 'The next year years they were the majority; but the last ten they have been the minority.' The other forces were external to the colony. The increase in population both in the Hudson's Bay territories and south of the border was gradually having its effect on the wilderness. Game was declining and Ross feared that within a few years this depletion, especially of the buffalo, would bring a crisis of major proportions to the Indian and the half-breed. He also worried that Red River would no longer have the comfort of isolation to work out its destiny, for 'the Americans are on the eve of planting their starry banner at the door.'[51]

Ross was all too aware that in its present state Red River would be overwhelmed by the forces that were forming around it. At the same time, any major change in the status quo implied the end of the experiment in the wilderness. Caught between a sympathy for the colony's unique identity and a sense of impending change, Ross vacillated. At times he talked of vast British immigration to counter-balance the growing American presence; at other times he urged moderate adjustments to the structure of the local government.[52] He was, like many around him, unable to resolve the dilemma that Red River faced in the middle of the century or to find a satisfactory course for the future. Caught between twin forces of the primitive and overwhelming change, Red River residents awaited, with expectancy or fear, an unknown future.

Alexander Ross died in 1856 and thus did not see the outcome of the crisis that he sensed in the colony's future. Two of the legacies he left the colony were, however, symbolic of the transitional age in which he lived. The first was a Presbyterian minister whom Ross had helped convince to come out. The Reverend John Black was educated not in Ross's native Scotland but in Canada and represented the new ties that were developing between that province and the Red River settlement. The second was a son, James, whom Ross sent east to the University of Toronto to acquire the education that Red River could not offer. When he returned, James Ross took up the editorship of a newspaper dedicated to a destruction of the old order and, consequently, to the end of any attempt to reconcile civilization and wilderness.

By the time Ross wrote his history of Red River there were a growing number of voices calling for change in the North West. For Ross the idea of change had necessitated a personal and agonizing decision, but for many others it did not. There had always been those who had found the wilderness representative of only savagery and material want: the man in it lived a life that degraded both him and his fellow men. Most adamant in this view were the Protestant clergymen who served in or took an interest in the North West. From the time they arrived their attitudes contained an explicit criticism of the wilderness and an implicit argument for the radical alteration of the social and economic structure of the Hudson's Bay territories.

The first Protestant missionary to come to Red River was the Anglican, John West. His arrival partly fulfilled the promise made by Selkirk to provide the settlers with a minister of their faith – only partly, of course, because the majority of the settlers were Presbyterian. With the arrival of West in 1820, whatever the original promise, the Anglican church became the first, and for a long time the only, Protestant church in the North West. In the 1840s the Methodists made their appearance under the direction of James Evans; and finally, as the era of the fur trade approached an end, a Presbyterian, John Black, came to Red River.[53]

The reaction of most of the Protestant missionaries to the wilderness was summed up by West early in his journal when he referred to the 'dreary wilds' of North America.[54] A later missionary, John Smithurst, echoed West's sentiment, commenting on 'this region of dreariness and desolation.'[55] There was little in the wilderness that appealed to these men. Rather, as missionary historian Sarah Tucker reflected in her description of Red River as it was in 1836, it was in progress that beauty existed: 'The once dreary swampy plains were now covered with herds of cattle, or adorned with waving corn; a church, school and parsonage house had been erected.' Similarly, when G.J. Mountain, the Anglican bishop, travelled from Montreal to Red River, it was not the wilderness that impressed him but his arrival at the settlement to see Christian Indians 'on the morning of the Lord's own blessed day ... gathering already round their pastor.'[56]

The missionary's attitude towards the wilderness was so negative because to him it represented a spiritual as well as a physical wilderness. The absence of Christianity throughout the region made the North West not only a physical but a 'heathen and moral desert.' To feel attracted to this land in its current state was to be attracted to paganism and it was impossible for the missionary to view the wilderness without remembering this fact: 'All nature appeared silently and impressively to proclaim the goodness and wisdom of God. Day unto day, in the revolution of that glorious orb, which sheds a flood of light over the impenetrable forests and wild wastes ... Yet His voice is not heard among the heathen, nor His name known throughout these vast territories by Europeans in general, but to swear by – oh! for wisdom, truly Christian faith, integrity and zeal, in this heathen and moral desert.'[57]

The close connection between the physical and spiritual connotations of wilderness also reflected the conservative and evangelical belief that the natural man would inevitably fall into evil. Man needed guidance and the wilderness could not provide it for, as Bishop Mountain put it, 'what kind of a moral nurse is mother nature, a Christian has no need to ask.'[58] The man who followed the dictates of the wilderness could not follow the teachings of God. The term 'wilderness' thus took on a metaphorical as well as a physical meaning to the Protestant missionary, and as such was invested with much more of a moral connotation that it was to the fur trader or explorer. The wilderness could not be a paradise until it was Christianized. Only then would 'this moral wilderness blossom as a rose, and the region of darkness and desolation become as the garden of the Lord.'[59]

The missionary's attitude to the wilderness determined his view of the Indian. Naturally, he lamented the Indian's lack of understanding of Christianity; beyond that, however, he felt that the Indian's material state reflected his degraded spiritual state. The Indian was not a noble and independent man but a degraded savage who 'endured all the miseries and privations inseparable from a state of barbarism.'[60] It was often debated in these years which had to come first, the civilizing of man or his religious conversion, but there was practically no doubt that the two were inextricably related.⁶¹ In fact, the Indian's spiritual and physical conditions were so closely tied as to be inseparable. The goal of the missionary was not just religious conversion but 'to raise the multitudes of this people in the scale of moral and intellectual existence, to surround them with the comforts of civilized life, to rescue them from the gloom of superstition, to mould their hearts to Christian purity and kindness.'⁶²

Given the connection that was drawn between spiritual and physical reform, it is not surprising that the missionary saw himself both as a secular and a spiritual teacher. John West set the example when, soon after his arrival in Red River, he set up a school so that the Indian child might be weaned away from the wilderness at the same time he was being brought to Christianity.⁶³ Much later Bishop David Anderson warned the ministers of his diocese not to become discouraged by the amount of time they were forced to spend on seemingly non-religious duties because this time was, in fact, an integral part of the missionary's work: 'But in the early history of all the churches of this diocese, has there not been a great amount of secular labour laid upon those engaged in the ministry of the gospel? And necessarily so. The minister is not only the pastor but the friend, – the promoter, not only of the spiritual, but of the temporal welfare of his people. His mental energies are anxiously devoted to the raising of the spiritual temple, but his hands assist at the same time in rearing the fabric of the material temple.'⁶⁴

For all these reasons, the missionaries had a particularly unsympathetic view of the wilderness. Alexander Ross, like them, felt that the wilderness could eventually erode the moral and religious fabric that was so important to man. The missionaries, however, felt no need to reconcile this belief with any feeling of attraction for the wilderness. Given their assumptions, there was no reason to try to do so. The attitude of the missionary was important; though the number of men involved in the missionary service in the Hudson's Bay territories was quite small, they had the potential to make a widespread appeal to British religious and humanitarian instincts. Those who accepted their message found that the idea of the North West as a missionary frontier clashed with the concept of it as a fur trade empire. The demand for reform lay implicit in the missionary's attitude long before the West was thought of as a commercial or settlement frontier.

By and large, the missionaries and the Hudson's Bay Company had lived in mutual tolerance. The company, as required by its charter, provided various forms of aid to the missionaries, and, on occasion, direct funding. The missionaries in their turn, whether because of a belief in the acceptance of constituted authority or because they too felt the fur trade company's paternal government best suited for present conditions, generally accepted the rule of the company.⁶⁵ There were exceptions to this general rule. Individual missionaries criticized the company for its refusal to give greater aid, accusing it of deliberate obstruction. The Methodists, particularly the Reverend James Evans, clashed with company officers on various occasions over the issue of Sunday travel.⁶⁶ For the most part, however, the missionaries accepted the company's existence, and if they rarely praised it, they also rarely criticized it – at least publicly.

The very dialectic which the missionaries perceived between the Indians' way of life and their spiritual and material condition, however, contained an inherent criticism of the Hudson's Bay Company. The wilderness was seen as a moral wasteland and the Indians' nomadic life and hunting-trapping economy were seen as part and parcel of this wilderness, and as one of the root causes of their miserable existence. From this it was only a short step in logic to conclude that the company was contributing to that misery by tying the Indians to an economic system that was based on an undeveloped land and a nomadic existence.

In 1847 a series of events seemingly unrelated to concern for the Indians brought the question of the Hudson's Bay Company's role to the attention of the British and Canadian public. In the debate that ensued, commercial interest mixed strangely with missionary concern and imperial strategy. At the centre of the whole debate, and more responsible than any other person for bringing it before the public, was a former native of the Hudson's Bay territory.

Alexander Kennedy Isbister was born at Cumberland House in 1822, the product of a liaison between Thomas Isbister and an Indian woman. He was sent back to his father's native Scotland to be educated; having completed his university training he returned, first to Canada, and then to the North West, where he entered the service of the Hudson's Bay Company. The many years abroad, seem to have whetted Isbister's appetite for a more civilized existence and after a few years he returned to Britain, where he became involved in education and was, among other things, editor of the *Educational Times*.⁶⁷

Isbister's return to England came at a troublesome time for the Hudson's Bay Company. In the Red River colony the growth of free trade had been aggravated by the approach of the American frontier and by the establishment, in 1844, of Norman Kittson's fur trading post at Pembina. In the face of this growing threat the company attempted to enforce its legal monopoly. Governor Alexander Christie of Assiniboia instituted a number of measures aimed at curbing the activities of the major free traders. James Sinclair and Andrew McDermot, two men especially affected by Christie's actions, objected and circulated a petition criticizing the actions of the company.[68] In their campaign these fur traders found a willing ally in Isbister. When Sinclair sent a petition to London, Isbister added his own comments and forced it on the attention of Earl Grey, the Colonial Secretary. He also published the petition and his remarks in pamphlet form in order to carry the complaints against the Hudson's Bay Company to the public.

The petitioners were, of course, opposed to the monopoly powers of the company and noted pointedly that it was 'the only survivor of the numerous exclusive bodies which at one time depressed almost every branch of British commerce.' They also reviewed the charter, the basis of the legal monopoly, and questioned its power. These arguments were to be expected in a controversy that surrounded the company's attempt to prevent the growth of free trade. The memorials, however, concentrated not on the legal rights of the company but on the effect that the whole system of government had on the native population. The Indians, they argued, were 'steeped in ignorance, debased in mind, and crushed in spirit.' The missionaries had been saying this for some time. Isbister, however, took the argument the final step and tied the Indians' condition directly to the policies of the company whose 'deity is gold, to obtain which they trample down Christianity and benevolence.' He portrayed the Hudson's Bay Company as a force acting to perpetuate all those evils which the missionaries were working to end. Whatever its charter might say, the company was not, and never had been, a force for civilization: 'That on the contrary, with a view to keeping the natives in a state of utter dependence, and of perpetuating the wandering and precarious life of the hunter ... they have permitted generation after generation of the hapless race consigned to their care to pass their lives in the darkest heathenism.'[69]

The way in which the memorial presented its case gave it the widest possible appeal. A question of commerce had been transformed into a question of justice to a people under British protection. At the same time it did not contradict the prevalent image of the North West as a wilderness. Isbister did not argue that any form of government would have created a settled, agricultural economy in the North West. He still saw the fur trade as the natural basis of the economy there and simply argued that free trade would return greater benefits to the natives and a free government make more effort to aid them.

Isbister called on British humanitarianism to ensure that justice was rendered to the native population of this far-distant possession of the crown. Supported by an appeal to this same spirit with nearly one thousand signatures attached, the memorial concluded with a call calculated to arouse British philanthropic instincts: 'Does it not behove every Christian man to demand that the British legislature should not continue to incur the fearful responsibility of permitting the extinction of these helpless forlorn thousands of their fellow creatures, by lending its countenance to a monopoly engendering so huge a mountain of human misery?'[70]

Diplomatic events ensured Isbister's memorial a high degree of attention in official British circles. The British government had already had its attention directed to the Hudson's Bay territory before the complaints of the free traders arrived. The influx of American settlers into Oregon had created demands by an expansionist President James Polk for territorial concessions that brought the two nations close to war. The Hudson's Bay Company was not a strong enough presence in the area to retain it for the British government in the face of such pressure. In 1846 the British conceded to a modified set of American demands and the international border was extended along the 49th parallel of latitude to the Pacific Ocean. The Oregon dispute had brought to the fore the question of the Hudson's Bay Company's role as guardian of British interests in the West, and even without the Isbister pamphlet there would have been discussions of the company. The pamphlet, however, turned the discussion into a debate.

The 1846 agreement by no means gave the British government an absolute guarantee that its control of the rest of the territory west of the Rocky Mountains would be permanent. The United States had often responded to pressures from its own population and even a formal treaty left the matter in a questionable position. The lesson learned from Oregon had been that in a confrontation between a fur trade presence and a settlement frontier the former would give way. Thus, as the British government turned its attention to Vancouver Island and New Caledonia, it began to consider setting up a colony to act as a bulwark against American expansion.

The question was whether or not the Hudson's Bay Company could act as a colonization agent for the mother country. Isbister argued, of course, that the priorities of such a commercial interest made a dual role impossible and to put either British subject or natives under company rule was dangerous both to the people involved and the British Empire generally. Isbister was able to keep his position before Parliament, and with the support of several humanitarian groups got an address to the crown asking for an enquiry into the company.[71] He also had the satisfaction of convincing several Members of Parliament that the grant of Vancouver Island to the company should be opposed.

Because Isbister's charges were receiving such widespread attention, the Colonial Office decided that some effort should be made to ascertain the facts of the case. Accordingly, in June 1847 Earl Grey wrote the Governor-General of Canada, Lord Elgin, to notify him of the charges that had been made and to ask his opinion on the matter. The very fact that Grey turned to Elgin for information reveals something of the absence of qualified and disinterested opinion on the region. As the Governor-General pointed out, he was not an expert, for 'the territory in question is so distant ... that it is by no means easy for me to obtain a perfect knowledge of their proceedings.' The conclusions that Elgin did reach, however, were highly favourable to the company. He dismissed the allegations of cruelty to the Indians and the major arguments of the Isbister pamphlet; considering the 'vast and inhospitable region' over which the company had to rule, he felt that its mixture of paternalism and commerce was 'on the whole very advantageous to the Indians.'[72]

Elgin's reply was not unnatural, given the image of the North West as a harsh and dangerous wilderness; the geography, isolation, and climate was thought to make the region suited for nothing but the fur trade and thus capable of supporting only a primitive state of society. Elgin's attitude, in fact, was not that different from Isbister's. Where they did differ was on the question of whether or not the Hudson's Bay Company was the best vehicle for making such improvements in the condition of the Indians as might be possible. Elgin argued that the monopoly was necessary in order to prevent both the violence and the use of liquor that had been a part of the fur trade before 1821, reflecting an attitude which had been standard for many years and which was still maintained by the British government. What was significant was not that he had reached these conclusions, but that they were, by 1848, being challenged.

Not the least portentous of these challenges came from within Canada. On 14 June 1848 the Toronto *Globe*, under the editorship of the Reform politician, George Brown, suggested that the British government send out a commission to examine the allegations that had been made. Concerned particularly with the religious and humanitarian aspects of the question, the *Globe* urged that greater effort be made to bring to 'those poor wanderers of the forest the truths of religion and the knowledge of such acts as will procure them the necessaries of life.' The *Globe*'s position was still tentative and qualified: it asked for an investigation rather than assuming the guilt of the Hudson's Bay Company – one of the last times it would do so – and looked upon the North West as a missionary frontier only. For all this, it was still a significant editorial, accepting the premise that the Indian was in imperative need of help, and thus implying a greater European presence in the region, even if only missionary, and an increased effort to aid the Indian to adapt to at least some sort of sedentary, agricultural mode of life. The editorial also indicated that the long ignored region was beginning to arouse interest among Canadians, not the least of whom was George Brown himself.

It turned out that Isbister was not the only former resident of the Hudson's Bay territory to have doubts about the rule of the company. The *Globe* editorial seems to have sparked at least two individuals to put their objections to the company in print. Captain William Kennedy, a retired fur trader and the uncle of Isbister, living in Canada, wrote Elgin in an attempt to awaken the Governor-General's sympathy for the Indian. John McLean, another retired trader living in Guelph, Canada West, followed Kennedy's letter, which had been made public, with a letter to the *Guelph Advertiser* urging concern for those 'wretched peole whose lives were devoted to the enrichment of their task masters.'[73] The next year he published a much more sweeping attack on the company with a volume of reminiscences highly critical of the condition of the Indians and the policies of exploitation perpetuated against them.[74]

If one was to judge by immediate results, it would have to be concluded that the flurry of debate brought on by Isbister and carried forward by the question of Vancouver Island was not very significant. The Colonial Office had felt impelled to make an investigation, but by 1849, with the aid of Elgin, had decided that 'no further interference ... ought to take place.'[75] Parliament, after much wrangling and debate, concluded in January 1849 that the Hudson's Bay Company should be charged with the settlement of Vancouver Island in spite of the accusations that had been made against it.[76] Even in terms of rhetoric the effect seemed limited. The arguments used did not vary a great deal from those Isbister had first presented. The *Globe*, Isbister, and Kennedy all remained concerned with the question of the North West as a missionary frontier. Isbister had talked briefly of the possible commercial advantages of the whale fishery but this was only a sidelight to the main thrust of his argument. No real challenge was presented to the image of the West as geographically and climatologically unsuitable for settlement. It was still, in 1849, perceived as an isolated and distant region with one valuable resource – furs.

To look at the immediate effects would be to underrate the significance of these years. The Isbister pamphlet had aroused the interest of men in both Canada and Great Britain and brought to the surface the instinctive dislike of monopoly that existed. The Hudson's Bay Company's rule over the region had been challenged on both legal and moral grounds. If the debate on the Isbister pamphlet died down in 1849, there were nevertheless other debates arising to replace it. In the future the North West would receive much more attention than it had in the past and that attention would include, as a matter of course, challenges to the Hudson's Bay Company.

31 A far and distant corner of the Empire

In the midst of this debate on the role of the Hudson's Bay Company there appeared a number of pamphlets and works that also concerned themselves with the future of the vast region to the west of Canada. These publications, though no doubt partly prompted by that debate, were only loosely related to those works primarily concerned with the North West as a missionary frontier. Most of the men who had initiated the debate on the welfare of the Indian had at some time been involved in the fur trade; their writings were based on at least some understanding, however biased, of the problems of the region. In contrast, the aims of this group of writers were not directly inspired by events in the Hudson's Bay territory; their purpose was not to solve the problems of the North West but to use the North West to solve the problems of the Empire. As befitted their goal and their background, none had been to the region, and the schemes they developed were both grandiose and visionary.

In 1849 Millington Henry Synge, a captain in the Royal Engineers, published a small pamphlet in which, undaunted by the implications of his proposal, he urged the construction of a mixed route of water, road, and rail transportation to the Pacific Ocean through the Hudson's Bay territory. At almost the same time another British officer, Major Robert Carmichael-Smyth, wrote a public letter to Thomas Chandler Haliburton, the author of the Sam Slick tales, urging a 'grand National Railway from the Atlantic to the Pacific.'[77] These two coincident pamphlets signalled the beginning of a series of overly imaginative proposals for the connection of the Atlantic and Pacific oceans.

The proposals were based on a European tradition that went back to Columbus. A western route to Asia would give access to untold riches and a trade of massive proportions. In recent years, in the wake of the failure of Franklin and others to find the mythical North West Passage, this dream had somewhat faded. These authors, however, offered a new route – one that would bridge rather than bypass the North American continent. 'It is,' said Synge of the route across the Hudson's Bay territories, 'the shortest route to Japan, Australia, and New Zealand, and all the countries contiguous to them.'[78] Two other writers, F.A. Wilson and A.B. Richards, picked up on the theme and wrote a work which described Canada as 'the high road to Asia.'[79] Once completed, such a transportation route would bring untold wealth in its wake. Carmichael-Smyth could already imagine his proposed railroad running to the shores of the Pacific, 'with the produce of the West in exchange for the riches of the East.'[80]

The idea of a land route to Asia was made possible, if not yet probable, by the technological developments that had taken place in the years immediately before the publication of these pamphlets. Only the rapid growth of the railroad as a practial means of communication and commerce made it conceivable to talk of an overland route to Asia. The authors were as much or more inspired to write their works by this technological revolution as they were by the empty spaces of the North West. Carmichael-Smyth, for instance, began his second pamphlet on the subject with a poem, 'Panegyric upon Iron':

> Hail Native Ore! Without thy powerful aid,
> We still had liv'd in huts with the green sod
> And broken branches roofed.

He later took another product of the industrial revolution, and another component of the railroad, and asked where can 'this wonderful discovery, this great power of steam, be called into action so effectually and so usefully.'[81]

To the man living in the middle of the nineteenth century the railroad seemed an almost miraculous invention. He was able to remember a much more rudimentary system of transport when a lengthy journey had very different implications. The technological breakthrough that made the railway possible and the revolutionary effect it had on society and the economy created a belief in the power of the railway that for some bordered on religious faith. It was no coincidence that the Canadian engineer, Thomas C. Keefer, would soon write his *Philosophy of Railroads* or that the American, Asa Whitney, would propose that his countrymen undertake a railway to the Pacific.[82] Their writings, as with those of Synge, Carmichael-Smyth, and the others, reflected the enthusiasm of the age for the new technology. The powers and possibilities of the railroad seemed to dissolve the transcontinental land mass of North America into insignificance. In its place, 'pictures of certain prosperity and grandeur and enterprise crowd upon the mind, with the prospect of a wilderness peopled – a remote ocean converted to an immediate and familiar high-road.'[83]

There were other, less optimistic, forces that made the transcontinental railroad seem not only desirable but necessary. The years in which these men wrote were ones of fluctuation and instability. Imperial relations had been completely transformed by Britain's decision, in the wake of the Irish famine, to abolish the corn laws. As a result of this decision Canada had entered a deep depression and was threatened by growing annexation sentiment. In Britain the philosophy known as Little Englandism encouraged this train of events as a means of ending the imperial burden. In Europe in 1848 revolutions had swept several nations. Britain had escaped, but even there such social movements as Chartism clearly warned that the danger did exist of forced social change from below. Recession continued in such a chronic fashion that many began to feel it was permanent, a reflection of Malthus's gloomy predictions of overpopulation. Behind the faith in technology was a growing fear that if some impetus were not found for British wealth and industry, England and its empire would sink into stagnation and poverty.

Those who wrote of a transcontinental route to Asia were very much aware of the crisis and looked to an imperial solution. Synge, who had served in Bytown, felt that the problems of the Empire were largely due to a failure to understand the important contribution Canada could make towards solving British distress. Carmichael-Smyth saw the railroad to the Pacific as the natural means of tying the colonies to the mother country. Most assertive of all in their insistence on the importance of the Empire were Wilson and Richards. Condemning Richard Cobden, whose 'paradise is a factory by a mill-stream,' they argued that to allow Canada to slip away would 'brand the Government of Great Britain with the stamp of immortal imbecility.'[84] The Pacific railroad was thus seen as the means of preserving both Britain and the Empire. England would have access to an important new trade and a productive outlet for both its capital and labour. The route would tie Canada to the mother country and provide a strong counter-balance to the growing power of the United States.

The concept of a transportation route across British North America thus took on vast imperial considerations. The importance of the route went far beyond questions of profit and loss and, it sometimes seemed, beyond questions of immediate practicality. If the power of the British Empire were combined with the possibilities of the railway the nation would be able to 'almost move the earth.'[85] With such power at hand and such important considerations at stake, the decision was imperative whatever the cost. The route would give Britain a new lease on life, and the Empire, rather than drift apart, would be pulled together.

The schemes developed at this time for a route to the Pacific were visionary rather than practical. The pamphleteers based their plans not on any understanding of the geography of the North West but on the need for some scheme that in its magnitude would equal the magnitude of the crisis which Britain and the colonies seemed to face. Wilson and Richards had so little knowledge of North American geography that they decided the railroad should run in a straight line from the Pacific until it reached a point east of Lake Superior and thence on an angle through the wilderness of Canada until it intersected the St Lawrence. In the face of anticipated objections that the railroad would not touch one community in Canada West, they replied nonchalantly that such considerations should not 'retard, for their provincial convenience, the direct traffic line of the whole world.'[86] Major Carmichael-Smyth equally easily dismissed the problems of constructing a railroad across the continent by pointing to the success of the Manchester-Liverpool Railway in negotiating Chat Moss.[87] Surely the nation that could conquer Chat Moss would have little difficulty with the Rocky Mountains or the Lake Superior muskeg!

Obviously, the works of these visionaries cannot be taken as representative of British opinion or considered too seriously as a set of proposals for the opening of the North West. They are, nevertheless, important in understanding the origins of the expansionist movement. In no matter how visionary a way these men did propose the opening of the Hudson's Bay territory. Furthermore, their schemes were closely tied to an imperial sense of mission and thus reinforced and added to the missionary impulse that had existed for some time and had been brought to public attention by Isbister.

The concept of a Pacific railroad, much more than the missionary concern for the Indian, challenged the existence of the fur trade empire; the empire would be subordinated to and eventually supplanted by the demands of the transcontinental route. Like Isbister, these writers saw the Hudson's Bay Company's system of trade and government as an obstacle to their plans; unlike Isbister they saw the company as not only harmful to the Indian but the whole Empire. Wilson and Richards referred to the 'Hudson's Bay Company, tenacious of its exclusive monopoly ... by which it would fair continue to assert the injurious and oppressive right of perpetuating a wilderness at the expense of the British nation and the entire civilized world.'[88] Thus self-interest joined philanthropic concern in the growing attack on the company.

Perhaps the most significant implication of these schemes for a transcontinental railway was the new perspective they invited on the land and climate of the North West. Any proposal for a transportation system involved, to some degree, the introduction of settlement into the region; people would be necessary to build the railway and their removal from the home country would, it was hoped, help relieve the chronic over-population that was thought to exist. The pamphleteers were somewhat defensive in making this proposal, seeming unable to believe that anyone would want to live in the North West. Undaunted, however, they put forth various schemes for the use of either convicts or paupers to settle the region.[89] Even Isbister picked up on the idea, proposing that two penal settlements be established in the territories.[90] The North West was seen as a suitably empty and distant place to send Britain's excess humanity. All of these plans were subsidiary to the proposals for a transcontinental transportation system but they were the first public suggestions for large-scale settlement in Rupert's Land since the time of Selkirk. Once people began to talk, even tentatively, of a through railroad and a settled population the preconception of the North West as a permanent wilderness was challenged. The questions of soil and climate, so often ignored in the past, became topics for discussion and evaluation.

Even a negative assessment of the North West when written in this climate of opinion contributed to the rapidly changing perspective on the region. In 1849 Robert Montgomery Martin, a well-known British author, wrote a work in which he denied both that the land in the Hudson's Bay territory was suited for settlement and that the company was deliberately preventing progress. Drawing on such sources as Thomas Simpson's *Narrative*, Martin concluded that the few spots capable of supporting European settlement were 'like oases in the desert,'; the prairies he dismissed as a mixture of 'sand and gravel, with a slight intermixture of earth.' The primitive society of the region was the result of the soil and climate, not of any conspiracy on the part of the company. The company, in fact, had 'prevented that destruction of the native population' which had been so common in other parts of North America.[91]

A few years earlier Martin's work would have received little attention; his arguments and conclusions had all been presented before. Times had changed, however, and before long a book appeared to challenge the conclusions he put forward. James Edward Fitzgerald, as he made clear from the outset, challenged Martin's bias and his description of the North West. Drawing from Isbister and others he argued that the Indians were being exploited and faced 'misery and destruction.' The company, rather than acting as the protector of British interests, had 'shackled the energies of Great Britain.' Most significantly, Fitzgerald took an optimistic view of the resources of the area and concluded that settlement had progressed slowly only because the company discouraged the development of settlement. 'The Question is,' he asked 'what has grown up? and, what might have grown up.' Such a position challenged not only Martin but a great deal of the previous literature on the West. In order to refute these words Fitzgerald offered a new and significant explanation for the harsh assessment of the North West; 'The power of the Hudson's Bay Company over hundreds of thousands of miles of North American continent is unlimited. Into these remote regions few ever penetrate but the servants of the Company. There is hardly a possibility of obtaining any evidence whatever, which does not come in some way through their hands, and which is not more or less tainted by the transmission. The iron rule which the Company holds over its servants and agents, and the subtle policy which has ever characterised its government, have kept those regions almost beyond the knowledge of the civilised world.'[92] It was an appealing explanation for those who sought to challenge the rule of the company. Little was known or thought of the region not because, as had previously been assumed, it was useless for settlement but because the company deliberately distorted information and withheld evidence. It was a conspiratorial view and it was to be widely accepted in future years.

The debate between Martin and Fitzgerald reflected the changes that had taken place in the attitude towards the North West in the previous few years. Religious mission and imperial concerns had raised questions about the role of the company in the North West. This debate, fuelled by events in Red River and Britain, had quickly broadened in scope until previous preconceptions about the nature of the region had been challenged. By 1850 the image of the West and thus its future role had become much more uncertain than even five years before.

Even if one looks only at events external to the territory itself, it is fair to say that the years 1846 to 1850 were important ones in the history of the West. The first words in what would later become an expansionist torrent came in this period. The initial statement of expansionist rhetoric came not from Canadians in 1856 but from expatriates of the North West and British visionaries in the later 1840s. Previous to these years there had been very little attention paid to the West. Those few people who did write about the region were pretty much unanimous in their belief that for geographical and climatological reasons the land would remain largely unsettled for the foreseeable future. Some concern had existed, especially on the part of missionaries, for the natives of the region. This concern, in turn, led to the conclusion that changes must be made in the social and economic life of the region. Before 1850, however, the whole missionary impulse was limited; most missionaries accepted the image of the land as inhospitable. They hoped for only semi-settled communities of Indians centred around churches in the more fertile spots that existed in the North West. The Hudson's Bay territory continued to be seen as a wilderness with a fur economy and fur-based government as the inevitable, if lamentable, result.

By 1850 such certainties no longer existed. The Hudson's Bay Company had been exposed to severe criticism from several sources, including, initially, residents of the Red River settlement. In its relations with the Indians, the European inhabitants, and the British Empire the company had been portrayed as tyrannical in its rule and opposed to progress. The question had been raised whether the Hudson's Bay Company was the natural result of the geography and climate of the region or, on the contrary, whether the company had deliberately 'retarded the progress of civilization and religion,' for the sake of the fur trade.[93] In the early 1850s the whole problem of the company's role in the territory was still a debate. The response of Elgin to Grey's request, the Colonial Office decision to end the investigation, and the grant of Vancouver Island to the company indicates that there was as yet little official suspicion of the company. A debate had been broached, however, where none had existed before, and by the early 1850s, in the face of troubles in the territory and criticism abroad, the company was already on the defensive.

Given the direction of institutional and commercial ties in this period it is not surprising that the centre of the debate was London. In Canada, however, John McLean and William Kennedy both took the Isbister allegations as a cue to voice their own opinions on the company and its treatment of the Indian population. George Brown, with a strong sense of reformist humanitarianism and an instinctive dislike of monopolies, had picked up the crusade. By 1850 his tentative concern of 1848 had been replaced by a firm conviction that the company's rule was 'injurious and demoralizing' and a less certain feeling that perhaps this monopoly was propagating a false image of the land as a 'frozen wilderness' for its own selfish interests.[94] Another Canadian, Allan Macdonell, with family ties to the fur trade, used the arguments of Synge and the others in an unsuccessful attempt to obtain a Pacific railroad charter.[95]

Even in this preliminary British-based challenge of the old assumptions about the North West, Canadians thus took an active interest. Moreover, once the colony's interest in the land was reawakened its particular relation to the region was again noticed. Macdonell appealed as much to Canadian hopes of supplanting Britain in the Asian trade as he did to imperial interests.[96] John McLean wrote George Brown after his editorial on the company to urge him to continue the campaign. Canada, after all, had a direct interest in the question: 'The interior of Rupert's Land belongs to the people of Canada both by right of discovery and settlement and it is therefore *our business* more than that of the people of England to claim the *restoration* of rights of which we have been so unjustly deprived.'[97]

In Canada, as in Britain, the initial crusade for the end of the fur trade empire was premature. The developing interest in the colony, however, and especially the concern for Canada's rights in the whole question, hinted at the future. Canadians had been exposed to and influenced by the changing image of the North West. When future demographic and political pressures again brought the question of the Hudson's Bay territories prominently before the public there was in existence, and ready for use, an initial expansionist body of literature and catalogue of anti-company rhetoric to draw from. And the next time the question arose Canadian involvement would not remain secondary to British; the province would assert in no uncertain terms an interest in the North West that forty years before Strachan had been unable to conceive.

2

New worlds to conquer: the opening of the expansionist campaign, 1856-57

In 1850 Sir George Simpson wrote Chief Factor Donald Ross of Norway House to tell him the good news that 'H.M. Government has put an extinguisher on the agitation respecting the Company's rights and management.'[1] Simpson's comment accurately summed up the conclusion of the attacks on the Hudson's Bay Company by Alexander Isbister and others. For all the doubts that had been raised concerning the future of the Hudson's Bay territories, British policy indicated that it was still felt that the North West would remain a fur trading empire for the immediate future and that the company was best suited to rule over the area. Both the Colonial Office and the British House of Commons had, after investigation, given the company a vote of confidence.

In Canada there had been even less reaction to the challenges to the Hudson's Bay Company. The only official Canadian involvement had been through the office of Lord Elgin, the Governor-General; and even that had been in response to a British request and favourable to the company. A few editorials by the Toronto *Globe* and letters from retired fur traders, while stirring interest in a few people, could hardly be said to have transformed the Canadian attitude to the vast region that lay to the north and the west. Over the next few years the occasional article or book was written on the company or the lands over which it ruled, but these elicited little response from the public.

This lack of interest did not last. Beginning in 1856 a new debate developed on the future of the Hudson's Bay territories, and, in contrast to the 1840s, this one aroused widespread Canadian interest. By the time it was over the company had lost any hope of retaining its exclusive position in the North West: Vancouver Island, its symbol of vindication a few years before, was taken away from it and raised to the status of a crown colony; the company's application for a renewal of the exclusive right to trade was refused; and, potentially most important of all, in 1857 a Select Committee of the British House of Commons accepted in principle Canada's 'just and reasonable wishes' to annex the North West.[2] By the end of the decade the debate on the Hudson's Bay Company had ended, because everyone, including its own officials, accepted the impending end of the fur trade empire.

From the Canadian perspective, the most noticeable characteristic of this successful assault on the position of the Hudson's Bay Company was the extremely small number of individuals who acted as its spearhead. In the later 1850s less than fifteen people formed the core of the movement that led Canada to assert its right to the region. This small group comprised those individuals who continually spoke or wrote of the potential of the West and of the crucial need for Canadian expansion. Together they were very quickly able to effect a profound shift in public and official opinion.

Perhaps the most committed of all these early expansionists was Allan Macdonell. His father, Alexander, had been in the employ of Lord Selkirk and it is possible that Macdonell first developed his interest in the North West through this connection. His belief in the potential of the West predated that of most other Canadians, and through the 1840s he had been involved in fruitless schemes to tap the wealth of the vast Canadian Shield north of Lake Superior. In 1851 the forty-three-year-old Macdonell took inspiration from the works of the British pamphleteers to apply for a Pacific railroad charter. The Canadian legislature, while it had granted somewhat dubious charters in the past, found Macdonell's proposal unacceptable. Undaunted by this rejection, he tried again in 1853 and 1855 only to be turned down both times. In August 1856 he began a series of letters to the editor of the Toronto *Globe* under the pen name of 'Huron' in support of Canadian interests in the North West. He was also the driving force behind the North-West Transportation, Navigation and Railway Company, the first substantial commercial attempt to reopen trade with the region.[3] In his enduring enthusiasm and endless schemes Macdonell did much to arouse interest in the possibilities of the North West, even though the company he initiated encountered difficulties making a profit.

Closely associated with Macdonell in the North-West Transportation Company was William Macdonell Dawson. As Dawson's middle name implies, he was connected with the same large clan of Highland Scots as was Macdonell. Until 1857 Dawson was an employee of the Crown Lands Department and used his official position to urge an expansionist policy on the government.[4] His two brothers, Aeneas Macdonell Dawson and Simon James Dawson, were soon to become committed to the vision of Canadian expansion and to use their considerable talents to support that policy.

Linked with the schemes of Macdonell and Dawson was a man who had long ago expressed his hostility to the Hudson's Bay Company. Captain William Kennedy had not changed his views since he had written the public letter to Elgin in 1848, and in his numerous articles and speeches he encouraged a favourable image of the North West and a hostile view of the Hudson's Bay Company. In 1857 he went to Red River and with his brother, Roderick, attempted to convince the residents of that isolated settlement to support Canadian expansion.[5]

Another person who had been interested in the North West from the 1840s was the powerful editor of the Toronto *Globe*, George Brown. The letters to his paper from 'Huron' in 1856 caught his attention and he soon became one of the most consistent advocates of Canadian expansion. A distrust of the monopolistic Hudson's Bay Company and a fervent enthusiasm for the spread of British institutions gave the movement a particular appeal to Brown. His commitment was further deepened by two factors which had little to do with the North West. First, his brother, Gordon, was involved with Macdonell and Dawson in the North-West Transportation Company and the fortunes of the Brown clan thus to some extent rested on Canadian expansion. Secondly, it was apparent to Brown that the annexation of the North West would imply a constitutional alteration for Canada and hence, he hoped, a political system that would ensure the dominance of English Canada and the Reform party.

Brown was joined in his enthusiasm for the North West by thirty-four-year-old William McDougall, who had previously been a Clear Grit and thus a political opponent of Brown. By 1857, however, the two movements of Reform and Clear Grit had effectively merged, and McDougall had abandoned his own newspaper, the *North American*, and merged it with the *Globe*. In 1857 he was on Brown's staff and it is possible that some of the editorials on the West in this period were written by him. In capturing the energies and abilities of Brown and McDougall, the expansionist movement gained two of its most powerful propagandists. Both were leaders within the Reform party and their influence would help to bring that party to a position of official support for the annexation of the North West as early as 1858.[6]

While the Reform party contained some of the most vociferous supporters of expansionism, the issue was not a partisan one. Within government circles Philip M. Vankoughnet, President of the Executive Council and a future Commissioner of Crown Lands, lent his support to the campaign for expansion as early as September 1856.[7] Other individuals within the government also came to advocate expansion and ensured that the Liberal-Conservatives of John A. Macdonald accepted the idea of expansion, albeit more cautiously.

The efforts of these prominent men were paralleled by more obscure figures. Typical of this group was Alfred R. Roche, another employee of the Crown Lands Department, who had been one of the first to express the new interest in the North West.[8] It is likely that he was the author of the numerous letters sent to the Montreal *Gazette* under the signature of 'Assiniboia,' thus performing a role in that paper similar to the one played by Macdonell in the Toronto *Globe*.

Perhaps the most important of all Roche's efforts on behalf of Canadian expansion was the key role he played in bringing the Canadian government to assert its historical and legal claims to the Hudson's Bay territories. In 1857 the British government appointed a select committee of the House of Commons to investigate all matters concerning the Hudson's Bay Company. The Canadian government appointed Chief Justice William Draper as its representative before the committee. At the time of his appointment Draper knew nothing of the question and admitted that he had 'the whole thing to study.'[9] The men who guided these studies were none other than William Dawson and Alfred Roche, and whatever tinges of expansionist thought coloured Draper's testimony before the committee can be attributed to them.[10] Moreover, Roche accompanied Draper to London and gave his own testimony before the committee. If Draper presented the position of the Canadian government, Roche represented the Canadian expansionist movement. Overall, he was a central figure in the early phase of expansionism and only his tragic drowning in 1859 has caused him to be noticed less than the rest.

Other individuals became associated with the expansionist movement in these years, though their primary participation would come later. Surveyors Alexander Russell and John Stoughton Dennis, both of the Crown Lands Department, seemed to catch the expansionist spirit which pervaded that organization. The rising railway engineer, Sandford Fleming, fresh from the construction of the Toronto Northern, began to consider the possibilities of even more ambitious railway projects. Alexander Morris, thirty-two-year-old son of the well-known Canadian politician, William Morris, wrote a pamphlet depicting an optimistic future for an expanded Canada.[11] In the coming years all of these men would have a great deal to do with the North West.

The expansionist campaign was effective only because it appealed to widespread hopes and fears within the Canadian community. In the 1840s attacks on the Hudson's Bay Company had aroused little interest in Canada. By 1856, however, when the issue was again raised, conditions had changed in such a way as to make the idea of expansion seem both desirable and necessary. The first half of the 1850s had brought tremendous growth in Canada. The economic dislocation that had accompanied the British shift to free trade in 1846 had given way to prosperity. The successful conclusion of a reciprocity treaty with the United States in 1854 and the beginning of the Crimean War the same year increased the market and demand for Canadian timber and foodstuffs. Immigration and a high natural birth rate continued to increase the population, and Canada West, which received the bulk of that immigration, surpassed Canada East early in the decade. By the middle of the decade Canadians had become accustomed to a degree of prosperity that few would have thought possible even a few years before.

The great symbol of Canadian prosperity was the railroad. The passage of the Guarantee Act of 1849 which, under certain conditions, provided a government guarantee for railway bonds, enabled years of schemes to assume more concrete form. Through the 1850s railways spread across the Canadian countryside at an amazing pace and within a decade the province's total railway mileage increased from 66 to 2066. Canadians enthusiastically welcomed the orgy of construction with its dizzying effects on society, economy, and, all too often, on politics. The same faith in technology and progress that had so marked the British pamphleteers of the 1840s was abundantly present in Canada. Individual cases of profiteering and jobbery did not alter this fact. Thomas Keefer's dictum, first written in 1849, that 'as a people we may as well ... attempt to live without books or newspapers, as without Railroads,' was still accepted in 1856.[12]

Of course, the reality of the railroad could never match the myth, but its arrival did have a profound effect on Canada. Goods could be transported more easily and cheaply and patterns of trade conformed to the lines of the railway. This, in turn, encouraged the dominance of those urban centres which had been able to attract railway depots. Industrial firms sprang up to service the new technology and this further aided the growth of these urban centres.[13] Most important of all, the railway expanded the horizons and the ambitions of Canadian manufacturers and entrepreneurs.

The optimism of the decade and the enthusiasm for railways were, in part, recognition that recent events signalled a new stage in Canadian development. It was hoped and believed that the progress of the early fifties would continue into the future. A new periodical, the *Canadian Journal of Science, Literature and History*, reflected the mood of 1856 when it saw fit to open its first volume with an eulogy to Canadian progress, past and future: 'The advancement of Canada in commercial and agricultural prosperity during recent years, is without parallel in the history of the British Colonies; and there is abundant reason for believing that it is even now only on the threshold of a career of triumphant progress.'[14] The Brantford *Courier* expressed the same theme a few months later when it stated that 'the prospect of Canada was never better or more encouraging than at the present moment.'[15] The development of Canada meant that the world would soon have to think of it as more than a backwoods colony, and then both Canadians and others would realize, as Alexander Morris put it, that 'her destiny is a grand one.'[16] A sense of immediacy overlay such thoughts and many confidently asserted that this destiny would become apparent in the near future.

Canada was outgrowing its previous status as a frontier colony. While this fact was a point of pride, it also forced Canadians to consider the implications of the changes that were taking place. A means had to be found to ensure that the transition from the frontier economy and society was smooth and successful. The problem was that Canada's past growth had depended to a large extent on the existence of an untapped frontier. Immigration from Europe and the settlement of the wilderness had been the basis of trade and prosperity. Canada, like the United States, had experienced and been shaped by the New World's peculiar economic resource, free land. Now, however, at the very time when the benefits of past growth were being felt, this resource was becoming scarce.

On 14 September 1855 the *Globe* noted that the last 'wild' land in the western peninsula of Canada West had been sold. With this sale Canadians were threatened with a new and possibly crucial factor – confinement. The problem was that for all the vastness of the Canadian territory the amount of suitable agricultural land was relatively limited. The great Canadian Shield arched over the province and severely limited the northward extension of settlement; with the settlement of the western peninsula the only place left to go was on to that shield. The implications of this fact were not encouraging. Joseph Cauchon, as Commissioner of Crown Lands, noted in 1856 that the western peninsula had been the scene of the greatest settlement of public lands. His argument that their sale did not signal the end of the Canadian settlement frontier was only partly successful, for, as he admitted, the remaining lands 'are not equal in climate nor in general fitness for cultivation to the western peninsula of Upper Canada.' What was fit for settlement was limited and before long, it appeared, 'the desirable lands in the sections described will be insufficient to meet the evident demand.'[17] The message was clear. It was only a matter of time before Canada ran out of wild land suitable for agriculture and when this happened its most powerful inducement to the immigrant would disappear. The worries expressed by Cauchon were firmly grounded in land sales. In 1856 some 140,520 acres of public land were sold in Canada West; in 1857 this figure dropped to 122,119 acres and by 1863 to

91,069.[18] Canada's settlement frontier had collided with the natural barrier of the shield.

It is doubtful that the later 1850s and early 1860s brought severe population pressure to Canada. There were still large areas of vacant land in the province in the hands of private individuals. Canada, however, needed not only land but an abundance of it. If it was to attract immigrants from Europe and prevent its own population from emigrating to the United States, it had to be able to offer a surplus of good land at nominal prices. By the later 1850s it could no longer do so, and more and more people, both European immigrants and Canadians, began to look to the United States. Cauchon concluded bluntly that 'they will continue to do so, much to the loss and injury of the Province,' unless lands can be found to compete with those available in the United States.[19]

Concerns for the future focused not only on settlement but on commerce. For more than a generation Canadian commercial schemes had centred on the St Lawrence–Great Lakes transportation network. The hopes for this trade artery had been badly shaken by the British shift to free trade, but by the early 1850s the faith in the system had been rekindled with a new rhetoric based on free trade and access to American markets. Unfortunately, the rhetoric could not disguise the weakness of the system. In spite of the reciprocity treaty, trade figures by the middle of the decade made it clear that the traffic of the St Lawrence system accounted for only a minute percentage of American trade.[20] If the great transportation system on which so much had been expended was ever to contribute to the further growth of the province a means would have to be found to increase the flow of goods through it.

The feeling that Canada had, for better or worse, come to turning point in its development was general to all regions of the province. There were certain areas, however, where this was felt more strongly than others. In two quite different regions, the city of Toronto and the Ottawa Valley, the hopes and fears for the future were felt with a special acuteness. Equally important were geographical and commercial factors which drew the attention of men in these areas to the upper Great Lakes and beyond. It is perhaps not surprising that the origins of much of the Canadian interest in the Hudson's Bay territories can be traced to these two centres.

Toronto, perhaps more than any other city in Canada, had felt the benefits of prosperity in recent years. When the town of York had become the city of Toronto in 1834 the total population had been only 9252. By 1851 the city had reached a figure of slightly over 30,000; the next decade, with the aid of the railway, would bring Toronto to a population of nearly 45,000 and give it ideas of competing with Montreal for the position of Canada's primary urban centre.[21] The residents of the 'Queen City of the West' had reason to feel proud of their city and its record of accomplishments. They were also anxious to ensure that the future would be as bright as the past.

Toronto, even more than Canada as a whole, had grown because of its ability to exploit an expanding western hinterland. The filling of the western peninsula thus posed serious questions concerning Toronto's future development. George Brown was one of many Torontonians who sensed the potential problems implicit in the closing of this settlement frontier. 'While congratulating ourselves on the rapid growth of the city,' he wrote in August 1856, 'it behoves us to consider well the circumstances that have produced that expansion.' The circumstances were many but Brown warned that one stood out above all the others – the progressive expansion and settlement of the western peninsula. That expansion had reached its limit and possibly so had Toronto's: 'Unlike the cities of Lake Michigan, our back country is comparatively limited, and unlike the cities of the south shore of Lake Erie, we have as yet no commerce with the distant states and territories of the United States to pour its riches into our laps.'[22] George Brown's enthusiasm for expansion has often been seen to derive from his adhesion to a frontier-based Reform party.[23] This enthusiasm, however, came not simply from the frontier but also from the city. It was the city of Toronto, not the farmer of the western peninsula, which had to find room for further growth if it was 'ever to rise above the rank of a fifth-rate American town.'[24]

It was natural that when Toronto began to cast about for a new frontier it should turn to the north and west. For a decade explorations had been carried out under the direction of the Geological Survey of Canada in the regions north of lakes Huron and Superior. The results had encouraged several mining companies to attempt to tap the wealth of the area.[25] In 1855 the completion of the Northern railroad to Collingwood gave the city direct access to the upper lakes and, potentially, control of any development in the area. The same factors which had led to this interest would soon lead to a call for the exploration of a more distant and vast potential hinterland for Toronto.

The communities situated in the Ottawa Valley were subjected to the same forces as Toronto but in a slightly different way. Toronto's aspirations were based on a desire to maintain its dominant position in Canada West. The Ottawa Valley, however, in the 1850s was a relatively remote hinterland – tributary to the St Lawrence system and the city of Montreal. If Toronto found its hinterland too small for its grand ambitions, the communities in the Ottawa Valley realized that, except for the timber trade, they had no back country at all. In fact, the settlement of such counties as Lanark and Renfrew reflected the population pressure which was forcing agricultural settlement on to marginal land. These counties were on the edge of the shield and residents of the area had to fight a stubborn and often rocky land in order to make a living.

The geographical position of the valley did offer at least the possibility of an escape from current conditions. In 1854 Thomas Keefer pointed to another, more specific application for the power of the railway. All that had to be done, he noted, was to 'burst the narrow belt between the upper Ottawa settlements and the broad expanse of Lake Huron' and a new and much more vast hinterland of the upper Great Lakes would become tributary to the valley.[26] Keefer's idea was not new and earlier plans to use either railway or canal had come to nothing. Two years later, however, such talk seemed much more meaningful. The government, concerned for the future of the St Lawrence system, sent an engineer, Walter Shanly, to investigate the feasibility of constructing either a canal or a railway between Georgian Bay and the Ottawa River.[27] The government's apparent interest in the long-standing idea encouraged a commercial speculation which stretched from the town of Perth down the valley to the city of Montreal. Through the early months of 1856 discussion raged as to the possibilities and implications of such a project as writers sought new adjectives to describe the numerous beneficial results that would come in its wake. Few, if any, of the citizens of the Ottawa Valley opposed the idea.

The trade possibilities of such a development were such that politicians dependent on votes from the region soon found it useful to give their support to the scheme. Philip Vankoughnet, running for a position on the newly elective Legislative Council in the autumn of 1856, was no exception. Speaking to a crowd of electors in September, Vankoughnet restated the traditional themes, pointing to the potential trade from Chicago and the Great Lakes. This trade alone would, if made to flow through the Ottawa Valley, give wealth to the region. Vankoughnet, however, did not stop with the possibilities of the American trade. There was no reason, he pointed out, to remain dependent on another nation as 'there was a great west to Canada as well as the United States.' That west, if only Canadians acted to open it, would provide an even greater and more certain source of wealth for the Ottawa Valley. It would also lead, inevitably, to that almost mythical source of wealth, Asia. Vankoughnet's speech called forth visions of the 'products of China and the East, journeying down the Ottawa valley, and the Gulf of St Lawrence on their way to Europe.'[28] Here was a hinterland large enough to satisfy even the most ambitious residents of the valley.

This vision of a vast new hinterland captured the imaginations of a number of people in the region, and before long the Ottawa Valley became a centre of expansionism rivalled only by Toronto. The town of Perth, for instance, was the first community outside of Toronto to adopt a public resolution calling for the annexation of the North West.²⁹ Various newspapers in that and other communities along the valley emulated the Toronto *Globe*, in tone if not in influence, in their insistence on immediate expansion. The spirit generated in 1856 was to have an influence for some time to come. Over the next several years such counties as Lanark and Renfrew were to have close associations with the expansionist movement. Alexander Morris and William McDougall both sat as members for the area. Other individuals – Charles Mair, Charles Napier Bell, and a future mayor of Winnipeg, Thomas Scott – hailed from the region. Years of discussion in their home towns had instilled an attraction for the West in all of them.

While Toronto and the Ottawa Valley were centres of expansionist sentiment interest in the North West was not confined to these regions. There was a provincial as well as a regional dimension to interest in the idea of expansion. A combination of pride in achievements to date and concern for the future led a good many Canadians to conclude that failure to expand would result in stagnation. Canada was outgrowing its boundaries; if room for Canadian energies was not found, the colony would sink into obscurity. The old Province of Canada was no longer sufficient for these energies, and, as the *Globe* put it on 10 December 1856, Canadians were 'looking about for new worlds to conquer.'

What gave the expansionist movement its power was a fusing of enthusiasm for the North West with a recognition of the crucial position Canada had reached. In a speech before the Toronto Board of Trade in December 1856, William Kennedy made the connection between the two explicit in order to show the importance of the campaign he and others were waging. Kennedy pointed out that since 1849 he had tried to arouse interest in the North West but had never had any real success. What had changed since then was neither the condition of the West nor the rule of the Hudson's Bay Company but the circumstances of the Province of Canada: 'But great progress has been made since then in railways, and other public works, and another aspect was given to the subject. Canadians now saw that the comparatively small fragment of this continent which they occupied would soon be both too narrow and too short for them, too small a field on which to exercise and develop their new born energies. It was the most notable work for the Canadians of the present day to undertake to bring within the pale of civilization the larger half of the North American continent, a country containing 270 millions of acres.'³⁰ The *Globe* echoed Kennedy's comments. Referring to Macdonell's unsuccessful bids for a transcontinental railway charter, it concluded that 'the circumstances of the country have materially changed' and urged acceptance of his latest application.³¹

Only possession of the North West could ensure that these changes would be allowed to continue to the benefit of Canada. The sheer size of the West encouraged Canadians to think that its development would allow them to rival the tremendous growth of the United States. In recent years Canadians had looked with envy on the flow of immigrants to the American mid-west while Canada backed onto the shield. The United States was a nation with seemingly infinite room for expansion and the Canadian desire for the North West was, in part, a desire to emulate the American experience. As Cauchon's 1856 report clearly revealed, a shortage of good land in Canada meant that it could not compete with the United States for immigrants; the report noted, as well that 'it is in the valleys of the Red River, the Assiniboine, and the Saskatchewan that such lands are to be found.'[32]

Agricultural settlement, however, was but a means to a wider end. As the references to the United States imply, Canadian expansionists were primarily concerned with the commercial implications of an expanding frontier. The tone was set by the North-West Transportation, Navigation and Railway Company, chartered in 1858 for the purpose of 'participating in the important and lucrative trade' which was thought to exist in the North West. The fur trade would provide the initial market but it was assumed that other markets would develop, giving 'an unlimited extent to Canadian industry, and to British commerce.'[33] The details of agricultural settlement were only vaguely conceived and even then were portrayed in terms of the production of goods for sale and as a market for eastern manufacturers. Expansionism did not contain any images of an Arcadian utopia such as ran through the American idea of the frontier.[34] Trade would precede settlement. The Canadian expansionist movement was essentially an attempt to increase the hinterland of such centres as Toronto and, more generally, to provide an extension for the great trade artery of the St Lawrence.

As was fitting for such a movement the potential for trade was almost invariably put in terms of the benefits that would accrue to the east. The concept of a vast agrarian empire, which emphasized the prosperity awaiting the farmer, had not yet developed. The editorials, speeches, and pamphlets of the first years of expansionism concentrated on the exploitation of a hinterland for the sake of a homeland. It was to the people of this homeland, Canada, that expansionist rhetoric was directed, not to those who might seek a livelihood in the hinterland. The North West was to be, in the words of the *Globe*, the 'back country' which Canada wanted.

The most dramatic, if still remote, expression of this commercial orientation was the idea of a transcontinental railroad system. Even the cautious William Draper expressed the hope that he would live 'to see the time, or that my children may live to see the time when there is a railway going all the way across the country and ending at the Pacific.'[35] Allan Macdonell reprinted his 1851 prospectus in his pamphlet on the North-West Transportation Company as an obvious indication of the ultimate goal of that firm.[36] George Brown reminded his readers in late 1856 that 'through British territory lies the best route for the Atlantic and Pacific Railway.'[37] No matter how remote the accomplishment or vague the conception, the transcontinental railway was always an integral part of Canadian expansion. Only with visions of such a railway was it possible to imagine a means whereby the vast North West could be developed and governed.

There were two alternate ways in which it was thought the railway would contribute to Canadian commerce. The first envisioned a hinterland carved out of the North West, supplying the railway with produce and returning eastern goods to the West. The other went beyond the North West in its search for wealth and looked, as had Synge, to the markets of Asia. The two ideas were not mutually exclusive for any railroad could serve both functions, but they did reflect different ideas as to the ultimate worth of the North West. It is indicative of the still limited faith in that region that, in the late 1850s and early 1860s, any transcontinental railroad was seen almost exclusively in terms of the Asian trade. As John Ross, the president of the Grand Trunk, said to the British select committee: 'the construction of a railroad is an important subject, apart entirely from the opening of the country through which it would pass.'[38] Ross was not an expansionist, but his comment did not bring forth any expressions of disagreement from those who were.

As a means of access to Asia, as a commercial hinterland and eventual settlement frontier, expansionists in 1856 and after looked to the North West as a potential answer to Canada's hopes and fears. The strength of the expansionist movement and the ability of a small number of individuals to influence public and official opinion was the result of various developments which made access to a large hinterland seem essential. Canada was at a crossroads. This fact had been sensed independent of the North West. The North West, however, made clear the choice that existed. In developing or not developing this region Canadians would make the choice 'whether this country shall ultimately become a Petty State, or one of the Great Powers of the earth.'[39]

Armed with varied arguments and supported, at least half-heartedly, by the Canadian government, the expansionists set out to convince the British government that the vast territory in question should be ceded to Canada by the Hudson's Bay Company. The company had faced challenges before and on those occasions it had employed its vast power, prestige, and political influence to shrug off such attacks. There seemed no reason for it not to do the same with the obviously self-interested expansionist criticisms. Canadian

50 Promise of Eden

expansionists, however, while they could not deny the selfish side of their campaign, argued that their commercial aims, unlike those of the Hudson's Bay Company, were complementary to other goals. The religious, humanitarian, and imperial themes of the 1840s had not been forgotten and it was not difficult to find reasons to justify the Canadian desire for the North West.

The first step for Canadians was to convince themselves that the act of expansion had some foundation in law. Canadians had often condemned the United States for its seizure of additional territory and were thus sensitive to charges they were adopting similar methods. Very quickly, the expansionist movement came to the convenient conclusion that there was no comparison between its aims and the American experience. Canada, it turned out, already owned the North West territory.

The legal claim to the territory was first detailed by Joseph Cauchon in the summer of 1857, though the ideas can be traced back to John McLean's writings in the 1840s.[40] While Cauchon signed the document in his capacity as Commissioner of Crown Lands, it is probable that the actual arguments were organized by William Dawson.[41] Canada's claim to the North West was based on the clause of the Hudson's Bay Company charter that excluded from its grant the territory of any Christian prince or state. Cauchon turned to the colonial era to argue that New France had comprised everything in North America above the British colonies in New England. The battle of the Plains of Abraham and subsequent cession of New France meant that Canada was the heir to these colonial claims.[42] Thus, in rather audacious fashion, Canada laid legal claim to the Hudson's Bay territories.

The exact boundaries of this extended Canada were uncertain. Draper, acting on instructions from the Executive Council, laid claim to all the territory south of the 'barren grounds' as far west as the Rocky Mountains.[43] The Toronto Board of Trade was less modest in its assertion of Canadian rights and claimed 'the whole region of country, extending westward to the Pacific Ocean, and northward to the shores of Hudson Bay.'[44] Whatever the actual extent of the claim, the fact remained that the legal fiction of territorial rights derived from New France allowed Canadians to covet the North West without any feeling of guilt. The expansionists argued that the officials of the Hudson's Bay Company were 'simply squatters' on Canadian land.[45]

The attacks on the Hudson's Bay Company were not confined to legal arguments. Expansionists turned to the ideas of Isbister and others in order to lay not only a legal but a moral claim for the transfer of the region to Canada. There was, however, a significant change in the rhetoric by the later 1850s. In the 1840s the assumption had been that the West would remain unsettled for some time to come and the primary concern was therefore a missionary one for the Indian. By 1857 the impulse was commercial and based on the belief that the region would quickly be opened up to civilization. This shift in assumptions drew attention from the Indians, those representatives of the wilderness, to the Red River settlement, that 'brave little colony of Britons' in the centre of the continent.[46]

It is true that some concern for the Indian population persisted. In England the Aborigines Protection Society continued to act as a lobby for what it perceived to be the interests of the Indian.[47] In Canada the occasional editorial by the *Globe* referred with concern to the Indian population and various individuals continued to call for aid to the native. But generally the exponents of expansionism in the fifties paid relatively little attention to the native population. This may have been because of at least a vague awareness that the plans to open the west were potentially harmful to the Indian. Allan Macdonell and others tried to convince the public that the release of the fur trade from the hands of a monopoly would ensure that the Indian was no longer 'compelled to submit to such terms as the Company may impose' and would thus benefit.[48] Men with a much more creditable background as humanitarians than Macdonell were not so certain. Even Isbister, pressed on the matter during the hearings of the British select committee, answered only that 'I should not like to express a very decided opinion on that point.'[49]

The decreased concern for the Indian was more than compensated for by a strong interest in the European and half-breed settlers of Red River. In shifting its focus the humanitarian motivation behind expansionism moved from a missionary concern for the native to a political movement aimed at aiding 'British subjects' who were currently 'vassals in a galling state of dependence on their lords of the company.'[50] Canada, as Macdonell wrote to the *Globe* on 30 September 1856, had a duty to stand 'between the oppressor and the oppressed.'

Expansionists argued that it was natural for Canada to be especially concerned with the plight of the Red River settlers, for their position was simply a more extreme example of what the Hudson's Bay Company had done to Canadians. Both groups had been hurt by the evil effects of monopoly. The Hudson's Bay Company was, in the words of the Toronto Board of Trade, 'injurious to the interests of the country so monopolised and in contravention of the rights of the people of the British North American Provinces.'[51] The company was harmful to Canada, and for that matter the British Empire, in that it opposed any attempt to develop the territory under its rule. Restating the arguments of the 1840s, expansionists claimed that the company deliberately sought to keep the territory a wilderness in order to preserve the fur trade. The progress of Minnesota, directly south of the Red River settlement, was both evidence of what could be accomplished and what the company had failed to accomplish. To fail to develop such a resource was to weaken the power and potential of the whole British Empire.

The Hudson's Bay Company was not just a passive obstacle to Canadian aspirations. Like Fitzgerald in 1849, Canadian expansionists explained the previous lack of knowledge of the region with a conspiratorial theory of Hudson's Bay Company policy. The company, it was said, had deliberately wrapped the country in a 'deep, thick veil of obscurity and darkness.'[52] Macdonell charged that it had perpetuated a false image of the North West as a region of 'barren lands, swamps, and granite rocks' in an attempt to make people believe the country was 'unfitted for civilization, and debased by nature from ever benefitting by its humanising efforts.'[53]

This conspiracy theory created a filter through which evidence about the company and the North West was viewed. The expansionists tended to suspect anyone who made negative comments on the North West to be a part of the conspiracy to keep the region a wilderness. The result was a strong selectivity in the use of source material. Increasingly the value attached to such material tended to be determined by its conclusions rather than the other way around. One of the more understandable examples was shown in the Canadian response to Sir George Simpson's attempt to explain away his earlier writings on the territory. His denigration of the land and the soil were seen as further proof of the company's willingness to distort the truth in its own interests. As the Montreal *Gazette* commented on Simpson's testimony: 'he must expect that people will be very ready to impute bad motives, for his change of opinion just at this particular time.'[54] Simpson was particularly vulnerable, but henceforth any person who undertook the task of defending the Hudson's Bay Company ran the risk of finding himself accused of being part of the conspiracy against the people of Red River and Canada.

The varied forms of the expansionist attack on the position of the Hudson's Bay Company left that company without any real defence. In earlier years there had been little question that the economy of the North West would remain based on the fur trade. Given that assumption, it was argued that monopoly was a necessary, if unfortunate, expedient in order to prevent the abuses and disorder that accompanied competition. By 1857, however, the assumptions were quite different. Canadians were now talking of opening the territory to settlement and, in spite of the vague nature of such statements, they proved irresistible. The company found it impossible to defend the mercantile empire in an era of free trade and the idea of a fur trade preserve in the face of agricultural settlement.

Even the representatives of the company dared not deny the desirability of opening the region. Edward Ellice, deputy governor of the Hudson's Bay Company, was suspicious of Canadian designs, but even he was forced to admit that if any of the company's powers were harmful to settlement they ought to be taken away.[55] Expansionists, of course, argued that the very existence of the company charter was a hindrance to settlement. In order to maintain its reputation as an honourable and patriotic firm the Hudson's Bay Company had to support the principle of development. In so doing it undercut its very reason for existence – the fur trade.

The Hudson's Bay Company was vulnerable because expansionists couched their arguments in terms of universally desirable principles. The opening of the West was to be in the name of progress and that progress would be to the benefit of the whole Empire and, for that matter, all of humanity. At the same time, as the basic legal claim put forward by Cauchon indicates, expansionists also looked to the particular interests of Canada. The specific right of Canada to participate in the development of the North West was seen to be as important as the principle of opening it for settlement. Any scheme that would have left the North West in other hands was rejected outright. In 1863 a reformed, newly progressive, and seemingly repentant Hudson's Bay Company received little sympathy from Canadian expansionists because, no matter how progressive, it did not represent Canadian aspirations.[56]

In order to assert Canada's particular claim on the North West, expansionists turned to history. Long after the fall of New France, it was argued, Canadians had been present in the North West. Various companies operating out of Montreal had competed with the Hudson's Bay Company for the wealth of the region. Then, in 1821, the merger of the North West Company and the Hudson's Bay Company had brought that Canadian presence to an end. In the climate of the 1850s this amalgamation took on a new and sinister significance. The natural course of history was said to have been diverted by the schemes of a tyrannical monopoly. The North West Company, for its part, assumed almost mythical stature as a symbol of the past that had been wrenched unjustly from Canada.

The main figure in this interpretation of events was Allan Macdonell. In his series of letters to the *Globe* he continually hammered home the theme that Canada had at one time had a direct and lucrative involvement in the North West. Not just a few traders in Montreal but 'Canada at large was benefitted by the trade,' he argued, 'for the wealth it brought back was freely flung back to circulate through those various industrial pursuits' associated with it.[57] Macdonell's argument was soon picked up by others, including George Brown.

At a public meeting in Toronto in August 1857 Brown called on his listeners to remember the 'immense traffic' of the 'hardy voyageurs.' The earlier wealth supposedly generated by the North West Company served as proof that 'every citizen of Canada is deeply interested in the opening up of settlement and commerce of those vast regions now held in the iron grasp of the Hudson's Bay Company.'[58]

In contrast to the years before 1821, the period after had left the wealth of the North West in the hands of what Alexander Morris termed 'a Company of London merchants.'[59] In spite of Canadian faith in the Empire, the Hudson's Bay Company, for all the benefits it conferred on Canada, might as well have been, as Alfred Roche termed it, 'a foreign body.'[60] In 1821 this foreign company had severed all connection with Canada and made Hudson Bay the main route of commerce between the North West and Europe. The expansionist distrust of the Hudson's Bay Company obscured the very real transportation problems which had led to this change of route. Rather, the switch to the bay was seen as a deliberate attempt to alter the course of history and to prevent Canadian influence in the region. From the time of the merger, 'no merchant trading along the St. Lawrence witnessed the imports for the west, nor the exports therefrom.' The Hudson's Bay Company closed the Superior route and the trade of the west was deliberately 'kept a secret from rising generations in Canada.' As a result, the wealth of the West, previously flowing into Canada, went instead to those 'who have never contributed one farthing to the revenues of this country.'[61]

George Brown saw evidence that this conspiracy against Canada continued even in the face of the expansionist campaign, In 1856 rumours spread that a contingent of troops was to be sent to Red River by the British government. When the government decided, not surprisingly, to use the normal route through Hudson Bay, Brown charged that the company had used its influence to prevent the use of the Superior route. 'It is beyond a doubt,' he concluded, 'that the troops could be transported with the utmost ease by that route; yet they are to be sent round by the frozen waters of Hudson's Bay, that the secrets of the Company may be kept.'[62]

The deliberate diversion of trade and the destruction of Canada's participation in the North West trade was, expansionists felt, sufficient to condemn the Hudson's Bay Company. But there was much more to it than that. Expansionists made the North West Company much more than a commercial organization. In their writings it became a specifically Canadian company, symbolizing Canadian enterprise and initiative. Its destruction by the Hudson's Bay Company thus also came to represent the destruction of the spirit of progress in the West. The difference in the two companies was apparent in their records in the opening of the West before 1821. 'The Canadian North West Company were everywhere in advance of their rivals,' and while the Hudson's Bay Company rested timidly on the shores of the bay these Canadians explored half a continent.[63]

Had the North West Company continued in existence, expansionists argued, this adventurous and progressive attitude eventually would have led to the opening of the West. Expansionists read into the North West Company their own goals and as such created a myth of it as the precursor of Canadian civilization. Macdonell told the Canadian Select Committee on the Hudson's Bay Territories that had the merger not taken place 'there is no doubt that the route via Lake Superior would by this time have been navigable all the way to the Saskatchewan.' William Dawson painted an inspiring, if romantic, picture of what might have been had the course of history been allowed to proceed unimpeded. The Fort William of the early nineteenth century, he stated, contained all 'the features of an embryo city, in strange contrast with the desolate and decaying loveliness which the blight of an illegal monopoly has thrown over it today.' Instead of this scene it should have been 'the entrepot of the trade of half a continent.'[64] Much more had been lost in 1821 than the profits of the fur trade.

The myth of the North West Company significantly reinforced Canada's claim to special rights in the North West. The West had all along been the means by which Canada might escape from the confines of the shield. In deliberately obstructing that development the Hudson's Bay Company had retarded Canadian growth and limited Canadian prosperity. The company was thus the enemy not only of the Indian and Red River settler but also of Canada. Expansionists were determined, now that the plot had been uncovered, that Canada's rightful destiny would no longer be blocked by a monopolistic trading company.

No conflict was thought to exist between these particular Canadian interests and the claims of the British Empire. From the time of Synge the closing of such a vast region had been seen as a hindrance to the development of the Empire and of civilization, and it continued to be so viewed. 'The time has come,' said Alexander Morris, 'when the claims of humanity and the interests of the British Empire, require that all the portions of this vast empire which are adapted for settlement should be laid open to the industrious emigrant.'[65] Canada, unlike the Hudson's Bay Company, would act not only in its own interests but in the name of progress.

While the opening of the West was for the benefit of the whole Empire, expansionists feared that only they clearly recognized this. They were, in fact, suspicious of the British government's ability to come to any objective conclusion on the whole question. In the same way that it was thought that Canada embodied the spirit of the North West Company, it was feared that at least the ruling circles in Britain had been tainted by the presence of the Hudson's Bay Company. The Canadian decision to send Draper to England was in part based on the fear that the British government would not take Canadian aspirations into consideration.[66] As the proceedings unfolded, expansionists were convinced that these precautions had been only prudent: 'Without the presence in London of some one to speak in our behalf the Committee would have been a sham; things would have "been made pleasant" for the Company; an unconditional renewal of the Charter would have been granted and we would have been sold.'[67]

This sort of bias on the part of the British government was not thought to be confined to the current round of hearings. Expansionists pointed to the stifling of attacks against the company in 1849 as proof that the British government could not or would not see the company for what it was. The refusal of the Colonial Secretary, Earl Grey, to act on Isbister's petition led Macdonell to ask in a rather far-fetched analogy whether 'the history of North America recall any ominous warning to deter that nobleman from pursuing his own selfish views?'[68] When it came to questions involving the Hudson's Bay Company, the British government seemed blind not only to the dictates of progress but also to the lessons of history. 'If history is of any value,' warned the *Globe* on 24 June 1857, 'even folly and infatuation must be made to hear the witnesses of the past.' The attitude of the British to date, however, led inevitably to the conclusion that it was 'in a mere death like sleep.'

The British government seemed unable to comprehend the dangers that the Empire faced. It delayed acting against a monopoly which, if removed, would have assured the Empire a great future. Canada, for its own sake and for the sake of the Empire, must force action if Britain would not. Its history gave it a right to the North West and its future seemed dependent on the region. It could not afford to stand by and watch an ignorant or corrupted mother country sacrifice its future. From 1857 on, Canada increasingly arrogated to itself the role of trustee of the North West in the name of the British Empire and civilization.

There was a certain expediency underlying the often shifting rhetoric of imperial and Canadian interests in the North West. When it came to matters of funds to develop the region, for instance, Canadians were quite willing to emphasize imperial interests. At the same time they continued to insist that whoever paid for that development it must ultimately be controlled by Canada. Beneath this expediency, however, a grandiose and significant idea was beginning to emerge. Many Canadians began to sense that the potential of the

North West not only guaranteed future Canadian prosperity but would also eventually alter in a fundamental way the relationship of the colony and the mother country.

At least since the 1720s when Bishop George Berkeley had written his famous and fatalistic line, 'Westward the course of empire takes its way,' the idea that power naturally moved westward from old seats of civilization to new had been commonplace. In the eighteenth and nineteenth centuries, at least in the English-speaking world, the word 'empire' as used by Berkeley implied the British Empire. Canada, as Britain's loyal offspring in the New World, liked to think of itself as the eventual successor to the mother country. Unfortunately, as Canadians were aware, that renegade daughter of the Empire, the United States, also had pretensions in this direction. And in the face of the tremendous growth of their neighbour to the south a good many Canadians might have concluded, as did one writer, that 'against such advantages possessed by the neighbouring states it seemed idle to compete.'[69] With a mixture of envy and fear Canadians noted the growing power of the United States, a power which might truly one day outstrip that of Britain.

As interest in the North West developed expansionists began to argue that there was no reason to assume the United States would inherit the British mantle. Alexander Morris, who developed the theme in the most detail, argued that if Canadian energy and vitality was focused on the vast potential of the North West, then British North America, not the United States, would be the scene of the 'new Britannic Empire on these American shores.'[70] If Canada was allowed to expand into the North West, it would continue to mature 'as surely as the child becomes the man, or the feeble sapling becomes the sturdy monarch of the forest.' With growth, its relationship to Britain would be transformed. Canada, not the United States, would ultimately inherit the British position as the centre of the English-speaking world. The British Empire would, of course, remain, for the connection with Britain 'will not be rudely severed.' The British North American confederation would remain true to British principles, 'reflecting the great parent country from which their inhabitants have mainly sprung, and rising to power and strength under her guiding influence.'[71] While the Empire would remain, however, the power relationships within it would inevitably shift and, ultimately, Canada would become the 'keystone of its strength.'[72]

Given these potential results of expansion it is not surprising that the North West took on an importance far greater than most hinterlands. In the future it was thought possible that the West would be the basis of power for the whole British Empire. This theme had been present in the writings of the British pamphleteers of the 1840s. Unlike the British pamphleteers, however, Canadian expansionists like Alexander Morris saw in their province the seed of an empire in its own right: 'With two powerful colonies on the Pacific, with another or more in the region between Canada and the Rocky Mountains, with a railway and a telegraph linking the Atlantic with the Pacific and absorbing the newly-opened and fast-developing trade with China and Japan ... who can doubt of the reality and the accuracy of the vision which rises distinctly and clearly-defined before us, as the Great Britannic Empire of the North stands out in all its grandeur.'[73]

In the 1850s this vision of a future Canadian empire was still very hazy. The nature of any empire was undefined and the achievement of imperial status reserved for an unspecified and distant future. Nevertheless, the rising importance of the North West in the minds of Canadian expansionists was clearly revealed when people like Alfred Roche could predict that Canada would 'become a mightier empire in the West than India has ever been in the East.'[74] Over the next few years, as Canadians grappled with the implications of expansion, such statements would become more common and possess a sense of immediacy which was still lacking in the 1850s.

Almost from the beginning the expansionist movement in Canada saw the North West as a means to empire. Given the enormous implications of this fact, it is perhaps understandable that expansionists insisted that the particular rights of their province be recognized. It is also understandable that their campaign should have met with such success and led the Canadian government to lay claim to the region.

3
A means to empire:
Canada's reassessment of the West, 1857-69

In a burst of enthusiasm Canadian expansionists turned their attention to the North West in 1856 and 1857. It had been eastern aspirations, commercial, moral, and national, that had led them to insist that the West should be opened up and claimed as Canada's inheritance. At the same time, even though they realized that the drive to the west obtained its impulse from eastern conditions, the nature of the land itself was important. Although Allan Macdonell might argue that the nature of the land was irrelevant, that 'even if the whole country from Lake Superior to the Pacific be a barren country, utterly destitute of any hope of cultivation' Canada should have the right 'to participate in the fur trade,' he and other expansionists knew that, in fact, the value of the region was crucial.[1] If the North West was really a barren tract, forever destined by its soil and climate to remain a wilderness, then Canada, if it could be roused to action at all, would find its acquisition of limited use. The fur trade was hardly the means on which to build the new power of the British Empire.

Expansionism had raised the question of the ultimate possibilities of the North West as an agricultural frontier. In an attempt to convince themselves, and the rest of Canada, expansionists soon began to make optimistic estimates as to the value of the land and climate. As early as 16 December 1856 the Toronto *Globe* stated hopefully that 'there is a stretch of country' between Lake Superior and the Rocky Mountains 'containing probably over two hundred million acres of cultivable land.' Others, re-reading earlier works on the Hudson's Bay territories, began to find evidence to show, as James Fitzgerald had said years before, that the North West was not a barren land but that its resources had been hidden from the world by the Hudson's Bay Company.[2] Canadian expansionists had to find good land in the West if their visions were to come to anything. In response to their needs, the existing sources began to yield new, optimistic information on the region.

One of the best examples of the changing perspective on the land came in a map drawn up in that centre of expansionism, the Crown Lands Department. The new map of the North West which Thomas Devine created in 1857 was based on the great works of Arrowsmith. Unlike Arrowsmith, however, Devine did not content himself with a delineation of the major physical features of the vast territory. His map was, in fact, as much a product of the expansionist impulse as was any editorial in the *Globe*. Even its title, 'Map of the North West Part of Canada,' reflected the new possessive attitude of the province to the Hudson's Bay territories. More basic to his purpose, however, was the running commentary, drawn largely from American sources, on the resources and capabilities of the region. The map was covered with such comments as the one placed between the North and South Saskatchewan rivers which described 'the scenery of these fertile valleys as magnificent, and the banks of the rivers on either side luxuriant beyond description.' Even that area that would soon be described as an extension of the Great American Desert was termed 'fine land.'[3] Devine's ability to reshape the map of the North West without any new evidence revealed the power which man's perspective has on his conclusions.

All the enthusiastic estimates by the *Globe* and descriptions on Devine's map could not hide the fact that Canadians were largely ignorant of the resources of the North West. Expansionists were all too aware that little was known of the region and that, outside of Red River, agricultural experiments had been spotty and inconclusive. Even Red River had a far from perfect record and 1857, at the very time when the region's agricultural capabilities were being extolled in Canada, brought the destruction of crops by the perennial pest, the grasshopper. Expansionists therefore could use those works that did praise the West with only limited effect. There was not enough evidence to conclude firmly that the West was capable of supporting agriculture.

If anything, all the hard evidence pointed in the opposite direction. When Sir George Simpson testified negatively on the resources of the West before the British select committee, his comments could be dismissed as coming from a man with an obvious bias. Simpson, however, was not the only man to make a pessimistic assessment of the region. The famous British scientist, J.H. Lefroy, concluded that 'agricultural settlement can make very slender progress in any portion of that region.' Sir John Richardson, equally well known and respected for his knowledge of the territory, testified that though 'the alluvial points on the Saskatchewan might be productive,' the prairie itself, 'although fit, probably for sheep pasture, is not a soil that I think would be productive for cereal cultivation.' Lefroy and Richardson were joined by Canadian John Ross and even by that original crusader, Alexander Isbister.[4]

61 A means to empire

While few in 1857 would deny Canada the right in principle to open the North West, there were still many who felt that right to be of questionable value.

The Canadian government, although it had laid formal claim to the North West, was especially uncertain as to the actual value of the region. Draper's testimony before the select committee clearly indicated that the position taken by the government in 1857 was essentially a holding action. It was a manifestation of the desire expressed some time earlier by the Montreal *Gazette* to 'see that the way is cleared,' should Canada decide it wanted to expand.[5] No legal or financial commitments had been made, nor were they likely to be until the government ascertained the nature of the resources and population of the region.

While the Canadian government's position in 1857 annoyed expansionists, it was, in spite of its limitations, a victory for their movement. The Canadian public and the Canadian and British governments had been made aware of the possibilities, and their interest guaranteed that further investigations would be undertaken. Over the next decade dozens of individuals would go west to look at this newly important region and would write of what they saw. Together they would dispel the ignorance of the North West that existed in 1857 and end for all time the negative assessments of the land and climate which had characterized the testimony of people like Lefroy and Richardson.

Those who went west over the next few years ranged from settlers in search of new land to merchants, adventurers, and tourists. Though there were probably as many reasons for going as there were people who went, it is possible to divide them into three general types. The first group to go, in time as well as classification, did so as a direct result of the claim that had been laid by the Canadian government in 1857. Canada had made a commitment and this, no matter how limited or hesitant, resulted, as Draper put it, in 'a desire to survey and explore before we do anything.'[6] Even as Draper presented the Canadian case in London, preparations were underway to follow up this resolution.

In July 1857 an expedition formed under the auspices of the Canadian government left Toronto for the North West. This group was formally under the charge of George Gladman, a retired fur trader whose primary qualification seems to have been his knowledge of the Hudson's Bay territories. Gladman had testified before the Canadian select committee on the Hudson's Bay Company and his stated opposition to that organization may have been seen by the government as additional qualification.[7] Gladman, however, proved to be only the nominal head of the party, a fact made clear when he was let go in 1858 as the expedition prepared for the second stage of its investigations.[8] The real charge of the Canadian scientific party rested in the hands of a professor from the University of Toronto, Henry Youle Hind.

Hind had been born in England and educated at Cambridge, emigrating to Canada in 1846. At the time the expedition was formed he was a professor of chemistry and geology at Trinity College. Hind was only thirty-four years old in 1857, but in spite of his relatively youthful age, he was well known in Canadian scientific circles. He was one of the earliest members of the Canadian Institute and had edited that organization's periodical, the *Canadian Journal*, from 1852 to 1855. He was the author of several articles and had firmly established himself as a leading figure in the Toronto scientific community. His work had brought him to the attention of the head of the Canadian Geological Survey, Sir William Logan, and Logan's recommendation had helped secure him a position on the North West party.[9] The expeditions of 1857 and 1858 were to make Hind's name familiar throughout Canada. At the same time, although he lived until 1908, these expeditions also marked the peak of his career. Hind seemed unable to refrain from attacking those whom he felt did not recognize his talents, and this inevitably had repercussions.[10] Most of his later years were spent as secretary of a women's school in Nova Scotia where, with one exception, he had little to do with the North West.

Another member of the Canadian expedition was to become almost as well known as Hind. Simon James Dawson was hired by the government to assess the potential of the territory between Lake Superior and the Red River as a line of communication. Dawson, a thirty-seven-year-old native of Scotland and brother of William Dawson, had emigrated to Canada and settled near Richmond in the expansionist Ottawa Valley. His position with the expedition marked his first senior appointment and began a connection with the region west of Lake Superior that was to last more than twenty years. On Dawson's shoulders fell the immense task of developing an initial transportation link between Canada and Red River.[11]

The Canadian expedition was not the only one to survey the West in 1857. The British government was also interested in the region over which it had ultimate, if remote, control. When a private exploration party was proposed by the prestigious Royal Geographical Society, the government picked up the idea and provided support. Midway through the hearings of the British select committee, authority was given to Captain John Palliser to proceed to the Hudson's Bay territories in order to make a scientific exploration of the country.

John Palliser was a member of the Irish gentry. At the age of forty, the only claim he could make to relevant experience was a hunting expedition he had made to the western United States a few years before.[12] No doubt he had learned something on that trip of the problems of wilderness travel and the necessity for tactful dealings with the Indians. The choice of Palliser as head of the expedition, however, can be most easily explained in terms of the interrelationships of upper class British society. In his initial support from the Royal Geographical Society and, eventually, from the British government, a string of influential people furthered Palliser's cause. It was influence that raised the Palliser expedition from the status of a private adventure to a major, official exploration under the auspices of the British government. Hudson's Bay magnate Edward Ellice commented caustically of the whole affair that Palliser simply had enough influence to allow him to indulge in his taste for buffalo hunting at government expense.[13] Ellice was too cynical, but only in his assessment of Palliser's motive, not in the degree to which the efforts of others played a role in the formation of the expedition.

Even Ellice could not challenge the credentials of the others who made up the party. A well-known botanist, Eugene Borgeau, was added to the group early in the planning stage and provided a high degree of expertise and enthusiasm throughout the exploration. Thomas Wright Blakiston, a British army officer, joined the group on the recommendation of Lefroy to act as magnetic observer; his scientific dedication and rigid personality soon brought him into conflict with Palliser. James Hector, only twenty-three years old and a recent graduate of the medical faculty of the University of Edinburgh, was perhaps the most important addition to the expedition; he worked closely with Palliser throughout and more than made up for his superior's lack of scientific training.[14]

The two scientific expeditions were perhaps the most important immediate consequence of the expansionist campaign. Others, however, had their interest aroused by expansionist writings and went west for very different reasons. In the years after 1857 the North West became almost fashionable as a destination for the young and adventurous tourist. With increasing frequency between 1857 and 1869, well-to-do young men from Britain headed to the far west in search of new game and new adventures. The purpose and attitudes of these men were in marked contrast to those of the members of the official expeditions. As one of them said, 'it was no definite purpose of mine to gather notes, nor closely record the geographical features of the country.'[15] Their aim was to experience the excitement of a wilderness before it succumbed to the forces of civilization. Many did not leave any records of their experiences and only the odd letter or other scrap of information indicates that they went west at all. Nevertheless, those who did write of their travels often provided some of the most acute and sensitive observations of a region in transition.

A third group had motives for going west and an attitude towards the region that distinguished them from both the scientists and the tourists. This group comprised those Canadians whose interest in the North West had been so aroused by expansionism that they emigrated to Red River, perhaps hoping to establish themselves before the rush began. Typical of them was a nineteen-year-old doctor, John Christian Schultz, who set up practice in Red River in 1859. Schultz hoped that the move would enable him to combine an interesting life with a successful career.[16] His hopes were to be abundantly fulfilled. While others were not always as successful as Schultz, they did resemble him in other ways. They were also well-educated, young, and from middle class Canadian families.[17] Like him they had accepted the promises of expansionism and based their lives on it. Their outlook and their published works reflected this fact.

Members of these three groups were, of course, far from homogeneous in their character or outlook. At the one extreme was the relatively high degree of scientific objectivity which Palliser brought to his examination of the region. Less swept up than others by the rhetoric of expansionism, Palliser refused to minimize those difficulties, particularly in the area of transportation, that would confront a transcontinental Canada.[18] At the other end of the spectrum were people like the young poet from Lanark, Charles Mair. When Mair visited the West in 1868 and 1869, he was already a complete convert to expansionism.[19] As a result he interpreted what he saw within the framework of expansionist ideals. On discovering, for instance, that the 'utopia' of Red River was experiencing famine, he tried to dismiss it. 'The half-breeds are the only people here who are starving,' he wrote, and 'it is their own fault – they won't farm.'[20] Though Mair's ideas on the famine were later to change, his initial attempt to minimize a major economic crisis indicates the way in which expansionist hopes biased his views of the West.

In spite of their differences, all these people did have one thing in common: they viewed the West in the light of the expansionist campaign. Even those like Palliser who did not completely accept the expansionist image of the West were influenced by it. The events of 1856 and 1857 made it apparent that the region was on the eve of a major change and this alone was sufficient to alter perceptions of the North West. Previously, the West had been viewed in the context of its existent wilderness state; as a result, the land and climate had been judged within the perspective imposed by the fur trade. The expansionist campaign of 1856 and 1857, however, challenged all of the traditional premises and brought a new perspective to bear on the North West.

The difference can be clearly seen in the writings and in the very travels of the men who went to the country after 1857. First, the focus of interest in the Hudson's Bay territories shifted to the south. Until 1857, as has been argued, the majority of scientific expeditions and a large proportion of the writings on the region had been concerned with the Arctic and sub-arctic; the region that was to become the agricultural heartland of the West had generally been traversed only in a perfuctory manner on the way to more northerly regions. This changed as questions of settlement and commerce came to the fore. Setting the new pattern were the two official scientific expeditions. Neither Hind nor Palliser went north of the 54th degree of latitude and both spent most of their time within two hundred miles of the American border.[21] As a result, the years after 1857 saw the North West become progressively less associated with the Arctic.

Second, and even more important in determining the image that was formed of the region, travellers after 1857 began with the assumption not of an economy based on the wilderness but of the potential of any economy based on agriculture. Once again the two official expeditions set the pattern for later observers. Both were instructed to look specifically at those economic questions raised by the idea of expansion. Hind, for example, was told that the 'character of the timber and soil [should be observed] and the general fitness of the latter for agricultural purposes ascertained.'[22] The instructions led to an examination of the potential of the region rather than its present state.

The questions asked altered the conclusions that were reached. The West was no longer seen through the eyes of the fur trader or the missionary but through those of the potential farmer. The possibility of agriculture was not only no longer ignored, as it had been in the past, but became the first priority to those who would make observations on the West. Once again man's tendency to find what he expected or wanted to find was revealed. This time, however, all the circumstances oriented the observer towards agriculture rather than the fur trade. None of the travellers after 1857 could really claim to be journeying through unexplored territory. Even the expeditions of Palliser and Hind travelled through regions that had been known to fur traders and buffalo hunters for generations. Nevertheless, their purpose in going over these routes and their perspectives on the country around them made those who went west original observers of the land.

The investigations of the North West that began in 1857 redefined the geographical and climatological structure of the prairie region between Red River and the Rocky Mountains. Newly acquired masses of detail made possible a type of description that had previously existed only for those well-travelled areas adjacent to fur trade posts. This additional information, set out by the Hind and Palliser expeditions, provided the basis for the redefinition of the geography of the North West. The work of Palliser and Hind, to which might be added the writings of the American, Lorin Blodgett, reshaped nineteenth-century geographical understanding of the region. Old generalizations concerning the hostile nature of the land were broken down. Such loose definitions and descriptions as had been circulated by fur traders and missionaries were given a new accuracy. The works of Blodgett, Hind, and Palliser became the new standard references for anyone who sought information on the North West.

The first of these men to come before the public was Lorin Blodgett. In 1857 he published his massive book, *The Climatology of the United States and the Temperate Latitudes of the North American Continent*. Blodgett offered little new hard evidence on the resources of the North West; he had only six sets of observations from all of British North America and not one of these was from the Hudson's Bay territories.[23] Nevertheless his work made a significant impact on both the scientific and popular mind. He was one of the first people to look at the West in terms of its agricultural possibilities, and his scientific method, no matter how limited his evidence, contributed to the expansionist campaign.

Blodgett appealed to those who would picture the North West as habitable because he challenged the assumption that latitude determined climate. As long as that belief was widely held, the North West could be viewed as suitable for settlement only with great difficulty. Canadians were aware of the harsh climate north of Lake Superior. The North West was just as far north and, it could be asked, even if the soil improved, was there any indication that climate would not prove an insurmountable barrier to settlement? Blodgett's answer was a resounding affirmative. Basing his work on the concept of the isotherm as developed by Alexander Humboldt, he concluded that such fears were groundless. Climate varies for reasons independent of latitude and any real understanding of a region has to come from following the isothermic temperature line rather than the degree of latitude. Specifically, in this case, the isothermic lines of the North West indicated the 'the increase of temperature westward is quite as rapid as it is southward to New Mexico.' It was not the climate of Lake Superior which was analogous to the North West but another and much more favourable region in the same latitude: 'The west and north of Europe are there reproduced.'[24]

Blodgett's work was especially significant because it appeared in time to influence those Canadians who were about to undertake their own investigations of the North West. *Climatology* included in its subscription list the University of Toronto, the Canadian Institute, and the Magnetic and Metropolitan Observatory of Toronto.[25] It was thus well known in Canadian scientific circles in Canada from the beginning and, by 1858 if not before, both Henry Youle Hind and Simon Dawson were aware of Blodgett's conclusions.[26] His optimism and the sense of destiny his style conveyed may have remained with them as they viewed the vast new territory which Canada claimed as its own: 'it is demonstrable that an area, not inferior in size to the whole of the United States east of the Mississippi, now almost wholly unoccupied, lies west of the 98th meridian and north of the 43rd parallel, which is perfectly adapted to the fullest occupation by cultivated nations.'[27]

For obvious reasons Blodgett's work had a great deal of prestige in expansionist circles and it was to be quoted repeatedly in the future. It was, however, hardly the detailed set of observations which were needed to counter years of scepticism as to the value of the North West. Blodgett's work was inspirational, but it was the evidence accumulated by the expeditions under Palliser, Hind, and Dawson that was to reshape the North West in a new image.

The initial contribution made by Hind and Palliser was their division of the region into identifiable sub-regions.[28] The three 'steppes' or levels described by others were confirmed and delineated and the resources of particular areas such as the valleys of the Swan River, the Assiniboine, and the Saskatchewan were recorded. Even the seemingly homogeneous prairie was found to contain very different conditions of soil and climate from place to place. The work of Palliser and Hind was influenced by the biases of their age, but this does not in any way depreciate the significant contribution to knowledge that resulted from their work in the North West.

What gave the work of Hind and Palliser such impact was the fact that, once they had torn apart old generalizations into more detailed observations, they reassembled the geographical picture of the North West into a clear and dramatic outline. Moreover, as suited their instructions, it was an outline based on the potential of the region rather than its actual state. The two terms which their expeditions made a standard part of geographical description in the West – 'the fertile belt' and 'Palliser's triangle' – were definitions that made sense only in terms of agriculture and settlement.

'Palliser's triangle' was an area of land 'forming a triangle, having as its base the 49th parallel from the longitude 100 degrees to 114 degrees W., with its apex reaching the 52 parallel of latitude.' It was a region characterized by the man who gave it its name as one of 'arid plains' and 'extensive sandy wastes,' unfitted in all probability for agriculture.[29] Hind was in full agreement, describing the region as 'not, in its present condition, fitted for the permanent habitation of civilized man.'[30] Both men thus virtually dismissed over 16,000 square miles of the North West. The lands of the Sioux and the Blackfoot, so long avoided by the Hudson's Bay Company, were now seemingly destined to be avoided by the settler and farmer.

Both Palliser and Hind believed this triangle to be but a sub-region of a much vaster area of poor land and climate. Beginning with the accepted premise that there existed in the United States 'a more or less arid desert,'

Palliser concluded that the area of bad land in the North West was in fact a northerly extension of that phenomenon. Hind, using American sources, came to the same conclusion, stating that 'this vast treeless prairie forms in fact the northern limit of the great arid region of the eastern flank of the Rocky Mountains.'[31] Whole areas including the upper Qu'Appelle Valley, the South Saskatchewan, and the prairies between them and the border thus became identified with the enormous wasteland which for more than a generation had been accepted as the heritage of the United States.

In such conclusions there was certainly nothing of great inspiration for the ardent expansionist. The identification of the prairie with the Great American Desert had existed long before Palliser and Hind made their trek west. If, however, the triangle did little to encourage the expansionists, the same can not be said of the fertile belt. It was this term that gave the expansionists what they needed, and ultimately it dominated the image of the sterile triangle in determining the Canadian assessment of the value of the North West. The concept of the fertile belt was essential to those who wanted to annex the North West. Presented most dramatically by Hind in a map in his 1860 *Narrative*, the area of fertility was depicted as a vast band of yellow sweeping in a giant arc from the American border at Red River northwest to the forks of the Saskatchewan and from there along the North Saskatchewan to the Rocky Mountains. As it approached the foothills of the Rockies it turned southward until it reached the border at 114 degrees west.[32] Here was scientific and dramatic support for those who would extend the proven fertility of the Red River valley to the west. The settlement was no longer an oasis in a desert but simply the small, easternmost portion of a vast area of land suitable for settlement.

Interestingly, neither the existence of the triangle nor the fertile belt challenged the older traditional relation between the absence of trees and aridity. The line between the fertile belt and the triangle was the region that Palliser and Hind felt divided the natural prairie from those areas that would support trees. Hind, in fact, began his definition of the area which he thought was an extension of the American desert by describing it as a 'vast treeless region.'[33] Equally, both parties went out of their way to explain the absence of trees in some portions in the fertile belt. Palliser dismissed the absence of trees in the Battle River area as artificial, pointing to the 'debris of large trees' as proof that the area could support vegetation. The lack of trees, both felt, was due to prairie fires, often set by Indians.[34] It was still felt necessary, then, to explain why trees did not exist in a supposedly fertile land.

Given the definition of Palliser's triangle and the caution with which both Hind and Palliser approached the prairie, it is perhaps surprising that they

69 A means to empire

played such an important role in changing the image of the West. Their impact came from the fact that, having accepted an extension of the Great American Desert, they then imposed definite limits on it. Furthermore, they inserted between that area and the other region that had tainted the image of the West, the Arctic, an extensive band of fertile land and appropriate climate. The fertile belt provided the agricultural hinterland and path to the Pacific which the expansionists sought. Hind was acutely aware of this and thought it of sufficient importance to set it down in block letters. 'IT IS A PHYSICAL REALITY OF THE HIGHEST IMPORTANCE TO THE INTERESTS OF BRITISH NORTH AMERICA THAT THIS CONTINUOUS BELT CAN BE SETTLED AND CULTIVATED FROM A FEW MILES WEST OF THE LAKE OF THE WOODS TO THE PASSES OF THE ROCKY MOUNTAINS, AND ANY LINE OF COMMUNICATION, WHETHER BY WAGGON ROAD OR RAILROAD, PASSING THROUGH IT, WILL EVENTUALLY ENJOY THE GREAT ADVANTAGE OF BEING FED BY AN AGRICULTURAL POPULATION FROM ONE EXTREMITY TO ANOTHER.'[35] This fact was what mattered to Canadians. The implications of the fertile belt made all the qualifications of both Hind and Palliser seem largely irrelevant. The point had been made that the North West was not a barrier to the Pacific and that it had resources which would allow it to become a valuable hinterland for Canada.

The importance of the two scientific expeditions was probably best summed up by Hind himself when he commented that 'the North-West Territory is no longer a *terra incognita.*'[36] The weakest link in the chain of expansionist arguments had been the lack of knowledge concerning the region in which they placed so much faith. Now, with the results of the expeditions, the expansionist could state with certainty that these reports 'have established the immediate availability for the purposes of Colonization,' of vast portions of the Hudson's Bay territory.[37]

The expansionists had not needed much convincing, of course. They simply found in the efforts of the scientific expeditions confirmation of what they had believed all along. The real importance of the two expeditions lay in the influence they had on those less committed. These people had needed proof, and in the seemingly objective assessments of Palliser and Hind they found strong evidence of the validity of the expansionist position. The work of these two parties provided sufficient material on the potential of the North West to shift the weight of evidence in favour of the expansionist argument. Over the next years it became standard in Canada to accept the conclusion that the North West was suitable for settlement rather than the reverse. By the time the Canadian government, in 1864, talked of the region as being 'fertile and capable of sustaining a vast population,' the comment was so commonplace as to be almost a cliché.[38]

Scientific reports alone were not responsible for the dramatic change in the image of the North West. While the volumes published on the two expeditions provided an essential basis of evidence, they were hardly the sort of material that could, by themselves, have wrought the transformation that took place in the public mind. Toronto scientist, Daniel Wilson, summed up their limitations when he commented: 'it is an old saying that Parliament can print blue books, but it is beyond its power to make people read them.'[39] In order to understand the change that occurred it is necessary to consider all those writings, whether by scientist or layman, that appealed, as one expansionist later put it, to the 'mind and emotion of the great agricultural community.'[40] The experience of the West after 1857 was as much an emotional process as it was intellectual.

Anyone who went west in the later 1850s or 1860s could not escape the feeling that he was entering a distinct environment. The Hudson's Bay territories were still isolated from the rest of British North America in terms of both trade and transportation. Most who journeyed to Red River had to go by way of the United States to St Paul in Minnesota and then northward. By the time they approached Fort Garry they had left behind such symbols of civilization as the railroad and the telegraph. Those who made the journey saw their own movement from civilization to wilderness as significant. Travellers gloried in their ability to return to a basic, primitive mode of existence and to thrive on it. The travellers of the 1860s, especially those tourists who had come to the West specifically for a wilderness adventure, recreated the sense of romance that had long been apparent in the writings of R.M. Ballantyne. The Earl of Southesk, on leaving Crow Wing, Minnesota, in May 1859, exulted: 'at last, I thought, as last the prisoner of civilisation is free.' British tourist, Doctor William Cheadle, was in a long-standing tradition when he concluded after his own trip on the prairies that 'truly the pleasures of eating are utterly unknown in civilised life.'[41]

In spite of the timelessness of such comments, the reaction to the wilderness was changing. In the wake of the expansionist campaign, explorers and travellers approached the wilderness in a manner that differentiated them from both the romantics and those earlier missionaries who had reacted so adversely to a heathen land. Gradually the very idea of the wilderness began to soften and change until it too conformed to the requirements of progress.

The changing approach was typified by the reaction of Henry Youle Hind, one of the first to reconcile the romance of the wilderness with the implications of expansionism. As had many before him, Hind found certain aspects of the wilderness life to be charming. His lengthy description of a camp scene early in the morning, where 'the stars are slightly paling,' and 'the cold yellow light begins to show itself in the east,' reveals that his sensitivity was not constricted by his scientific purpose. It was a description, more than anything else, of a peace inherent in nature, where 'no sound at this season of the year disturbs the silence of the early dawn.'[42] Such scenes and experiences of 'boundless prairies, sweet scented breezes, and gorgeous sunsets,' made a trip to the North West an emotional as well as an intellectual experience for Hind.[43]

If the beauty and peace of the wilderness were impressive, so was its power. The incredible forces that often shattered the peace of nature were awesome to Hind. 'The grandeur of a prairie on fire belongs to itself,' he wrote. Only unchecked nature was capable of creating such an impressive sight, since, 'like a volcano in full activity, you cannot imitate it, because it is impossible to obtain those gigantic elements from which it derives its awful splendour.' Even the tiny grasshoppers, massed in quantities appropriate to the vastness of the West, became an awe-inspiring, if destructive, manifestation of the power of the wilderness: 'Lying on my back and looking upwards as near the sun as the light would permit, I saw the sky continually changing colour from blue to silver to white, ash grey and lead colours, according to the numbers in the passing cloud of insects ... the aspect of the heavens during the greatest flight was singularly striking. It produced a feeling of uneasiness, amazement and awe in our minds, as if some terrible, unforeseen calamity were about to happen.'[44]

While Hind was awed by the wilderness he felt no temptation to ascribe to it moral attributes superior to civilization. His enthusiasm, for instance, did not extend to the men who lived in the wilderness. His attitude to the Indian, in fact, resembled the disdain and pity of the missionary more that it did the praises of the romantic. The native, he felt, was not in harmony with nature but degraded by it. When Hind visited an Indian village he thought of the comparison 'between the humanizing influence of civilization and the degraded, brutal condition of a barbarous heathen race.' The power and beauty of the wilderness was indeed impressive, but it was too powerful for man to accept unaltered without becoming dominated by it.

Hind's whole reaction to the wilderness and to the North West rested on his awareness and acceptance of Canadian expansionism. The power and beauty of the wilderness were, for him, inseparable from his hopes for the movement. In fact, it simply demonstrated the importance of expansion: 'the vast ocean of level prairie which lies to the West of Red River must be seen in its extraordinary aspects, before it can be rightly valued and understood in reference to its future occupation by an energetic and civilised race, able to improve on its vast capabilities and appreciate its marvellous beauties.'[45] Hind felt none of the conflicts of Alexander Ross, because for him the romance of the wilderness was not in its own intrinsic beauty but in its potential.

In the wake of the expansionist crusade the land began to be viewed in terms of agricultural potential not only in the scientific but in the aesthetic sense. Descriptions of present scenes of beauty became prophecies of future development. 'I stood upon the summit of the bluff' near the Qu'Appelle, wrote James Dickinson, a member of the Hind expedition, 'looking down upon the glittering lake 300 feet below, and across the boundless plains, no living thing in view, no sound of life anywhere.' It was a romantic scene in itself, but for Dickinson the romance was as much in the mind as in the scene, for he 'thought of the time to come when will be seen passing swiftly along the distant horizon the white cloud of the locomotive on its way from Atlantic to Pacific, and when the valley will not resound from the merry voices of those who have come from the busy city on the banks of the Red River to see the beautiful lakes of the Qu'Appelle.'[46] Similarly, while traversing a series of hills the English tourists, Milton and Cheadle, 'remarked to one another what a magnificent site for a house one of the promontories would be, and how happy many a poor farmer who tilled unkindly soil at home would feel in possession of the rich land which lay before us.'[47]

In the later 1850s and 1860s man's reaction to the North West began increasingly to be determined by his sense of its potential, in the same way that, in previous years, the missionary's reaction had been conditioned by the fact that it was a heathen wilderness. The prairie took on a new beauty because of the resources it contained. As S.J. Dawson said of Red River, 'if the scenic beauty which characterizes the region so near it to the eastward is wanting, this country is incomparably superior in all that can minister to the wants of man.'[48] Charles Mair said almost the same thing a decade later when he enthused that 'there is, in truth, a prospective poetry in the soil here – the poetry of comfort and independence.'[49] It is not surprising that expansionists paid little heed to the costs that civilization would impose on the North West, for to them the charm of the wilderness lay mainly in its potential for development.

The expansionists' belief that civilization was, unquestionably, preferable to wilderness placed them closer to the missionary than to the romantic. Even the rhetoric of expansionism often resembled the earlier missionary tracts. Both groups looked forward continually to a time when 'the deserts of the North-West shall blossom as a rose where now a few thousand savages drag out a miserable existence.'[50] The views of the two groups were, however, far from identical. The missionary had found little beauty or romance in the wilderness. Landscape had, for him, been viewed against the heathen and miserable condition of the Indian. The expansionists, on the other hand, enthused over the land and scenery even as they looked to the time when it would be transformed. Whereas the missionary had found the wilderness a reproof to the moral sensibilities of man, the expansionist saw as positive the very fact that the land was still a wilderness.

The fact that vast areas of good and habitable land still existed was in fact providential. The region had been kept isolated from the rest of the world until Canada had been prepared to occupy it.[51] Now, however, its potential was becoming known. As George Brown pointed out, it involved an area 'greater in extent than the whole soil of Russia,' and that vast resource would be 'opened up to civilization under the auspices of the British American Confederation.'[52] The millions of acres available for the farmer were valuable precisely because even after centuries of expansion and settlement they lay 'free and unoccupied.'[53] The missionary had felt blocked and frustrated by the isolation, emptiness, and seeming permanence of the wilderness in which he worked. In contrast the wilderness state added to the expansionist's estimate of the region. 'Man is a grasshopper here,' wrote Charles Mair, 'making his way between the enormous discs of heaven and earth. And yet man is master of all this.'[54]

This reaction to the wilderness was reinforced by the fact that the North West was in a state of flux. The wilderness, as if preparing for things to come, already seemed to be receding. 'The days when it was possible to live in plenty by the gun and the net alone, have already gone by on the North Saskatchewan.' wrote Milton and Cheadle. While the disappearance of game signalled the end of the wilderness, other developments predicted the coming of civilization. 'The river communication has been opened up,' Bishop Anderson noted in 1860; 'the road over the prairie has been traversed; and the appliances of modern science have rendered more easy the production of some necessities of modern life.'[55]

Observations such as these, and the continued orientation towards the potential of the region, began to diminish the image of the wilderness in the minds of those who observed the North West. Wilderness, by definition, implied a region where the natural dominated the works of man, whether those works be put in technological, legal, or spiritual terms. This view was common to Hind, Ross, and the early missionaries. Where earlier observers differed from the expansionists, however, was in the implication they drew from this fact. In various ways both the missionaries and Ross had tended to see the wilderness as irreconcilable with civilization; there was, in a sense, an adversary relationship between the two states. To Hind and the expansionists no such implication was thought to be necessary; rather civilization, the works of man, were a superstructure to be imposed on nature. The only necessary question, therefore, was whether the natural environment was suitable as a base for European society. The re-evaluation of the climate of the North West had, seemingly, answered that question, and thus in a very real sense the distinction between wilderness and civilization was reduced to matter of time. The only difference between the resident of the North West and that of Europe was, 'if the greatness of his country is past or passing, ours is yet to come.'[56]

The more that men viewed the North West in terms of its potential, the more they began to concentrate, either inadvertently or deliberately, on those attributes of the region that reinforced the new image. Those facets of the North West which had previously been used to emphasize its wilderness state – isolation, savagery, harshness – were downplayed and replaced with quite different attributes. Ruggedness of land and climate was scarcely mentioned; instead, the North West began to be described in terms more appropriate to the estate of a well-to-do landowner than to a vast unpeopled land: 'There are many delightful spots in the belts, the herbage is clean as well shaven lawn, the clumps of aspen are neatly rounded as if by art, and where little lakes alive with waterfowl abound, the scenery is very charming, and appears to be artificial, the result of taste and skill, rather than the natural features of a wild, almost uninhabited country.'[57] While the harsh and wild aspects of the North West were not ignored, there was an increased tendency, from the time of Hind on, to look on the North West as a rather tame wilderness.

Man's work in this vast land was not overlooked in the process. The expansionists turned to Red River as proof that men could live in the North West; even in the midst of an empty land it was possible to develop a comfortable and civilized way of life. By its very nature the expansionist approach challenged Ross's argument that this isolated settlement was in danger of being overwhelmed by the wilderness that surrounded it. Rather, Red River was viewed as a somewhat quiet place with all the basic attributes of a civilized community: the people were 'hardy, industrious, and thrifty,' living in a settlement with 'churches many; and educational advantages which will endure comparison with those of more pretentious communities.'[58] In going to Red River the Canadian was not entering the howling waste that had been imagined. Comfort was not just a thing of the East for, as Charles Mair wrote of Red River, 'they live like Princes here.' Houses were 'all snug and respectable' and there was even 'an hotel with two billiard tables.'[59]

Canadians wished to see Red River as a civilized community and every opportunity that allowed them to do so was given great play. Typical of this was the attention given to the formation of the 'Institute of Rupert's Land,' a western version of the Canadian Institute. The *Nor'Wester*, that western voice of Canadian expansion, devoted columns to the event while the meeting itself attracted most of the leading members of the community. In Toronto the *Canadian Journal* noted the event and well-respected Daniel Wilson wrote a long and laudatory article on its importance.[60]

The significance attached to the formation of the institute was very much a by-product of the Canadian expansionist outlook. The expansionist perspective had altered the social image of the region; in the most basic sense it can be said that those interested in or affected by expansionism had ceased to see the region as a true wilderness at all and were, instead, judging it as the outpost of an expanding and powerful civilization. Events that reinforced this image became, in themselves, further proof of the expansionist argument. As Daniel Wilson pointed out, the importance of the formation of the institute lay as much in the principle as in any contribution which might actually be made in the field of science. Its very existence was proof 'of the changes which are slowly but surely revolutionizing this vast continent; and giving evidence of an intellectual dawn which heralds the period when states and empires of the great northwest are to claim their place in the world's commonwealth of nations.' Given the historical significance of the occasion, it was somewhat unfortunate that the *Nor'Wester* referred to a number of stuffed animal specimens presented to the institute as 'tastily arranged.'[61]

If civilization triumphed over savagery in Red River it was in part because that settlement was no longer an oasis in a dangerous and hostile wilderness. If one accepted the existence of the fertile belt, it was simply the eastern point of a vast region suited for the settlement of man. In social and political terms it was no longer viewed as an island of civilization in the midst of barbarism, but simply the first of many centres of civilization. In fact, it came to be seen as the natural staging ground for other communities in the North West. As the *Globe* suggested as early as 13 December 1856, it could be made 'the *point d'appui* for the Canadian government's operations in opening up the Hudson's Bay Territories for settlement.' The more evidence that accumulated on the resources of the West, the more common this idea became. Expansionists began to realize that the presence of the settlement would make their task all that much easier. As S.J. Dawson argued in 1859, 'There is already a nucleus where the wants of settlers may be supplied in the first instance, and the population of ten thousand ready to welcome them and give them the advantage of their experience.'[62]

The new role which expansionists envisaged for Red River also meant that that community ceased to be seen in terms of its own history or society.

Instead it came to be viewed, in the same manner as the wilderness, in terms of its future potential and in relation to Canadian expansion. 'This settlement,' wrote one George Le Vaux in 1869, 'now surrounded by a vast wilderness, and far removed from the civilized world, is nevertheless destined to become the nucleus of a new empire.'[63] That empire was to be the product of Canadian expansion, and, from at least 1860 on, Red River was viewed as the outpost of Canadian-Britannic civilization. Such an image not only had no place in it for the concept of an oasis but equally made impossible Alexander Ross's hope that it might serve as a link between the wilderness and civilization. Red River was to represent the force of civilization and the wilderness was to be subjugated.

Cumulatively, the writings on the West in this period shifted the tone of the expansionist campaign. Previously, the expansionist image of the settlement frontier had always been left ill-defined. In the wake of the exploring expeditions and the increasingly optimistic reports on the region, however, more attention began to be paid to the potential benefits of agricultural settlement. The populating of the prairies, rather than a hazy by-product of expansion, became an immediate and major reason for it. As early as 1865 George Brown talked ambitiously of the North West as the key factor in a scheme to establish 'a government that will seek to turn the tide of European emigration into this northern half of the continent.'[64] Such statements revealed that by the mid-1860s the idea of the West as an agricultural empire was becoming an important part of expansionism. Minerals, furs, and even the route to Asia began to be subordinated to the hope that the North West would become 'the seat of an industrious, prosperous and powerful people.'[65]

As agriculture assumed greater importance, expansionists began to appeal not only to those in the East who would benefit from annexation but to those who would go west to take up farms. The land began to be talked of as a place where 'millions yet unborn may dwell in peace and prosperity.'[66] Once it was ascertained that the North West did have resources to offer 'temptation to the emigrant nowhere excelled,' that fact became central to the expansionist campaign.[67] At the same time, this emphasis on the farmer did not alter the commercial orientation of the movement. The farm, rather than the fur trade or Asia, was now seen as the primary source of trade, but it was still trade that was discussed. There would be a 'joint extension of settlement and commerce.'[68] The future farmer of the North West was to be a man who bought and sold goods, not one leading a self-sufficient existence.

The idea of an agricultural empire significantly reinforced and extended the importance of the North West in the Canadian mind. More and more, in a time of uncertainty, it was looked to as the most important single guarantee of

Canada's future existence. In terms of external relations it would permit the development of a British North American nation with enough power to withstand any hostile pressures from the south. An one anonymous writer put it, the possession of the North West would make Canada 'an almost impregnable military post in an enemy's country' and would be 'the best possible barrier against aggression.'[69] Charles Mair's friend, the formidable George Denison of Toronto, agreed. 'I am very glad to hear such good accounts of the resources and fertility of the great North West,' he wrote Mair in 1869, for 'I have every confidence in time it will prove a great source of strength to the Dominion and together we men of the North (as Haliburton says) will be able to teach the Yankees that we will be as our ancestors have always been[,] a dominant race.'[70]

Denison's interest in the whole question reveals the broadening appeal of the expansionist movement by the later 1860s. As estimates of the importance of the North West increased, the idea of expansion became a sort of umbrella solution for all of Canada's problems. As such, it appealed increasingly to all those Canadians who considered themselves ardent nationalists. Denison saw the region as the means by which his particular phobia, American annexation, could be avoided, but others, with different concerns, also looked to expansion as a solution. The response of the Canada First group, formed in Ottawa in 1868, was typical. Its members included, initially, Denison, Mair, R.G. Haliburton, W.A. Foster, and H.J. Morgan.[71] Of all these men only Mair could be considered an expansionist; the others had different causes to keep them occupied. Yet all of them seem to have felt that the annexation of the North West was a necessary corollary to the preservation of the Canadian nation.

By the later 1860s expansionism had become intertwined with nationalism. The very definition of the young Dominion of Canada and its hopes for the future were increasingly thought to be inseparable from the opening of the West. An editorial entitled 'Patriotism' in the Toronto *Globe*, on 16 February 1869, summed up the relationship. In order to build a great country Canadians had first to understand that their nation, while just emerging, was inferior to none, and, the *Globe* argued, there was no reason to feel ashamed: 'There are few countries, indeed, on the face of the earth of which the inhabitants have more reason to be proud.' The source of that pride was the 'mighty resources of the North West.' Thomas D'Arcy McGee, Canada's most eloquent nationalist, put it even more succinctly when he concluded in 1868 that 'the future of the Dominion depends on our early occupation of the rich prairie land.'[72]

In the 1850s Canadians had sensed, or hoped, that they were on the threshold of some new stage in their evolution as a people. In their efforts to assure that this new stage would be attained, a number of them turned to the North

West. By 1869 these expansionists had determined that future development to their own satisfaction. For them, the years between 1857 and 1869 simply brought confirmation of the belief that Canada's route to greatness was through the opening and settlement of the North West. The next stage had been defined, and in that definition the expansionist saw, as Mair put it, 'the significance and inevitable grandeur of his country': 'Far behind him are his glorious and old native province, the unsullied freedom of the North, the generous and untiring breed of men. Before him stretches through immeasurable distance the large and lovelier Canada.' Mair's description of man's movement onto the prairies contained within it the expansionist vision of Canadian development. It was an image of history and destiny, for by imposing the traditions and energy of Canada's past to the potential for the future that existed in the North West lay 'the path of empire and the garden of the world.'[73]

4
Conspiracy and rebellion: the Red River resistance, 1869-70

By September 1869 the long campaign of the expansionists seemed on the verge of triumphant success. After a number of proposals and counter-proposals, Canada and the Hudson's Bay Company had come to terms on the transfer of Rupert's Land. Canada, for its part, had already passed the legislation necessary for the extension of its control and only the date of the official transfer remained to be set.[1] William McDougall had even been named as the territory's first governor and was in the midst of preparations for his long journey. Canadian expansionists predicted that annexation marked the dawn of a new era for, as Alexander Morris wrote, 'the history of the territory is yet to be made.'[2] The nature of that future history, now in the hands of Canada, seemed to be assured, and the *Nor'Wester* on 21 September, could not resist writing its outline before it had actually begun: 'The NOW of this country finds a territory of immense extent occupied by about 14,000 civilized people; the THEN of ten years shall see a population of 500,000 – Now we are almost isolated from the rest of the world; then we shall have a large and energetic population upon our southern border, extending from Lake Superior to Puget Sound ... Now the eye wanders, without a resting place over our unoccupied plains, then it shall be arrested by the happy homes of thousands which dot the horizon.'

The *Nor'Wester* should have looked a little more closely at the immediate future. If it had, it might have seen that in a little over a month William McDougall would be forcibly prevented from entering the country and that within two months the paper itself would be closed down. It would take almost nine months, the creation of a new province, and the presence of a military force before the North West truly began its history as a part of Canada.

By 31 October McDougall was able to pen his 'first report from the North-West Territories' to the Prime Minister. Unfortunately, to McDougall's amazement and chagrin, he had to state that it 'announces insurrection and possible bloodshed.'[3] A group of French half-breeds, headed by John Bruce and Louis Riel, had blocked the road from Pembina to Red River. The barring of McDougall from the territory he was supposed to govern marked the opening of what was to become known as the Red River resistance.

In retrospect the action of the Métis is understandable. Canada, the Hudson's Bay Company, and the British government had all shown a singular lack of concern for the interests of the inhabitants of the North West in arranging the transfer. Even as William McDougall approached the border, no one in Red River had received any official information or statements regarding the terms of the transfer or the nature of the new government.[4] Resentful of the treatment they had received, concerned for the future, and possessing a strong sense of identity, the Métis decided to act. They would force consideration from those who would shape their future.

While there had been no official comment on the transfer or its implications, there had been numerous private opinions expressed. These, however, rather than dispelling public concern, served to increase it. Beneath the confidence and optimism of Canadian expansion lay an implicit threat to the type of society with which Red River was familiar. As early as 14 January 1860 the *Nor'Wester* had warned that after annexation 'the indolent and the careless, like the native tribes of the country will fall back before the march of a superior intelligence.' By 1869 several incidents had brought this type of intolerance clearly before the people of Red River. The attitude of the *Nor'Wester*, the actions of the Canadian road party under John Snow, and then of the surveying parties under J.S. Dennis, had not helped to bring about a peaceful meshing of old and new cultures in Red River. Forceful introduction of new systems and rash remarks with racial and religious overtones 'seemed to confirm a growing suspicion amongst clergy and Métis that English, Protestant, Orange Ontario, not the Dominion of Canada was to annex the North-West and swamp its people.'[5]

If the resistance is understandable in retrospect, there are also many reasons to believe that it should have been foreseen. In the years before the official sale of the territory to Canada, several knowledgeable individuals had warned that the settlement was in a turbulent state.[6] The repeated warnings, however, had no discernible effect on Canadian policy, and when the resistance came the government acted as if it was totally unexpected. In actual fact the government was probably not so surprised as it let on, but the expansionists were. A number of presuppositions and biases in their image of the West had blinded them to the danger signals and made them incapable of comprehending the resistance when it did occur. They clung to their preconceptions and thus insisted on interpreting events in such a way as to make them agree with earlier assumptions. As a result, new and disturbing elements were introduced into the expansionist process.

The expansionists' reaction to the rebellion can only be understood if one basic fact is recognized: they seem to have sincerely believed that the inhabitants of Red River fervently desired annexation. From the beginning Canadian interest in the North West had been predicated on the assumption that the inhabitants of the region were unhappy with government by the Hudson's Bay Company. The petitions presented by Isbister, the Métis hostility to company control expressed in the Sayer trial, and other signs of opposition to company rule, had been factors in the stirring of Canadian interest. In 1857, as the expansionist movement in Canada came into its own, the link between Canadian desires and supposed discontent in Red River had grown even stronger. The assumption developed that there was a community of interest between Canada and Red River. It was truly, if conveniently, believed that, as Isbister said, 'the unanimous desire of the inhabitants of the Hudson's Bay Territories, is to have the entire region annexed to Canada.'[7]

The expansionists were reinforced in this belief by the numerous petitions from Red River. The pattern was set in the summer of 1857 when Roderick Kennedy sent a petition to Canada from Red River with some 574 signatures praying for the development of the region.[8] Between then and 1869 numerous other petitions flowed east to Canadian and British authorities. Resolutions, such as the one of January 1867 asking 'to be united with the Grand Confederation of British North America,' encouraged the idea that the extension of Canada's frontier was a two-way process.[9] Of course, a good many of these petitions were of a questionable nature. Their supporters were but a relatively small segment of Red River's population, and, as with the Kennedy petition of 1857, were often initiated by a small group of Canadian expansionists. Those who received the petitions, however, were not aware of this, and few in Red River who disagreed with the resolutions made any public statement concerning them that reached the East. The origins of the petitions were not apparent to those in Canada and they had neither the reason nor the desire to suspect their authenticity. Canadians eagerly jumped to the conclusion that the settlers of Red River wanted annexation.

Actively encouraging this assumption were those expansionists who, as has been mentioned, migrated west in the wake of the expansionist campaign and settled in Red River. They were to become known both by contemporaries and by historians as the 'Canadian party.' This party's membership was succinctly defined in 1869 as being 'those who favor annexation to Canada.'[10] These individuals, centred around the young Dr Schultz, had been the force behind many of the petitions that had originated in Red River. Having made a material and personal commitment to the development of the North West, it is not surprising that these men attempted to encourage annexation.

This group had an especially strong influence in shaping the Canadian image of Red River because they controlled the only newspaper published in the North West. In 1859 William Buckingham and William Coldwell arrived in Red River from Canada. Both had previously worked for George Brown at the *Globe* and when they moved west took not only their type and their practical experience in journalism but a set of attitudes formed in Canadian expansionist circles. They founded Red River's first newspaper in order to spread further their expansionist views. Over the next several years the editorship of this paper would change hands many times, but it would remain a consistent advocate of the idea of Canadian expansion.

It is questionable whether the *Nor'Wester* did much to encourage support for Canada among the inhabitants of Red River. The *Nor'Wester*, like the Canadian party itself, proved a disruptive force in the already unstable society of Red River in the 1860s. The newspaper's intemperate attacks on the Hudson's Bay Company alienated many. For all its imperfections, people realized, the company was the only barrier to the total collapse of law and order in the region. Further, the Canadian party became a faction in its own right and in many instances found its outlook antagonistic to other groups within the settlement. Ironically, it was a Canadian emigrant, Alexander Begg, who, in a satire on Red River, gave the most cynical description of the *Nor'Wester*. It was, he said, 'the organ of a few ambitious intriguing men in the settlement ... who, while working for a change of government, calculated upon a large benefit to themselves personally, without taking into account the welfare and condition of the settlers at all.'[11] Begg's description gives a picture of the paper as a force acting to alienate rather than promote support for annexation to Canada.

Even if such was indeed the case, the influence of the *Nor'Wester* on Canadian expansion cannot be discounted. As every editor of the paper sensed, as much could be accomplished in the name of Canadian expansion in the East as in the West. The real impact of the paper was not among its readers in Red River but in a constituency thousands of miles away. John Schultz summed up the real purpose of the *Nor'Wester* in a melodramatic editorial that left no doubt as to the importance he attached to its mission: 'I am penetrated, deeply penetrated with the importance which attaches to the integrity, high character, and literary reputation of our paper. By it we are not only influenced here but judged abroad. Far across our broad expanse of plains, dense woods – our hermit lakes – ah, who would not be a hermit amid such lakes to dwell –

83 Conspiracy and rebellion

far across the mighty sea – to where the roar of men goes thickest up, – even there can be seen the lighthouse on our coast – the beacon that lets men know that we are here, a healthy seedling for a brave old tree. And what is it? Why our paper. Nothing but that.'[12]

From Buckingham and Coldwell, through James Ross, Schultz, and W.R. Bown, the editors of the *Nor'Wester* realized that their paper could act as a spur to the eastern expansionists and their style reflected that fact. As the only newspaper in the North West between 1859 and annexation, the *Nor'Wester* had a near monopoly on the interpretation of events. Expansionists in the East, in turn, welcomed the information which the *Nor'Wester* provided as reliable and interesting. The relationship of the Toronto *Globe* to this small paper could almost be described as that of parent to child, which in some ways it was. Editorials and opinions of the *Nor'Wester* were frequently printed in the Toronto paper and often served as the basis for its own editorial stance. Among Canadian expansionists a subscription to the *Nor'Wester* became a badge of membership in the campaign for annexation.[13] At times it even seemed as if the papers real readers were not the inhabitants of Red River at all but the eastern expansionist community. When the *Nor'Wester*, on 5 March 1862, ran a special supplement on the formation of the Scientific Institute in Red River, none of the supplements reached the local populace, for, as the paper unapologetically pointed out, 'the whole impression [has] been mailed to foreigners.'

The *Nor'Wester* and the Canadian party worked consistently to convince their eastern audience not only of the potential of the land but of the urgent desire of the people to cast off the yoke of the Hudson's Bay Company. Attacks on company rule were a consistent part of the paper's policy and, at least by the later 1860s, it repeatedly argued that the best solution was annexation to Canada.[14] Further, many of the petitions that reached the east from Red River had their origins, and much of their support, from among the group surrounding the paper. The petition presented by Sandford Fleming to the Canadian and British governments in 1863 was a case in point. The meetings that led to this petition were headed by none other than the two current editors of the *Nor'Wester*, James Ross and William Coldwell.[15]

Thus, if the Canadian party was less than successful in its attempt to convert the people of Red River to annexation, the same cannot be said for its mission to convince Canadians that the settlement was ready and willing to join their province. Alexander Begg's fictional and malicious character, Cool, summed it up when he said that 'Canada has had an eye to the North West for some years past, and is only too ready and willing to swallow anything that is said against the Honorable Company, whether true or not, and is willing to accept any statement that tends to show us in the light of downtrodden people.'[16] Expansionists had long believed that by bringing British progress and liberties to the North West they were a 'ray of light' in a dark region.[17] They wanted to believe this, of course, and when the *Nor'Wester* confirmed their opinions they found no reason to doubt that it represented the wishes of the people of Red River.

The expansionist belief that there existed a community of interests between themselves and the citizens of Red River made them feel that it was unnecessary to ask the inhabitants of the settlement for their opinion on Canadian annexation. Expansionists were certain that they desired, in the words of Charles Mair, 'the unspeakable blessings of free Government and civilization.'[18] It was symptomatic of the misunderstanding with which Canada approached annexation that when the Toronto *Globe* commented on 2 June 1869 that 'we hope to see a new Upper Canada in the North West Territories,' expansionists probably thought of it as a promise rather than a threat.

A second factor in determining the expansionist response to the rebellion was that it was primarily a movement of the French half-breed population. The warning to McDougall had been in French and the men who had prevented his entry into the North West had been French speaking, Catholic, half-breeds. Throughout the rebellion McDougall and those who shared his outlook saw the Métis as acting alone. It was believed, whether accurately or not, that the Canadians, English half-breeds, and Europeans in the settlement were opposed to Riel; the resistance had its origin and support in only one section of the population of Red River.

Until the rebellion, neither the Canadian government nor the expansionists had paid much attention to the Métis. The Sayer trial and the appearance of French names on various petitions had encouraged the assumption that their opinions were indistinguishable from the other segments of Red River's population. Given the general ignorance in Canada of the political climate of Red River, it is not surprising that the Métis were ignored. With the exception of the Canadian party, the opinion of everyone else was equally ignored. Nevertheless, the failure to recognize this powerful and distinct faction in Red River was a tragic and costly blunder.

Contributing to the lack of understanding of the Métis was the image this group had in the Canadian and European mind. In spite of the fascination travellers had shown for the organization of the buffalo hunt, they had consistently failed to follow the implication of such organization through to its logical conclusion. Those who wrote of the North West did not relate, or did not themselves perceive, the powerful sense of identity and ability to work in concert, which had been a part of the Métis tradition from the troubled days of Cuthbert Grant and Seven Oaks. Rather, the writings in the years before annexation consistently portrayed these people as rather quaint and undisciplined individuals whose habits and character placed them somewhere between the Indian and the European peasant. Thus, when the time came for the transfer of the territory, it was hardly deemed necessary to consult these 'semi-savages and serfs of yesterday,' as William McDougall had described them.[19]

While the Métis had been ignored as a political entity, their character and appearance had been the subject of much description in writings on the West. In Alexander Begg's novel, for instance, the Meredith family, in St Cloud on their way to Red River from Canada, see 'a number of peculiarly dressed men standing in groups upon the platform.' It was the first time they had encountered French half-breeds and Begg makes it a highlight of their journey: 'All of them had sashes round their waists, some of which were of the brightest hues. A few, spotted leggings highly ornamented with bead work. One or two wore long blue coats, with bright buttons, while others were in shirt sleeves; and most of them had moccasins on their feet. As a general thing, they showed great strength and activity of body; their features were chiefly dark, but regular – mild and pleasant in appearance. As a rule they were what could be considered handsome, although many of them gave indisputable signs of Indian origin.'[20] Begg's image of the Métis was typical of his age. In fact, unlike many other interpretations of western land and life, the attitude towards the Métis did not change significantly as a result of the expansionist campaign. From the time of Paul Kane through to the Red River rebellion, the Métis were pictured as a quaint, colourful, and somewhat romantic people.

The romantic and positive aspects of the Métis derived from their connection with the wilderness. They were seen by observers as a people whose way of life reflected the influence of the empty lands of the North West. Functioning within the framework of the environment, they were an adventurous people, admirable for their abilities. They were, said one writer, 'the wildest, gayest, and most reckless set of dare-devils that ever scattered death and destruction among the terrified buffalo.' In their work as voyageurs they were routinely able to handle rivers 'that would seem to deny the utmost powers of men.'[21] Man's survival in such a land demanded hardiness, and in facing the challenges of the wilderness the Métis had become 'a very hardy race of men.'[22] S.J. Dawson was impressed by their physical characteristics and felt that they 'are far superior to either of the races to which they are allied.' This he attributed to 'their leading a life favourable to the development of the human frame.'[23]

As hunters and trappers, as voyageurs and guides, the Métis had no superiors. The wilderness, however, had shaped their character in other, less desirable, ways. Those characteristics which European man viewed as essential to success within a civilized society seemed lamentably absent in the Métis. They exhibited a lack of restraint which made them 'as volatile as children,' with all the immaturity such a comment implied.[24] Lord Milton concurred, noting that while they were exceptionally skilful in the hunt they were also 'hasty, frivolous in the extreme and thoroughly untrustworthy.' Many complained, as had Alexander Ross, that they could not be induced to farm in a serious manner or to undertake regularly any other type of steady employment. Milton commented that 'a casual observer would think that they only played at them.'[25] Wilderness activities such as the hunt continually drew them away from more serious pursuits and this, more than any other factor, separated them in the European mind from 'civilized peoples.' Agriculture was the basis of settled society and the Métis had not accepted that fact. In this area at least, they, like the Indians, had failed to rise above barbarism.

The association of the Métis with the wilderness led observers to emphasize his Indian ancestry. Thomas Simpson, a man who had little liking for the Métis, felt that the 'uncontrolled passions of the Indian blood' determined their character. Paul Kane concluded that it was their Indian ancestry that drew them continually back to the wilderness and 'consequently they make poor farmers, neglecting their land for the much more exciting pleasures of the chase.'[26] John Palliser, who did so much to reshape the image of the North West, did not differ from those who had preceded him in writing of the Métis. 'The Canadian or French half-breed,' he wrote, 'become more and more Indian'; in the contest between the two races from which he has sprung, 'his sympathies are all toward his mother, squaw, and especially his (belle mere) mother in law.'[27]

In this tendency, many writers argued, the Métis was distinct from his English half-breed counterpart. The English half-breeds had established themselves within the society and economy of agricultural Red River. Alexander Ross, himself an English-speaking European who had married an Indian, had emphasized this fact at great length.[28] The many comments by others indicated that Ross's view was not unique. Once again Palliser was simply reiterating the common wisdom when he stated that 'there is a very remarkable difference between the Scotch half-breed and the Canadian or French half-breed; the former is essentially Scotch.'[29] Lord Milton also judged the English half-breed as 'capable of far greater improvement socialy [sic] than their French brethren': 'They are much better at farming being steadier, far more honest and trustworthy and not quite so much given to drunkenness ... They are not superstitious like their other friends who hold many of the Indian superstitions and many more of their own. They are far more virtuous, though the settlement and indeed all the Hudson's Bay posts are famous for immorality.'[30]

This composite portrait of the Métis served to accentuate their Indian background rather that their French language or Catholic religion. Even among French Canadians, where the identity of religion and language produced some sympathy for the Métis, there was a general belief that these people were a poor semi-nomadic group whose only link to civilization was through the church.[31] English Canadians, while they recognized and noted the French language and religion of the Métis, interpreted their character as a product of the wilderness.

The Métis were still distinct from the Indians. It was believed, for instance, that the Métis would have little trouble in adapting to the coming of civilization. The same certainty was not felt about the Indians whom Canadians had watched being continually pushed back by advancing frontiers of settlement. As anthropologist Daniel Wilson speculated as early as 1856, the Indians 'may remain uncivilized and perish before the advance of civilization.' European society and the Indians, he felt, were essentially incompatible. Wilson, however, argued that 'such was not the case with the half-breed.' In the mixed race of the North West would remain traces of Indian blood long after European society had extinguished the last true Indian culture. 'Much, perhaps all of their aptitude for civilization may come by their European heritage of blood, but the Indian element survives even when the predominant Anglo-Saxon vitality has effaced its physical manifestations.'[32]

The survival of the Métis within the European framework was qualified for, as has been seen, it was thought that the character of the Métis limited their capability outside of the wilderness. The assumption was that they would adapt to onrushing civilization but that they would fill the role of a lower socio-economic group. They 'will be very useful here when the country gets filled up,' noted Charles Mair, for they are 'easily dealt with and easily controlled.'[33] The image of the Métis, and their role for the future, thus resembled that of peasant as much as it did Indian. Strong but docile, able to cope with European civilization but unlikely to thrive on it, they were expected to accept passively their new lot. It was a convenient image that allowed English Protestant expansion to dismiss the Métis as political nonentities while retaining them as a pliable pool of labour.

Even the limited economic prospects which the Métis were expected to have in the new Canada were regarded by Canadians as an improvement on the life they had led under the rule of the Hudson's Bay Company. For both economic and political reasons Canadians expected to receive the gratitude of these people in the same way they expected the gratitude of all Red River. At the same time, it was hardly to be expected that the Métis, as either peasant or Indian, would be consulted in such a major transaction as the transfer of the North West. They were at best a 'wretched half-starved people' whose comprehension of such matters would be feeble.[34] Even in the face of armed resistance, William McDougall could not understand that the Canadian image of the Métis was distorted and incomplete: 'The Canadian Government and Canadians have done nothing to injure these people, but everything to benefit them. They helped to save them from starvation, gave them good wages for their labour – very poor labour too, and by competition in trade and farming, enabled them to obtain better food and lower prices than ever before. They cannot specify a single grievance against Canada in the past, and I have not heard of any they apprehend in the future except that they – 3 or 4000 semi-savages and serfs of yesterday – will not be entrusted with the government and the destiny of a third of the American continent!'[35] McDougall's commentary typifies the Canadian expansionist's failure to understand the French half-breed. The Métis were more misunderstood and their sense of identity more underestimated than any other group in the North West; as a result, the expansionists were never able to comprehend the reasons for their decisive and successful resistance.

The first reaction of the expansionists to this seemingly meaningless resistance was one of ridicule and contempt. McDougall initially predicted that the 'insurrection will not last a week.'[36] The *Globe*, on hearing of the activity, scornfully commented on 17 November that 'it is altogether too much of a joke to think of a handful of people barring the way to the onward progress of British institutions and British people on the pretence that the whole wide continent is theirs.' As autumn moved into winter, however, and Louis Riel's provisional government gained rather than lost strength, such offhand comments dwindled in number. Gradually expansionists were forced to take the whole issue more seriously.

In attempting to analyse the situation and thereby reach a possible solution, the expansionists were at a disadvantage. Their image of the Métis and their continued belief that the majority of Red River was in favour of annexation made them unable to accept the arguments of the rebels at face value. Only by portraying the Métis as puppets in the hands of artful manipulators, whose real purpose was not being revealed, were they able to find an explanation satisfactory to their own presuppositions. The *Nor'Wester*, in its last issue on 23 November 1869, maintained that the Métis had been 'imposed upon' and led into rebellion. McDougall concurred and wrote to Macdonald that 'the half-breeds were ignorant and that parties behind were pushing them on.'[37]

89 Conspiracy and rebellion

The *Globe*, on 13 November, referred vaguely but pointedly to 'certain persons in their settlement, who are hostile to the Dominion' as the ones who 'have made it their business to stir up discontent among the most foolish and ignorant of the population.' As the expansionists, and those who agreed with them, developed this conspiratorial interpretation of the rebellion, they began to focus on three individual but interrelated groups as the real instigators of the Métis resistance.

The conspirators that figured most prominently in expansionist thoughts came from south of the border. 'It was well known at Fort Garry,' McDougall commented in the fall of 1869, 'that American citizens had come into the country.' Ostensibly they were traders but that was merely a mask for their plans to 'create disaffection, and if possible, a movement for annexation to the United States.' These men and their allies 'had been actively engaged in circulating stories, absurd as they were unfounded, to alarm the fears of the half-breeds, and excite their hostility against the Canadian government.'[38] It was not surprising that American designs on Red River should be seen as a force behind the Métis resistance. Canadians, and particularly Canadian expansionists, had long worried about American pretensions to the North West. The *Nor'Wester*, throughout its existence, had urged Canada to act quickly before Red River was forced into 'annexation with the United States.'[39] Also, as those interested in the North West were well aware, Canada was not the only home of expansionists. The effective monopoly which the state of Minnesota exerted over trade and transportation with Red River gave its own expansionists some hope that the North West would drift into the American political orbit.

The activities of Americans like Oscar Malmros, the United States consul in Red River, Enos Stutsman, and James Wickes Taylor, gave some reality to the charges of American encouragement of the Red River resistance. What Canadians, and particularly expansionists, failed to realize, however, was that these annexationist forces were auxiliary rather than basic to the Métis resistance. Ironically, they failed to perceive that the Americans who hovered around Riel suffered from the same lack of perspective that they did. As was said of Malmros, he persisted in 'seeing everything and everybody in Rupert's Land through the eyes of a Minnesota expansionist.' As a result, 'his image of Red River and the rebellion was usually shortsighted and often distorted.'[40] The presence of some annexationists in Riel's provisional government and the creation of the *New Nation* gave the American party some influence in Red River in December 1869 and January 1870. Thereafter, however, this influence rapidly declined. Both Canadian and American expansionists failed to understand the purpose of the Métis; the Americans assumed their dislike of

Canada could be transformed into American annexationism, while the Canadians feared such a goal was all too probable.

The second force which expansionists perceived behind the rebellion was the Hudson's Bay Company. When McDougall met resistance his first reaction, besides perplexed surprise, was to warn William McTavish, governor of the Council of Assiniboia, that 'you are the legal ruler of the country, and responsible for the preservation of public peace.'[41] It was, however, not that simple. As McTavish well knew, the Hudson's Bay Company had no force with which to assert its authority. This had been apparent as far back as the Sayer trial and it would have been both impossible and dangerous for the company to have attempted to face such a determined group as the Métis. Canadian expansionists, however, had a different explanation. 'The Hudson's Bay Company are evidently with the rebels,' Schultz wrote in November 1869. 'It is said the rebels will support the Government of the Hudson's Bay Company as it now exists.'[42] McDougall, perhaps because he was an official representative of Canada, was more circumspect that Schultz, but did point to 'the complicity of some members of his [Governor McTavish's] council with the insurrection.'[43]

There were two variations on this theme of company involvement in the rebellion. One charged that the Hudson's Bay Company's inaction during the crisis was the culmination of a deliberate plot on the part of its officials to block annexation. The member of Parliament for Brant North, J.Y. Bown, passing on the opinions of his brother, the deposed editor of the *Nor'Wester*, warned Macdonald that before the rebellion 'certain parties then in the pay of the Company and holding office under it made threats of what they would do.'[44] The second variation had local officials acting on their own in order to improve their benefits under the transfer negotiations. They encouraged the Métis out of spite towards the company only to find later, as Riel's power increased, that they had lost control.[45] Whatever variation was used the basic theme remained the same: the current government of the North West had actively encouraged opposition to the lawful transfer of the territory to Canada.

Though a few individuals in the Company showed some sympathy for the Métis, the charges of expansionists were based on little evidence. The expansionists had proclaimed for so long that the company exerted an oppressive tyranny over the people of Red River that they could not now accept the fact that it was powerless. Those more detached from the expansionist perspective tended to have a more realistic analysis. John A. Macdonald sharply disagreed with McDougall's condemnation of McTavish and at no time did the Canadian government accept the theory that there was any Hudson's Bay Company involvement in the rebellion.

The third conspiratorial force perceived behind the rebellion was to prove the most dangerous in its implications for Canada. The Roman Catholic church, or at least its representatives in Red River, were also accused of aiding the Métis in their resistance. 'The worst feature in this case,' McDougall told Macdonald, 'is the apparent complicity of the priests.' Rather than support constituted authority they had openly supported rebellion. 'It appears certain that at least one of them has openly preached sedition to his flock and has furnished aid and comfort to the parties in arms.'[46] By December 1869 the Toronto *Globe* had singled out Father J.N. Ritchot as the 'head and font of the whole movement by the French half-breeds.' The Catholic clergy joined the rapidly swelling ranks of those who were seen as the instigators of rebellion, having 'worked upon the ignorance and fears of the French speaking portion of the people to such an extent as to lead them to armed resistance.'[47]

The Catholic clergy had long been concerned for the future of the Métis in the event of the opening of the Hudson's Bay territories and had shown little enthusiasm for rapid settlement. Expansionists remembered this when the rebellion broke out and pointed to works by Alexandre Taché, bishop of St Boniface, such as *Esquisse sur le nord-ouest de l' Amérique Septentrionale*, with an accusing finger.[48] The negative and cynical assessment of the North West in this and other works was sufficient proof to the expansionists that the Catholic clergy of Red River was implicated along with the Hudson's Bay Company in the attempt to keep the North West isolated from the rest of the world.

Expansionist perceptions of the relationship between the Métis and the clergy gave them further reason to suspect the priests. The Métis were viewed as a superstitious and ignorant people and, as every good Ontario Protestant knew, the Roman Catholic church exercised totalitarian control over its membership. It thus followed that, had the clergy wished to stop the rebellion, they could have. Further, no individual priest would dare work in opposition to his own church hierarchy and thus the ultimate conclusion had to be, as the *Globe* decided in the spring of 1870, 'that Bishop Taché holds the whole threads of the affair in his hand.'[49] At any time he could have commanded the Métis to cease resistance but he consistently refrained from doing so. This was the best proof of all that the church was in league with the rebels. 'A word from their Bishop,' McDougall charged, 'would have sent them all to their homes and re-established the lawful Government of Assiniboia, but that word was not spoken.'[50] Having been in Rome during much of the resistance, Taché would have had to speak very loudly indeed.

Not all the charges against the clergy were as unfair as those against Taché. J.N. Ritchot and Georges Dugast were sympathetic to the resistance and, on occasion, acted as advisers to the provisional government.[51] Nevertheless, the expansionist charges were distorted and exaggerated by an almost instinctive suspicion of the Roman Catholic church. The expansionist movement and their nationalist allies consisted largely of English-speaking Protestants. French-Canadian Roman Catholics had played little part in the effort to acquire the North West and thus had no spokesmen within the ranks of the movement. Moreover, many expansionist leaders, such as William McDougall, had long viewed the Catholic church as some sort of hostile foe conspiring against Canada. The religious and political controversies of Canadian history had paved the way for the expansionist reaction to the clergy in 1869. Many English Canadians were all too ready to involve the Catholic church in any activity directed against the Canadian nation or British Empire.

Such conspiratorial explanations enabled the expansionists and nationalists to reconcile the rebellion with their belief that the population of Red River favoured entry into Canada. The rebellion was not a popular uprising at all. The majority of the people opposed the resistance, but 'the Yankee, the Company and the Priests had a fair field; whilst the loyal English natives, comprising about two thirds of the population, without arms and ammunition, cursed their own helplessness, and shrunk from the guns of Fort Garry.'[52] The rebellion was the fault neither of Canada nor the Canadian expansionists and was not supported by the people of Red River. Foreign elements had manipulated an ignorant segment of the populace in order to gain their own nefarious ends.

The analysis of the rebellion had obvious implications for the policy to be pursued in bringing it to an end. For John A. Macdonald, who saw expansionist arrogance and Métis suspicions behind the outbreak, the best solution seemed to be to 'behave in as patient and conciliatory a fashion as possible.'[53] The rebellion was essentially a movement that aimed at political guarantees and to Macdonald that implied a political solution. Compromise with the Métis would allay their fears and allow the peaceful acquisition of the territory before American expansionists could exploit the situation. He even suggested bringing Riel into the police force which was planned for the region as 'a most convincing proof that you are not going to leave the half-breeds out of the law.'[54] It was an approach reminiscent of the Hudson's Bay Company's decision to make Cuthbert Grant, the Métis responsible for the Seven Oaks massacre, warden of the plains. Macdonald, however, had a more recent precedent – his successful attempt to bring Nova Scotia's famous anti-confederate, Joseph Howe, around to support of the government through a seat in the cabinet.

In contrast to Macdonald, those who saw the rebellion as a conspiracy felt it was dangerous to assume the matter could be resolved by conciliation. They perceived the ultimate goal of the rebellion to be the disruption of Canada and perhaps the whole British Empire. Attempts to reconcile the Métis were pointless for they were not at the base of the rebellion. The problem went much deeper and had much more important consequences. As George Denison melodramatically stated, 'a half a continent is at stake.'[55] Given the aims of the conspirators and the importance of the result, the only possible response to the rebellion, the expansionist argued, was to use force in return. As the movement was not a popular uprising, the Globe concluded as early as 24 January 1870, the use of troops would not put Canada 'in the unpleasant position of oppressors forcing an unpopular government upon a protesting people.' Rather, the troops would be received by the majority in Red River as 'defenders of British authority and British freedom against those who for merely selfish purposes seek to overthrow both throughout a wide sweep of country.' Military action would simply ensure the wishes of the majority of the people of Red River were carried out while, at the same time, preserving Canada's rightful heritage on the North American continent.

The use of force was encouraged by the tendency to depict events in Red River in terms of the classic struggle for the preservation of empire. Honour and pride became entangled with questions of proper policy. When, for instance, Schultz and Mair returned to Toronto from the North West they were greeted as loyal Britons who had faced hardship and possible death for Canada and Great Britain. Indicative of the widespread support for this view was the presence of some five thousand people at an open air meeting on the steps of city hall. In keeping with the mood of the moment the two expansionists were introduced by the mayor of Toronto in sentences replete with the rhetoric of imperial honour and power: 'He felt confident that the same power which had been able to make itself felt at Lucknow and Delhi would be sufficient to put down that miserable creature (cheers) who attempts to usurp authority at Fort Garry and establish again the supremacy and glory of the British flag.'[56] The rhetoric prevalent in Ontario by the spring of 1870 portrayed the rebellion as a test of nationalism and depicted the situation as a microcosm of the great struggle waged by the British Empire for survival in the face of hostile and malignant forces. The Métis and those behind them symbolized all those enemies that threatened Canada's efforts to survive and expand in North America. The expansionist and the nationalist grew even more closely together.

The Red River rebellion altered the relationship between the expansionist movement and Canada as a whole. Expansionists had previously felt, with some validity, that they were but the vanguard of a general consensus of Canadian opinion on the question of the North West. Now, however, widely differing interpretations of the rebellion had led to equally divergent proposals for bringing it to an end. Further, many government officials blamed leading expansionists – William McDougall, Charles Mair, John Schultz – for their provocative actions.[57] In turn, the expansionists strongly criticized Macdonald's abandonment of McDougall and refusal to accept the transfer of the territory until peace was restored.[58] In this climate of bitterness and mutual recrimination expansionists began to think of themselves and their supporters as a minority within the nation. Only in Ontario did there seem to be enough national patriotism to create a forceful demand for the suppression of the rebellion. Other parts of the Dominion, indeed the government itself, delayed and hesitated, while Canada's future remained in jeopardy.

As this mood took hold, enemies of the country began to be found not only on the banks of the Red but in Canada itself, often in the very offices of the government. Joseph Howe, for instance, was suspected of secretly supporting the rebellion. He had visited the settlement shortly before the outbreak of violence and, so it was charged, had propagated his anti-confederation views throughout the colony; the results of his work were shown a few days later when McDougall was forbidden entry. McDougall himself, who felt he had been betrayed by the Secretary of State for the Provinces, was especially bitter in his denunciations of Howe.[59]

Even more serious were the charges that began to circulate in the spring of 1870. In the wake of the execution of Thomas Scott by Riel the Canadian government reluctantly decided that a military expedition to the North West was necessary. From the expansionist perspective such an expedition was of the utmost importance; they had called for a show of force from the beginning and Scott's death added a new emotionalism to these demands. Scott had been martyred for his loyalty, and 'humble though his position was – yet he was a Canadian; his mental gifts may have been few – yet he died for us.'[60] As preparations were undertaken for the expedition, however, many individuals began to suspect that there was an element in the government working to hamper it. Singled out were prominent French-Canadian politicians, including the Minister of Militia, George-Etienne Cartier. Those who supported the use of force saw in Cartier and his allies a 'party which opposed in every possible manner the departure of the expedition.'[61]

Complicating matters was an increasing public opposition in French Canada to use of such force. As attitudes grew increasingly militant in Ontario in the wake of Scott's death, many French Canadians became wary of the motivation that lay behind such vehemence. Naturally sensitive to the arrogance and intolerance often exhibited by English-Canadian Protestantism, they had little difficulty in accepting the Métis rationale for the rebellion at face value. French Canadians needed no devious conspiracy theories to explain the Métis position: they were, with good reason, simply seeking guarantees that their religious and language rights would be protected under the new order. A military expedition seemed both unnecessary and oppressive and many French Canadians protested against the decision to send one.

While it was natural that French Canada protested against the use of force, it was also, to the expansionists and a good many other English Canadians, treasonable. More and more the wrath of Ontario public opinion turned its attention from foreign agents to those within Canada who would oppose their militant brand of expansion. French-Canadian opposition to the expedition, the *Globe* warned on 2 May 1870, contained within it an ominous principle: 'If British troops cannot go on British territory wherever the authorities desire to send them without being denounced as butchers and filibusterers by fellow subjects, things must be in a poor way. If that can't be done in Red River, it can't in Quebec, and if the latter doctrine is held, by all means let it be advanced, but it is just as well to have it understood that a good many pounds will be spent, and a good many lives lost before it will be acquiesced in.' Howe and others may have, for personal reasons, worked to thwart the interests of Canada. In the growing hostility of French Canada, however, expansionists perceived a movement of much larger proportions and much greater significance.

The racial and religious implications of the Red River rebellion had never been far below the surface. The priests, accused of participation in the insurrection, had brought the issue of the Catholic religion into the controversy from the beginning. The Métis had often been rather loosely referred to as the 'French party' and that term, in turn, used as a description of the rebellious elements in the settlement.[62] On the other hand, expansionists had tried to play down the popular support for the rebellion by portraying the rebels as a small segment of even the French half-breeds. John Schultz, for instance, made a point at the public rally in Toronto of distinguishing between the rebels and the loyal French half-breed elements in Red River.[63] Also, as will be remembered, William McDougall had initially seen the clerical involvement in the rebellion as a result of the fact that most of them were foreign-born.[64] Thus, if religious and racial overtones were present throughout the rebellion, they were muted.

The debate over the militiary expedition brought these overtones to the surface. The process was a dialectic one. French Canada objected to Ontario demands for the use of force against a people which it felt was, whether in a correct manner or not, simply trying to protect itself; Ontario expansionists, seeing the complaints of the Métis as a subterfuge for more malignant ends, took the French-Canadian opposition to the rebellion as a sign of disloyalty. The muted racial friction grew in strength and increased until it became a dominant ingredient in Canadian politics.

By July 1870 it was being argued not only that French Canada opposed the expedition but also that unless 'loyalists' acted quickly the force would never reach Red River. Canada First members, Denison and Haliburton, saw a devious plot on the part of Cartier and his cohorts to give Riel an amnesty and recall the force before it reached Red River. Warning was given by these 'loyalists' that any such attempt would meet massive resistance from Toronto, and that Cartier and Taché, scheduled to arrive in Toronto, would be confronted by hostile crowds. Shortly afterwards another huge rally was called and there the honour of the Empire and the suppression of rebellion were again demanded. 'Men of Ontario! Shall Scott's blood cry in vain for vengeance?'[65] Once again the cry of treason had been raised, but in this case the traitors were identified as French-Canadian cabinet members rather than the rebels themselves.

The slightly ludicrous hysterics of Denison and Haliburton indicate the change that had taken place in the analysis of the rebellion by the summer of 1870. Between March, when news of Scott's death first created widespread support for the use of force, and July, the focus in the conspiratorial analysis of the rebellion shifted. Americans and Hudson's Bay Company officials remained under suspicion, but it was the role of the priests that was assuming the greatest significance. Their role in the rebellion became much clearer once it was understood that French Canada was also involved. The two forces, linked through their common language and religion, were in league. Their joint goal was, as McDougall warned his constituents after his return to Canada, to have 'the North-West made into a French Catholic Colony, with special restrictions on all their inhabitants.'[66] The Toronto *Globe* on 14 April, replying angrily to criticism of Ontario's militancy in the Quebec press, charged that 'if anyone is fanatical in the matter, it is certainly not the people of Upper Canada, who desire merely to see law and order restored in the Territory.' Rather, 'the fanatics are the French Canadians, who are striving to obtain for themselves peculiar and exclusive privileges.'

In a complex psychological process brought on by French-Canadian opposition to Ontario militancy, the conspiratorial figures of Red River were transferred from the North West to Canada. It was the story of the established church, clergy reserves, and anti-democratic privileges for the minority all over again. French Canada had allied itself with the priests of Red River in order to prevent the natural development of British civilization and to preserve autocratic rule. For, the expansionists argued, as surely as the Hudson's

Bay Company, rule by the Catholic church would 'lock up the splendid country under a more odious tyranny than that which has long ruled it.'[67]

These fears were reinforced when the government introduced the Manitoba Act to Parliament on 2 May 1870. When the bill was presented to the House of Commons, Macdonald accompanied it with a map showing the proposed boundaries of the new miniature province of Manitoba. McDougall, on looking at this map, noticed 'that an important Canadian settlement containing some five hundred families, namely: Portage-la-Prairie, had been left beyond the limits of the Province.' This was suspicious to McDougall and proved to his satisfaction the degree of French-Canadian and priestly influence in the counsels of government. Over shouts of opposition from French-Canadian members, he went on to interpret this omission of a Protestant stronghold as a direct extension of the conspiracy: 'It is just as well that there should be a little plain speaking on this point at an early day. It was known by the Government and the country that the rebellion in the North West originated with the Roman Catholic priesthood ... The priesthood desired to secure certain advantages for themselves, their Church or their people. And they advised the people to take the course they did.'[68]

The government hastily altered the bill to include Portage la Prairie, but this did not end the controversy. Other clauses, especially those which set aside blocks of land for the Métis, were looked upon as part of the same plan to give the French language and Catholic religion privileged places in Manitoba. 'The setting apart of lands for one part of the people,' the *Globe* commented on 23 April, 'was not to be thought of.' Captain G.L. Huyshe, a member of the Red River expedition, envisaged dire consequences in such a policy for 'it is probable that a large portion of it will eventually fall into the hands of the Roman Catholic church'; this would give the church in Manitoba 'an undue preponderance of wealth and power.'[69] To many, the overall implications of the Manitoba Act were clear enough: its designs threatened by Colonel G.J. Wolseley's advancing troops, French Canada had attempted one final time to gain what it had sought from the beginning. The Manitoba Act was nothing more than 'a Bill to establish a French half-breed and foreign ecclesiastical supremacy in Manitoba.'[70]

Throughout the expansionists' shifting of attention from conspirators in Red River to those in Ottawa and Quebec, one point remained constant: the Métis continued to be seen as dupes being used by others for their own ends. Rather than the servants of the Hudson's Bay Company or Americans, however, they were seen as the instruments of French-Canadian and Catholic imperialism. This fact in no way changed the fears of the expansionists and nationalists. In its social outlook, exclusiveness, and tendency towards a state church, French Canada appeared to possess the same unprogressive tendencies as did the Hudson's Bay Company. Most importantly, both the company and French Canada were threats to the triumph of the sort of British Protestant commercial society which expansionists desired to see established in the North West.

Two implications flowed from this distrust of French Canada. First, the French Catholic nature of the Métis was emphasized. Previously, as has been mentioned, the Métis' ties to the wilderness were seen as the dominant factors in shaping their character. In the wake of the rebellion, or, more accurately, in the wake of the controversy surrounding the rebellion, this changed. As agents, whether wittingly or unwittingly, of French Canada and the Catholic church, the Métis' connection with French Canada began to be stressed. This shift was apparent in both French and English Canada. The continual references by the Ontario press to the 'French party' had led French Canadians to identify with the Métis to an extent unknown previously.[71] The year 1870 did not mark a complete reversal of French Canada's position but, rather, began a trend which was increasingly to identify the cause of the Métis and their leader, Louis Riel, with the cause of French-Canadian rights.

The second implication for the expansionists was that only in Ontario had there been strong support for annexation of the North West and forceful suppression of the rebellion. From this it followed that only Ontario possessed the true spirit of Canadian nationalism and thus sensed the importance of the North West. If necessary, that province would have to arrogate to itself the development of the North West in the name of Canada in the same way that Canada had claimed it in the name of the Empire. It was Ontario, as Schultz pointed out, from which 'this movement to add Red River to the Dominion commenced; it was in Ontario this expression of indignation was expressed.' It was therefore, he concluded, 'to Ontario the Territory properly belonged.'[72] The resistance made explicit what had been implicit all along – the regional nature of Canadian expansionism.

While the arrival of the expeditionary force in Red River in August 1870 ended the actual resistance, its legacy was to be felt for many years to come. The soldiers of that force and those immigrants who followed them brought to Manitoba a set of suspicions that continually threatened to destroy the racial and religious balance the Canadian government had recognized in Manitoba.[73] Contributing to this tension was the tendency of the Canadian volunteers stationed in Winnipeg to assume the right to mete out justice to those associated with the Riel. As one immigrant of those years later recalled, 'during the fall and early winter of 1870 we could always rely upon several exciting fights between the soldiers and the half-breeds any afternoon after three o'clock, by which time the soldiers not on duty were at liberty to come down town.'[74] The tragic climax of such vigilante action occurred when Elzéar Goulet, a half-breed and former supporter of Riel, drowned in the Red while attempting to flee pursuing militiamen. Thereafter violence declined but broke out sporadically as religious and racial frictions prompted individuals to fight again the resistance of 1870.

Such individual violence was only a symptom of a general suspicion that French-Canadian attempts to turn Manitoba into a Catholic province had not ended with the collapse of the resistance. Expansionists and nationalists continued to watch for signs of government or individual activity against English Canadians in Manitoba. Typical was George Denison's warning to Schultz that the Ontario troops would be sent back east on some pretext rather than be allowed to disband in Manitoba and thus contribute to the permanent English population there.[75] R.G. Haliburton, not to be outdone, wrote Macdonald angrily when he heard that a French Canadian was to be appointed to the bench in Manitoba. Such an appointment, he argued, would simply aid Quebec in its attempts 'at making Manitoba a New Quebec with French laws.'[76] Suspicions of racial favouritism in Manitoba, distrust of the federal government, and the question of amnesty for Riel, perpetuated and deepened that attitude created by the events of 1869-70.

Many saw in such attitudes an unhealthy sectionalism and bigotry which threatened from the outset to pervert the social and political character of the developing Canadian West and eventually the whole nation. As one anonymous writer commented, the 'people who strongly condemn the insurrection of the Half-breeds of Red River have succeeded in justifying it.'[77] There was a fair bit of truth in this statement. The intolerance of Ontario immigrants in the West and the bigotry against the Métis revealed why Riel had felt it necessary to gain some guarantees for his people.

Those who were so determined to read the Métis out of Manitoba's future held a radically different perspective. The Red River resistance, they felt, had proven that various elements in Canada were willing to sacrifice or distort the development of the West for their own selfish ends. The North West was Canada's guarantee of future greatness and such policies thus became dangerous to the very survival of the nation itself. These people could not be trusted with control of such a valuable heritage; in the province of Manitoba was being determined the future not only of that province, important in itself, but the future of the whole of the North West and, ultimately, of Canada. Eastern politics and prejudices had not only been taken west but found in the West an ultimate test of the strength of the various factions: 'Manitoba has been to us on a small scale what Kansas was to the United States. It has been the battle-ground for our British and French elements with their respective religions, as Kansas was the battle-ground for Free Labour and Slavery. Ontario has played a part in contests there analogous to New England, Quebec to that of the southern States. The late government ... was, with respect to the Riel affair, in the position of an American Government, resting at once on Massachusetts and South Carolina, would have been with respect to Kansas.'[78]

The violence and racial strife which marked Manitoba's entry into the Dominion gradually subsided. The settlement of the question of amnesty for Riel, whether to anyone's satisfaction or not, removed the issue from the daily press. In the same period Manitoba saw the establishment of political and legal institutions under the governorship of Adams Archibald and his successor, Alexander Morris. Most importantly, the continuing inflow of population from Ontario made the English-Canadian element dominant in Manitoba and thus eased fears of a French-Canadian plot on the North West.[79] It was perhaps symbolic of the triumph of the Canadian party in old Red River that as early as 1872 Alexander Morris recommended that John Schultz, implacable enemy of the Métis and the old order, should be appointed a member of the North West Council.[80]

The Red River resistance had brought to the fore a new element in the expansionist campaign for progress and civilization – a racial and social expansionism based on British Protestantism. Thus, while the new province of Manitoba was able to incorporate many elements of the old Red River colony into the social order of the 1870s, the French half-breeds were not among them. In increasing numbers the Métis sought refuge both from the civilization of Red River and the intolerance of its new inhabitants. This had a double significance: first, if, as Daniel Wilson thought, the Métis represented the link between civilization and wilderness, then the failure of Manitoba to make room for them indicated that the province was not going to be a link between civilization and the old order; second, it revealed the expansionist insistence on uni-racial society. Moving to the still empty banks of the North Saskatchewan, the Métis remained a separate and distinct representative of the old order. Alexander Morris's warning to Macdonald in 1873, that 'the Saskatchewan will require prompt attention, or we will have the same game over again there,'[81] went unheeded in the same way as had the warnings of the 1860s.

5
The geography of empire: the quest for settlers in the 1870s

The entry of the expeditionary force into Fort Garry in August 1870 made Canada's annexation of the North West a reality. Canada now possessed the vast hinterland which it had sought for so long. In the preceding years the stereotype of the region as a wasteland had been replaced by an image of a fertile and empty land covering thousands of square miles. The problem for Canada after 1870 was to convert the visions of earlier years into concrete and detailed policies and to make the region a centre of growth and population.

The analysis of the task before Canada was affected by two factors, both products of the expansionist campaign. First, over time the expansionists had attached ever-increasing importance to the opening of the West; in many minds, by 1870, Canada's future as a nation seemed to rest on the development of the region. This new transcontinental Canada was thought capable of achieving national and even imperial stature, and the centre of this empire would be the newly annexed West. 'These North West Territories,' the *Nor'Wester* wrote on 24 August 1869, 'constitute the body of the Dominion and the outlying provinces are but the acorns or branches.' It was a pointed comment for, the newspaper concluded, 'as long as the body is undeveloped we cannot reasonably expect that the branches will thrive.' The expansionist campaign had been so successful that it encouraged the belief that the rapid development of the North West must be the first priority of national development. The idea of a hinterland to be tapped by old Canada had been replaced by the notion of the West as a potential empire; Canada's growth seemed dependent on the rate at which that territory was developed.

The expansionist rhetoric had also introduced a second and somewhat paradoxical factor into the Canadian approach to the West. The writings of nearly a generation had exalted the whole process of western expansion to an almost mythical plane. The talk of expanding civilizations and settlement had developed, in Canada as in the United States, overtones of a national manifest destiny and providential design. Expansion was an irresistible force over which man had little control. 'The impulse of emigration to the westward cannot be arrested,' Allan Macdonell had written. The best that man could do was to take a position in accord with this impulse, for if he did not he would certainly be swept aside. 'Circumstances may indeed retard its course but it cannot prevent it from ultimately fulfilling the destiny which is reserved for us. No power on earth can close upon the immigrant that fertile wilderness which offers resources to all industry – an oasis and refuge from all want.'[1]

The settlement of a region as vast as the North West was a complex and challenging process, comparable in magnitude to the expansion of the United States across the continent. The expansionist campaign, however, had both compressed the time frame expected for its accomplishment and minimized the difficulties involved. Following the Palliser and Hind expeditions, expansionists insisted that the removal of Hudson's Bay Company control over the region would result in almost immediate and automatic development. As annexation approached, the prediction by Charles Mair that the North West 'is destined, before ten years, to contain a larger population than Canada,' was not an isolated one.[2] Natural providence, manifest destiny, and the hopes of expansionists all pointed to the rapid settlement of the region. Many concluded, as did British Columbian Gilbert Malcolm Sproat, that 'population ... must naturally concentrate in Central Canada, even without great effort to make it do so.'[3]

These factors tended from the outset to oversimplify the Canadian approach to the settlement of the North West. On the one hand, the importance attached to the region led to an insistence that it be rapidly developed; on the other, the whole process of westward expansion and settlement was seen as an inevitable fact of history. As a result, few questioned whether rapid settlement could be made to work for the benefit of both the nation and the settler. It was assumed both that the frontier could be readily incorporated into the rest of the nation and that the man who went to that frontier would have little problem earning a livelihood. The very real difficulties that were involved in opening and developing such a vast territory would dawn only slowly on those Canadians who accepted the idea of western expansion. The disillusionment which their understanding brought would be accentuated by the fact that it had been so long delayed.

The United States was the natural example for Canadians when they talked of the wondrous impact that immigration could have. Now that Canada possessed the North West, it hoped to recreate the American experience of rising to the status of a great power through rapid immigration and an expanding frontier. The recent past of the United States became a guide for Canadian expectations of the future: 'All that Illinois, Wisconsin, Iowa, Nebraska, Kansas, and Minnesota are now combined, our own North-West may be within the lifetime of many amongst us.'[4] By 1870 Canadians had convinced themselves that the envied growth of the United States was the result of neither wise government policy nor the attractiveness of American political institutions; rather, they felt it was, as immigration agent and future Minister of the Interior, Thomas White, put it, the result of 'that inevitable hankering after western homes.'[5] Now, however, that attraction to the west could be turned to Canada's advantage. Thomas Spence, clerk of the Legislative Assembly of Manitoba, summed up expansionist hopes when he stated that 'the grooves worn smooth by the millions tramping westwards will hereafter change in the direction of Canada's boundless prairie lands.'[6]

The American process of expansion had occurred over half a century as internal migration and large-scale immigration pushed the frontiers of settlement westward. This process, while an essential part of the American experience, was not the result of a deliberate policy; there were no timetables and repeatedly the nation found that it had underestimated the rate of western expansion. Canada, however, had acquired its great western frontier in one giant stride. The suddenness of Canadian expansion and the insistence that it be developed rapidly made it almost as if the nation wished to make up for lost time. As the Presbyterian minister, George Grant, commented while travelling through the North West, 'we must do, in one or two years, what had been done in the United States in fifty.'[7]

If Canada was less patient than the United States, it was also more confident than its neighbour had been through much of its history, of the desirability of rapid expansion. In the United States the passage of a liberal land law for the frontier had been preceded by years of debate as to the implications of such rapid settlement. Not until 1862, with the southern secession having removed some of the strongest opponents of expansion, was a liberal homestead law passed. Canadian policy-makers seem to have had no such qualms about the rapid development of the West, and readily accepted suggestions such as the one by William J. Patterson that Canada should imitate 'in its details, as far as may be desirable, the policy of the United States.'[8] Practically without discussion, Canada adopted a set of homestead laws comparable to the ones which had proved so contentious in the United States.[9]

Other, less concrete, differences existed between the Canadian and American approaches to the settlement of the frontier. In Canada, for instance, the concept of 'seeding' the North West with reliable men was a recurring theme in the rhetoric of Canadian expansion. When the captain of a militia company in Ontario proposed that he and five hundred of his men emigrate to the North West in return for a grant of land, John A. Macdonald commented enthusiastically to McDougall that 'these are the kind of men you want.'[10] Similarly, when Captain William Butler proposed the establishment of a police force in the North West, he pointed out that an additional benefit could be derived from the formation of the force through incentives to encourage these men to remain in the West at the expiration of their enlistment 'to become military settlers.'[11] The plan was as old as 1668, when the Carignan-Salières Regiment had been disbanded in New France.

Also characteristic of Canada's policy in this period was the encouragement given to whole communities who might be tempted to settle in the North West. As early as 1863 Sandford Fleming had proposed support for a group of Norwegians who were thinking of moving to the region.[12] Nothing came of that plan, but after annexation the encouragement of the Canadian government towards the Mennonites in 1873 and to the Icelanders a short time later brought more concrete results. The expansionist movement had begun by requesting that the immigrant's right to settle in the North West be guaranteed. By 1870 that request had been transformed into an urgent demand that the region not only be settled but that the government become actively involved in promoting that settlement.

The rapid development of the North West would be achieved only if large numbers of individuals could be prompted to settle in this vast region which, for the most part, remained in its natural wilderness state. Immigrants had to be convinced of the advantages of the North West in the 1870s in the same way that Canadians had had to be convinced of the value of the region in a more general way in the preceding decades. For this reason, the promotion of immigration became a central theme of expansionist rhetoric in the 1870s. Those who urged rapid development turned their efforts from attacks on the Hudson's Bay Company to bringing news of the North West to anyone in Canada, Europe, or the United States who would listen. The career of Thomas Spence is a case in point. Spence, a Scottish emigrant to Canada, had moved to Red River in 1866. He became known in expansionist circles in the later 1860s for his efforts to set up an independent government of Portage la Prairie in defiance of the Hudson's Bay Company. His project quickly collapsed when the British government pointed out the illegality of the move, but the attempt had shown Spence's good intentions among expansionists.[13] In the 1870s, however, Spence's involvement in the North West was on a quite different level. While clerk of the Legislative Assembly of Manitoba, he spent much of his time writing immigration pamphlets that were both readable and enthusiastic. The agitator of the 1860s became the immigration promoter of the 1870s.

Over the decade Spence and numerous others produced dozens of works aimed at the potential immigrant. The number of titles, however, were not nearly so revealing as the circulation that some of these works were able to obtain. The well-known writers of Canada in the decade were not those struggling authors of serious literary works who managed to publish but rather the popularizers of the North West. The names of Thomas Spence and Acton Burrows were probably more widely known in Europe than were those of Charles G.D. Roberts or Charles Mair. *Our Great West* by Thomas White, for instance, had fifty thousand copies printed and distributed by the Canadian government. Even this respectable figure was dwarfed by the circulation of the official government immigration pamphlet, *Information for Intending Emigrants*, which, in its various forms and editions, had more than a million copies in circulation as early as 1873![14]

While the emphasis on the promotion of immigration was relatively new to Canadian expansionism, some of the techniques employed were as old as the practice of salesmanship. The pamphlets always began with the strongest promises of realism and then continued with descriptions of prosperous and contented farmers living amidst slightly unreal fields of golden grain. As was perhaps inevitable, the attempt to sell the North West led to an often one-sided and over-enthusiastic picture of the region. In the extreme this bordered on outright fraud. One particular map of the North West, for instance, seems to have been especially popular in immigration literature. This map, which first appeared in 1874, optimistically showed a Canadian Pacific railway running the breadth of the land; in contrast, it carefully differentiated between those railroads in the United States that were complete and those that were only 'projected.'[15] But then, perhaps, the pamphleteer should not be faulted for using the map so readily: it was, after all, an official publication of the Canadian government, which itself distributed five hundred thousand copies.[16] In another and earlier instance railway promoter Alfred Waddington carefully marked down the numerous and presumably hostile Indian tribes in the United States for the benefit of the immigrant; Canada, however, at least to judge by Waddington, had only one tribe of Indians – the Blackfoot – and they were thoughtful enough to reside exclusively within the confines of Palliser's triangle.[17]

Such obvious misrepresentation was not really all that common in the first decade after annexation. More typical were those instances where descriptions of the West simply reflected the enthusiasm of the writer. The Canadian expansionists had spent a great deal of time convincing Canadians that the North West was not a barren desert and it is almost as if the writers of the 1870s still marvelled at the new-found resources of the region. Each man who aspired to be considered an expert on the North West had to demonstrate his own knowledge of the quality and variety of attractions which the region had to offer.

On some occasions this enthusiasm would become almost ludicrous. In 1877, for instance, Spence was called to testify before the House Committee on Immigration and Colonization. The supposed purpose was to acquire information but, as there were members on the committee who felt themselves every bit as well versed as Spence, the sitting resembled a joint affirmation of faith in the new land rather than a serious inquiry. The chairman was James Trow, member of Parliament for the expansionist constituency of Perth South. Trow had made a pilgrimage west some years earlier and had written of his experiences. Another member of the committee, A.G.B. Bannatyne, had been a merchant in Red River before annexation and thus could also claim considerable knowledge of the North West. When Trow asked Spence if he thought the climate was healthy, the resultant exchange indicates that the question was purely for the record:

Chairman: 'You consider it a very healthy country?'
Witness: 'Very much so.'
Chairman: 'I have seen some very old stones in grave yards there, 72 and 78 quite often.'
Bannatyne: 'And 99.'
Chairman: 'Yes, and 102 years.'
Witness: 'Hardly a year passes but two or three of those who die are 100 years old.'

Unfortunately, before the committee could confer immortality on the healthy citizens of the North West, a more cynical member interjected with the comment that such longevity was 'partly accounted for by the fact that none but those who have good constitutions go there.'[18]

Enthusiasm rather than fraud typified the writings on the North West in the 1870s. Canadians, slightly startled by the tremendous growth of their nation, were not at all reticent to talk of the wonders of the new transcontinental Dominion. The North West seemed to offer Canada great opportunities, and expansionists confidently expected that 'a tide of emigration will flow through Canada as fast as a convenient channel can be opened for it.'[19]

Canada's hopes of emulating the experience of the United States were based on the assessment of the resources of the North West that had formed during the expansionist campaign. This assessment was the product not only of the scientific expeditions that had gone west but also of fifteen years of expansionist rhetoric. Over the preceding years the image of the North West had changed from that of howling wilderness to fertile garden. The 1870s saw a continuation of this type of imagery and in this sense there was no sharp break in the image of the West as a result of annexation. Myths of an agrarian empire flourished in the literature of the 1870s as they did in that of the 1860s.

In two ways, however, annexation did alter the nature of expansionism and the image of the North West. In the first place, actual possession significantly accentuated the relationship between national and western growth; indeed, nationalism and expansionism became so closely entwined that many individuals saw them as identical. This same factor also made the expansionist movement more widespread and more diffuse. Canada was committed to development of the North West and no one, not even Alexander Mackenzie's cautious cabinet minister, Edward Blake, denied that this development should be pursued. After the transfer the term 'expansionist' has to be defined on the basis of commitment to the policy of development rather than the principle behind it. The line between Blake and someone like Mair was defined by the rate with which it was thought development should proceed.

Annexation also brought a new sense of rivalry with the American frontier. Canada not only wanted to emulate the United States but now had to compete directly with it for immigrants. British railway promoter, Edward Watkin, summed it up in rather cynical fashion when he commented that Canada was a nation 'barely feathered, which seeks already to fly in rivalry with the eagle.'[20] Only by convincing potential immigrants that Canada had more to offer could it be hoped that the American experience would be equalled. This rivalry forced Canadians to upgrade their own assessment and to denigrate the resources of their neighbours. The image of the North West always had to meet the standard set by the image of the American West.

The initial point of comparison between Canada and the United States was sheer size. Until recently, as railway surveyor, Charles Horetzky, pointed out, 'Canada represented but an insignificant portion of the North American continent.'[21] Confederation and annexation changed all of this, however, and the very size of the Dominion of Canada quickly became an integral part of the nation's self-image:

O'er our rich acres of vast prairie,
Our hopes as boundless, and our souls as free,
Far as the heart can wish, the fancy roam,
Survey our empire, and behold our home.[22]

Long before the North West actually contributed to national strength, it contributed to national self-esteem. The feeling of confinement that had characterized the writings of the 1850s disappeared with the annexation of the West. 'Our country,' wrote H.B. Gates in 1872, 'has expanded into a broad empire.'[23] Writers, in Gates's time and since, have never tired of pointing out that Canada, whatever else it might be, is one of the earth's largest nations. And perhaps more relevant to Canadian aspirations, annexation made it the largest nation in North America. As one government publication exclaimed, 'it occupies a greater area than the United States of America.'[24]

While size claimed its own place in the lexicon of Canadian nationalism, the area of the country was really pertinent as a measurement of potential. After 1870 Canada was ready to claim that it matched the United States not only in size but in resources. In Manitoba alone nearly nine million acres of land were available for settlement, and, it was pointed out, Manitoba was 'comparatively a speck on the map of the vast territory out of which it has been formed.'[25] The vastness of the empty territory implied a great potential for the future. Size could be equated to potential because of the vast resources which were thought to exist in the North West. Minerals, commerce, manufacturing, and even the fur trade were still a part of the vision of the future. By the 1870s, however, these were seen only as secondary resources; the real hopes for the North West had come to rest pretty much exclusively on the agricultural empire which Canadians envisaged. The doubts of earlier years had vanished and expansionists confidently asserted that the West had been designed by a wise providence to supply the wants of man. The Red River Valley, pictured in different times as a marginal agricultural region amidst a vast desert, now became one of the best farming regions in the world, with soil 'exceeded by none and only equalled by the alluvial delta of the Nile.'[26] The land in Red River and elsewhere in the fertile belt was so rich, government pamphlets proclaimed, that fertilizer was not necessary. It was 'inexhaustible.'[27] George Grant found it so rich that the only equivalent in the East was the special soil used in garden pots; it was a soil, he concluded, 'capable of raising anything.' His only criticism was that it was too rich, leaving the farmer with nothing to do with his manure except dump it in the nearest river.[28]

George Bryce, a Presbyterian minister newly settled in Winnipeg, pointed out that such soil gave Canadians reason to expect much from the West. 'In Canadian eyes the great recommendation of any soil is its capability to produce marketable grains.' In these terms there was much to recommend the West, for the crops produced there were enormous by eastern standards. James Trow gave perhaps the best reason for the continued interest of Lanark in the North West when he commented of Manitoba that 'half a crop is

109 The geography of empire

much better here than what we considered a good crop in Lanark, Ontario.' The productivity of the West was reflected not only in the yield but in the size of the plants. Charles Horetzky noted that 'the fertility of the soil is so great in certain localities that beets, carrots, and other vegetables grow to an enormous size.'[29] The earth itself was the greatest asset of the North West, for it was a soil that 'drops fatness and hoards up wealth.'[30]

The fertility of the soil was matched by a beneficent climate. The taming of the climate had been an important part of the transfer of the image of the North West from wilderness to potential garden. Most importantly, it was repeatedly emphasized, the northerly position of the North West did not imply an arctic climate. The writings of Blodgett, Hind, and Palliser were reprinted with frequency, edited slightly to meet the more enthusiastic demands of the 1870s. Charles Mair, for instance, writing from Portage la Prairie in 1875, reiterated Blodgett's famous dictum that 'It is an agreeable hyperbole to say that a degree west is equivalent to a degree south.' It might be hyperbole in some cases, but, said Mair, 'as far as the north-west climate is concerned, there is not only an atom of truth in the saying, but, in some respects, it falls short of the truth.'[31] The North West, the immigrant was assured, held no terrors for the prospective farmer because of its northerly position. It was commonly asserted as proof of this that animals could be left out to graze in the dead of winter.[32]

Appropriate temperatures were not all that was required of a climate if it was to be suitable for agriculture. The other major necessity was a sufficient rainfall. It was known that the North West had less rainfall than Ontario and pictures of arid plains had been passed down through the 1850s and 1860s, in spite of the expansionist campaign, thus making aridity a more difficult image to dispel than that of harsh temperatures. The admission that there was, in Palliser's triangle, a section too dry for cultivation further tended to cloud the image of the North West as an agricultural Eden. Conscious of this fact, those who urged the immigrant to go west emphasized the retentive qualities of the soil, the regularity of rains, and the advantages of the numerous rivers flowing through the North West. Charles Mair even added dew to those natural resources working actively on behalf of the farmer: 'The average rainfall is much less in the Fertile Belt than in eastern Canada, the showers being frequent but not abundant. Nightly, however, during the dryest season of the summer, the sprouting grain is literally drenched with dew, and the spongy earth takes in sufficient moisture to maintain its powers of reproduction and stimulation to the utmost.'[33] The prospective settler was thus assured that he had no reason to be concerned with lack of rain. Nevertheless, the writers of the 1870s were less convinced and less convincing in their dismissal of aridity than they were in dealing with other obstacles to settlement.

The transition in the image of the soil and climate of the North West had been underway from at least the time of the Palliser and Hind expeditions. The change in attitude towards the prairie was more rapid and thus more dramatic. Palliser and Hind both remained wary of the treeless plains and as late as 1860 it had been common for Canadians to condemn the American West because it was treeless.[34] The early years of expansionism thus did not see the development of a positive image of one of the most prominent features of the North West. As annexation approached, and with it Canadian possession of a prairie region, such an attitude became increasingly unacceptable. In response, the image of the prairie began to change and by the later 1860s its positive benefits began to dominate its negative. Suddenly one of the attractions of the West was the fact that it was largely prairie, thus drawing 'many immigrants who go to a foreign country to obtain such prairie land.'[35]

The major single advantage of the prairie was that a man settling on previously wild land could do so without 'spending the best part of his life cutting down forests.'[36] As one anonymous writer pointed out, in eastern Canada 'to reclaim a farm of 100 acres was the work of a long and laborious life-time.' In contrast, in the North West 'no clearing of bush, grubbing of stumps and roots, or making ditches' is necessary.[37] On the prairie the farmer thus avoided the 'exhaustive labour of clearing the land.'[38] The settler, already burdened with the difficulties of starting a new farm would, the argument went, find his work that much easier. Young men who, as one writer asserted, became 'prematurely old and stooped in the shoulders' while clearing farms in the East, would find life much easier and their efforts more quickly rewarded if they went to the North West.[39] The forests of eastern Canada, which had always been seen as an essential element of agriculture, were discovered to be, after all, a liability.

There were subsidiary advantages to the prairie. The level terrain and its openness allowed the farmer to employ the latest machinery. 'The prairie land is the place for steam ploughs,' wrote George Grant. Not only, it appeared, could the farmer avoid the drudgery of clearing his land, he could also avoid much of the effort in working it. 'With such machinery one family can do the work of a dozen men.'[40] These conditions further served to support the contention that the North West was perfectly adapted for agriculture. As one anonymous writer said, 'nowhere on this continent can steam ploughs, sowing machines, reapers and threshers, be employed with so much profit and ease; and the inducements to engage in this pursuit on such a scale are surely sufficient to induce all who possess the necessary means and skills to do so.'[41]

While the prairie had many advantages it had also been seen traditionally as having many drawbacks. In particular the absence of wood, even if it did not imply infertility or aridity, created immediate problems for the settler in terms of shelter and fuel; if the immigrant was to be attracted to the prairies, solutions would have to be found for these problems. This was satisfactorily accomplished by the generalization of the theory enunciated by Palliser and Hind that much of the baldness of the prairie was the result of artificial occurrences such as prairie fires. It followed from this that when the land was settled and the number of fires decreased it would be possible to grow trees successfully. James Trow concluded that trees planted by settlers 'will in a few years grow large enough for fuel and fence timber, and will add very materially to the health of the inhabitants, attracting moisture and rain, embellishing the landscape and giving shelter to man and beast.' Trees, conveniently absent so that the settler might begin a farm in ease, could afterwards be grown on the prairie at the farmer's convenience. 'The settlement of the territory and its cultivation,' wrote immigration promoter and newspaper editor, Acton Burrows, 'puts an end to these prairie fires and a fair proportion of wood growth naturally follows.'[42]

For those who remained unconvinced by such theories in the face of such a vast, treeless land there was always the possibility of alternate sources of fuel. From the time of the Hind expedition the presence of coal in the North West had attracted a considerable amount of attention.[43] During the 1870s, as further discoveries of coal deposits were made and as the need for an alternate source of fuel to wood became more apparent, coal began to be viewed as a resource wisely deposited by nature for the convenience of the farmer. Several writers emphasized, as did George Grant, that 'The simple fact is that the coal deposits of the North-west are so enormous in quantity that people were unwilling to believe that the quality could be good.' It was good, however, or at least good enough for private use, and this had important implications. 'Here then,' said Grant, 'is fuel for the future inhabitants of the plains.'[44] The farmer, whether he planted his own trees, hauled wood from nearby river valleys, or exploited the coal seams that existed throughout the land, had nothing to fear in the supply of fuel, just as he had nothing to fear from climate or soil. Given the variety of attractions which the North West held for the immigrant who sought a farm, it is perhaps not surprising that writers talked readily of the 'hundred million of population which is eventually to inhabit the West.'[45]

What made such predictions all the more amazing was the assumption that the livelihood of so many people was expected to derive not only from agriculture but essentially from the cultivation of one crop. The greatest asset of the North West was that it possessed 'lands which are probably more favourable for the growth of wheat in greater abundance and perfection than those of any other country in the world.'[46] From the time that the West had begun to be viewed as a potential agricultural region the greatest attention had been paid to the possibility of wheat cultivation. Its ability to produce wheat, more than any other single feature, would determine its worth to Canada. By the 1870s, with the agricultural potential seemingly established, the estimates of the region's potential as a wheat-growing region became equally optimistic. By 1877 the Department of Agriculture could confidently predict: that 'the North-West of British America is destined to become the granary of the continent is clear beyond all doubt. Nature has done her share, and done it well and generously; man's labour and industry are alone required to turn these broad rolling prairies to good account.'[47]

Wheat was not the only crop that could be grown, of course. Other crops, from barley through potatoes, beets, and even peaches, were felt to be well adapted to conditions in the North West. From the time that the region began to be viewed as an agricultural frontier, however, it was wheat that dominated the minds of Canadians. 'The grand staples of the North West of Canada,' said Thomas Spence, 'will be Bread, Beef and Wool.'[48] Writing before the establishment of a large ranching economy in the extreme west of the prairies, there was no doubt why Spence had put bread first on the list.

The climate and soil of the North West were believed to have characteristics that ensured the wheat grown would be of the highest quality. The type of wheat grown, it was asserted, would soon set a new standard of excellence in the world's markets. Railway magnate James Hill testified before a house committee that in Minnesota and a few other select districts a quality of wheat had been produced which, in competition with other types, 'heads the list by fifty cents or a dollar a barrel.' The United States was restricted in the amount of wheat of this quality it could grow, however, for 'the farther north it is raised, the better wheat it is.' In this context the northerly position of Manitoba was an asset rather than a liability, for its position made it a country 'peculiarly adapted to the growth of that quality.' Moreover, Canadian farmers would find no problems of excess supply no matter how much they grew. 'The whole country might go to the growing of this wheat,' Hill concluded, 'and it would not even affect the price, because there is always a demand for good flour.'[49]

The supposed perfection of the North West as a region for wheat production had enormous implications. Wheat, with beef, was the basic staple of the Anglo-Saxon and European world and as such had special qualities attributed to it. It is, said Spence, 'pre-eminently the food of civilized nations; and perhaps there can be no surer measure of their civilization' than its use as a staple. There was proof of this, Spence continued, for 'scientific analysis confirms the indications of history. Anatomy and chemistry show that food to be best which gives toughness to muscular fibre, and tone to the brain.' In fact, the reliance of northern Europeans on wheat helped to explain why they had for so long dominated the world's affairs: 'That wheat fulfills all these conditions, is not only attested by the character and fate of nations, but it is susceptible of scientific demonstration. The nice adjustment of its vital properties, supports brain, and blood and muscle, in just the proportion requisite for the highest type of manhood. Refinement, fortitude and enterprise, most distinguish those nations which most consume wheat. Beef eating and wheat-consuming races, at once dominate and elevate the rice and pork consumers with whom they come into contact.'[50] Wheat thus assumed racial, historical, and almost mystical overtones as a source of both individual and national strength.

The elevated place assigned to wheat in determining the fate of nations put Canada in an enviable position. If wheat was the staple of the world's dominant nations, then Canada, as a potential foremost producer of wheat, could expect to assume an important position in world trade. Wheat was also important within the context of the British Empire, for with the West as a granary of that most strategic of all materials, food, the Empire would be self-sufficient and this would 'render that Empire able to defy the world.'[51] This single crop could lift Canada to imperial greatness and truly make it the equal of Great Britain. Charles Mair summed up the numerous implications of this train of logic in three words: 'Wheat,' said Mair, 'is Empire.'[52]

Moving from the level of rhetoric and imagination to the concrete questions of the nature and direction of settlement in the North West, one finds a much greater degree of caution. The expected direction of settlement and the formation of the policies that would allow that settlement to proceed, rested on the general geographical and climatological assumptions that had been set down by Palliser and Hind more than a decade before. For all the talk of the benefits of open prairie it was readily apparent that neither Canadian immigration promoters nor the settlers themselves were ready to commit themselves to too complete a change in their way of living and practising agriculture.

Manitoba was the first area to receive settlement. The fertility of the soil and suitability of climate along the banks of the Red River had long been accepted. Moreover, it was the most eastern and thus most accessible to immigrants. As settlement moved west from Manitoba, however, account had to be taken of regional geographical and climatological conditions. As had Palliser and Hind, travellers of the 1870s noted a sharp change in the nature of the land as they approached western Manitoba. This change had implications for the future of settlement for, as Commissioner G.A. French of the North West Mounted Police commented in 1874, 'I think civilization will be hard pressed for room when it requires the coteau of the Missouri, at least for agricultural purposes.'[53]

This change in the height of land, crossing the border at about 104 degrees west, was thought in the 1870s to mark the eastern limit of Palliser's triangle. The triangle itself was still assumed to be unsuited for agriculture and that implied that settlement would not push indiscriminately westward from Manitoba. It was still believed, as Captain William Butler put it in 1870, that 'alone from Texas to the sub-arctic forest, the Saskatchewan valley lays its fair length for 800 miles in unmixed fertility.'[54] As long as this was assumed, then settlement would turn north as it went west, following the 'fertile belt' which Hind had described years before. Five years after Butler made his observation, the respected geologist, George Mercer Dawson, headed a party surveying the boundary line between Canada and the United States. After extensive observation and analysis, Dawson concluded that 'the progress of settlement will follow the valley of the Saskatchewan River to its head, and then spread north and south along the eastern base of the mountains.' The vast southern prairies might eventually be settled but it would be a long time before they were and even then 'the fertile belt to the north must form the basis for settlement and utilization of the western plains.'[55]

These assumptions were reflected in and encouraged by government policy. The survey, that necessary prerequisite of land ownership, was planned on the basis of the existence of the fertile belt. As J.S. Dennis, who by 1877 was Deputy Minister of the Interior, said: 'the country embraced in the Saskatchewan valley possesses immense agricultural resources and is rapidly attracting settlers.'[56] The Dominion Lands Survey, attempting to predict the demand for land, worked out from Manitoba not in a westward but in a northwestward direction. The Assiniboine Valley, Fort Pelly, Prince Albert, and Edmonton marked in succession the advance of the survey in the 1870s. Year after year the progress maps of the Department of the Interior revealed this movement to the north and west. The lines of the survey, as shown on these maps, had they been placed over Hind's original map, would have traced his fertile belt almost exactly.[57]

The acceptance of Hind's interpretation of the West was equally revealed in the projected route of the Canadian Pacific Railway. When Sandford Fleming and George Grant made their famous scouting tour through the West in 1872, the route they chose reflected the assumption that the railway would head through the fertile belt. Four years later the official map of the railway showed the projected route as heading northwest from Manitoba to Edmonton. The lands to the south were marked as 'more or less barren.'[58] It was a route that, as Fleming was probably aware, had been suggested more than ten years before by Hind.[59] Through the 1870s, as discussion raged over the choice of a Pacific terminus, the projected prairie section of the line remained largely unchallenged. Even those who did call for a change in the prairie route looked to the north of the Saskatchewan River rather than to the south.[60]

The whole shape of the developing prairie economy of the 1870s was thus determined by the assumption that there existed in Canada an extension of the Great American Desert. The arctic image of the region had collapsed with the explorations of Hind and Palliser. The question of aridity, however, had lingered on to qualify the worth of the garden. Fortunately, Palliser and others had restricted this aridity to a particular geographical area and thus made it avoidable.

In fact, while the continued belief in Palliser's triangle indicated a certain caution in the Canadian approach to the prairies, it might also be said that the triangle served a useful purpose. Speaking of the southern Canadian prairies Charles Mair reminded his readers in 1875 that 'a wide extent of these plains is of much the same desolate character as the great American desert to the south.'[61] While this fact condemned that particular section of Canada to remain empty, it also did a much more important thing: it condemned the frontier lands of Canada's chief rival, the United States. Throughout the 1870s, as Americans sought to revise their image of the great plains beyond the 98th meridian, Canadians held firmly to their belief in the uselessness of the American West. George Grant, returning east from the Pacific, felt assured that Canada had little to fear from American efforts to attract immigration:

The American desert is a great reality. It is utterly unfit for the growth of cereals or to support in any way a farming population, because of its elevation, its lack of rain, and the miserable quality, or to speak more correctly, the absence of soil ... In a word, after reaching the summit of the first range of mountains, from the Pacific, the railway in the United States has to cross more than a thousand miles of desert or semi-desert. According to the evidence of our senses, whatever guide books may say to the contrary, we discovered on the home stretch that the great west of the United States, practically ceases with the valley of the Missouri and of its tributary the Platte.[62]

This commonly held belief significantly reinforced hopes that Canada might supplant the United States as the major receptacle of European immigration. The historical dominance of the United States in the field of immigration was coming to an end, it was argued, not only because Canada now possessed the

North West but also because the United States had little left to offer. 'What a proud position the United States once occupied in the eyes of the world,' Thomas Spence proclaimed. Spence could afford to give such praise to his American neighbours because he felt that their role as provider of comfort for the landless of Europe was finished. The continual flood of immigrants over the past years had taxed even the mighty resources of the United States and gradually these immigrants found less opportunity for 'most of the public domain that is worth anything has been absorbed.' Just as this moment in history arrived, however, 'our vast virgin prairies are thrown open to the world, while there is little good land left in the United States.'[63] The existence of Palliser's triangle and an area of bad land within the North West was not really all that unfortunate when in turn Canadians were able to assert the existence of the American desert and the impending end of a frontier of open land in the United States.

Reputable scientists judged the American plains and Palliser's triangle on what they thought to be objective criteria. The geographical configuration that they drew of the North American West in the 1870s was no doubt sincere, but there are indications that the Canadian image of the North West had evolved over time not only to conform to scientific evidence but to meet the perceived needs of the nation. This was as true of the 1870s as it was of other decades. The image of the North West, including the qualification implicit in the notion of Palliser's triangle, neatly suited Canadian expectations and hopes. The condemnation of the American West was as much a matter of emotion as it was of science.

Canadian writers tended to project the comparison between their West and that of the United States beyond such phenomena as climate and soil as it pertained to agriculture. It was a common theme throughout the decade that Canada possessed in the Noth West a climate ideal not only for crops but for man. It was a land where 'humidity is absent; the air is bracing and dry; stagnant waters and their poisonous exhalations are unknown.'[64] Even the admittedly cold winters had few bad effects on the constitution, for it was not long before Canadians discovered what westerners have been maintaining ever since: 'In the winter the thermometer sinks to thirty or forty degrees below zero; but this degree of cold in the dry atmosphere of the North West does not produce any unpleasant sensations.'[65]

Most importantly, this beneficial climate, it would seem, was confined to the North West. Although Canadian expansionists had long ago accepted Blodgett's argument that latitude did not determine climate, one would never have guessed it by the magic powers they assigned to one degree of latitude – the 49th parallel. Weather in the 1870s seemed to have a very strong respect for the international boundary. When, for instance, J.Y. Shantz travelled to Manitoba in 1872 as the escort for some prospective Mennonite settlers, he found that by early November the state of Minnesota 'snowed continually with drift.' The border, however, marked a turning point, for north of it there was 'very little snow, and on arrival at Fort Garry on the 17th of November, there was not enough snow to cover the ground.'[66] On another occasion Daniel Gordon, Presbyterian minister in Winnipeg, wrote his friend Sandford Fleming in a light-hearted vein to say that Manitobans did not mind a strong northerly breeze but that they abhorred one from the south: 'I don't know what the Yankees do with our breezes when they get them across the line but when they send them back to us they are much less pleasant than when they left us. Like some of our people they get sharpened up a little in the States. If this is a specimen of Yankee methods of raising the wind the less of such reciprocity the better. Kindly ask the Finance Minister to lay a tax on wind coming from the States.'[67]

While Gordon treated the question lightly, others warned immigrants that the climate of the two countries was of the utmost importance. The weather in the United States was not only less pleasant than in Canada but also much more dangerous. The prairies of Manitoba, James Trow noted, were free from the stagnant ponds which were present in Minnesota and other western states. 'The effluvia arising from these low places poisons the atmosphere, and fever and death frequently result.' Such facts, and stagnant ponds were but one of them, meant that to settle in the United States could be a tragic and even fatal error for the immigrant. What use to the farmer, Alexander Begg asked, 'are fair fields and meadows, beautiful crops and the acquisition of wealth, if to obtain them he is obliged to sacrifice his own health and that of his family.' It was far better to settle in Manitoba where 'the almost total absence of fog or mist; the brilliancy of the sunlight; the pleasing succession of the seasons, all combine to make Manitoba a climate of unrivalled salubrity, and the home of a healthy, prosperous and joyous people.'[68]

The American climate was so virulent that even in Canada it provided some secondary danger. Charles Mair warned the settler to beware of the southern wind for it had 'danger on its breath, and anything but healing on its wings.' Fortunately the wind rarely blew from the south, for when it did 'it brings with it the dim edge of fever, the dread of pestilence and famine.'[69] In the mind of the Canadian expansionist it would seem that all the negative aspects of the North West, from Palliser's triangle through pestilence and famine, had their origins in the United States.

Canadians developed a well-defined set of comparisons between their own West and that of the United States during the 1870s; the comparison began

118 Promise of Eden

with questions of rainfall and soil but went far beyond such relatively scientific matters. The concept of climate as a determinant of health, with the north healthier than the south, is really better explained in terms of myth than science. It was a part of the Canadian folklore that those who yielded to the temptation of the United States and went south to seek wealth would find that the climate threatened them; in contrast, it was argued, the northerly climate of Canada offered a man better chances of good health.[70] In 1869 this conventional wisdom had been systematized to some extent by Canada First member, R.G. Haliburton. He had argued that the northern races, as a result of climate, proved to be more powerful and resilient than southern races. Canada, Haliburton had said, need not lament the fact that its crops could not compare in size to those of the United States for the nation would be amply compensated in its northerly position with a 'healthy, hardy, virtuous, dominant race.'[71]

The addition of the North West to Canada allowed the myth of the north to gain in appeal. Haliburton had depicted a nation and people trading off some of their material wealth for continued health and hardiness. As a myth this was not completely satisfactory, in that it reminded Canada of its materially inferior position relative to the United States. The application of the myth to the North West, however, resolved this dilemma. The North West was not only healthier than the United States but it was, as the Great American Desert proved, capable of reproducing greater wealth for the settler. For one of the few times in Canadian history, Canada was able to claim confidently not only greater virtue and character than its southern neighbour but greater potential wealth as well.

The favourable image of the North West, the expectations of the expansionists, and the importance that was attached to the region led to both the demand and the assumption that the West would be rapidly developed. The West, it had been concluded, was the garden which thousands sought, and it was thus assumed that its opening to immigration would result in a sudden burst of activity. George Denison, writing in 1870 as a member of the North West Emigration Aid Society, noted optimistically that 'we have already had applications from many parties about going West although we have not advertised at all.' He confidently concluded that 'there will probably be 1500 to 2000 persons going out next summer.'[72] S.J. Dawson, still in charge of the mixed land and water route that bore his name, was even more optimistic; when the Dawson route opened for traffic in 1871, it was organized to handle fifteen hundred immigrants a month.[73]

Such expectations were unrealistic. To coax settlement into a new and largely untested land would take time and money. The majority of European immigrants continued to follow the well-trodden path to the United States. While many Canadians and some Europeans, most notably the Mennonites in 1873, did move west, the actual rate of immigration fell far below that which was expected. The Dawson route, prepared for such a large influx of immigrants, carried only 136 bona fide settlers by the end of 1871.[74] Nor did things improve greatly over the next few years. In 1873, it is true, Canada could boast some 50,000 immigrants. That year, however, proved to be a peak, for as depression settled over the world the immigration figures dropped, to 39,373 in 1874 and to only 25,633 in 1876.[75] These figures implied that it would be a very long time indeed before the North West reached the millions of population that had been so confidently predicted for it.

The disappointing immigration figures did not destroy Canadian optimism or faith in the North West. Expansionists continued to predict that the great wave of immigration was just around the corner. John Schultz typified the mood of the 1870s when he wrote in 1877 that 'times have not been very brisk this winter,' but 'there is reason to expect a large immigration in the spring.'[76] There were always reasons to explain the lack of immigration, from grasshoppers through rain, and every negative factor was seen as exceptional and thus as only a temporary deterrent. Increasingly, as the decade went on, these problems were thought to centre on one factor. All the other deterrents retarding the inflow of settlers seemed to pale in comparison to the overriding fact that the North West remained isolated and difficult of access. Only the railway promised an end to this isolation and therefore the beginning of rapid settlement. As J.S. Dennis concluded in 1877: 'with the facility of access by railway ... a rapidly and constantly increasing traffic will pour into the country.'[77] Only give men the means to get to the North West and to sell their crops and they would surely come.

The question of some form of transcontinental transportation had been around from the time that men had first begun to consider the possibility of developing the West. In fact, it could be argued that the idea of the railroad preceded the idea of western development. The English visionaries and pamphleteers of the 1840s had concentrated their thoughts and their somewhat vague plans on the idea of a route to Asia; the North West was simply something to be traversed on the way. The mystical markets of the Orient had drawn men to the idea of a transcontinental railroad long before it had been firmly believed that the North West could support an agricultural population. In the wake of the Palliser and Hind expeditions, however, this began to change. Their positive assessments of the resources of the West led people to think in terms of tapping the wealth of the region itself. By at least 1863 Hind could argue for a transcontinental railroad not on the basis of Asian riches but on the strength of 'the remarkable fertility of forty million acres in the valley of the Saskatchewan.'[78]

Moreover, Hind believed such a scheme was practical and revealed his faith in it when Sir Edward Watkin moved to buy out the Hudson's Bay Company. Watkin planned to develop the region and his schemes included a transcontinental railroad.[79] Unlike the pamphleteers of the 1840s, Watkin was, as president of the Grand Trunk, an established, if ambitious, railway promoter and there was thus at least the possibility that his plans might develop into something concrete. Henry Youle Hind was only too eager to help. 'I take a deep interest in everything connected with the North West,' he wrote Watkin, 'and I should be sorry to see any enterprise begun without assisting in carrying it out.'[80] Nor were Watkin and Hind the only men who saw such a project as practical. Experienced engineers like Sandford Fleming and S.J. Dawson were, by the middle 1860s, presenting their own ideas for a system of transcontinental transportation.[81] Within less than two decades the idea of a railroad to the Pacific within British territory had moved from the fantastic scheme of a few dreamers to the point where it was assumed by most expansionists that it would eventually be a reality.

Underlying the question of the economic possibilities of such a railroad was the more abstract consideration of national unity. The expansionist movement had had from the beginning a very strong understanding of the geo-political aspects of expansionism. The North West, isolated from Canada by thousands of miles of unsettled territory, had to be shown to be assimilable into the Canadian economy and body politic if the case was to be made for extension to the West. Crucial to this question was the problem of access to the region. Traditionally there had been three routes to the North West: one through Hudson Bay, another from the south via St Paul, and the third via Lake Superior and eastern Canada. Each of these routes had their own implications for metropolitan control of the vast region. The Hudson Bay route, as expansionists pointed out in the 1850s, directed the trade and attention of the North West to England; the continued use of that route implied continued dominance by the London-based Hudson's Bay Company. The route from the south was, naturally, seen as the forerunner of American control. As the *Nor'Wester* warned on 28 July 1860, the placing of a steamboat on the Red River indicated 'a complete revolution in the trade of this settlement.' Trade with the United States, as much as with England, implied political control.

The Superior route, unused and largely overgrown, was the only one of the three that implied Canadian control. The expansionists had been acutely aware of this during their campaign for annexation. The myth of the North West Company had been useful, not only for the moral claim which it gave

Canada to the North West but also as proof that that route was feasible. In order to make the North West Canadian it was necessary to make it accessible from Canada and early expansionist conclusions on the Superior route were very much influenced by this fact. S.J. Dawson, the man who had the responsibility for assessing the potential of the route, was no exception:

> It has been said, indeed strongly urged, by interested parties, that the route through the State of Minnesota by St. Paul and Pembina would afford the best means of communication with the Red River Settlement. But I do not see how this opinion can be reasonably entertained. Under any circumstances there would be a greater extent of land carriage by the Minnesota route, I should say twice or perhaps three times as great as by the Canadian route, so that the time occupied in travelling it would be greater, unless a railroad were constructed, and it will be borne in mind that the extreme western limit of the United States railway system does not as yet approach within seven hundred miles of the Red River settlement.[82]

For national reasons Canadian expansionists had to believe that the Superior route could be made to compete with the American one. In much the same way that the expansionists set out to challenge those who presented the climate of the North West as hostile, they challenged those who saw an east-west trade axis as impossible. Even the cast of characters was similar. Men like Sir George Simpson and Henry Lefroy scorned the idea of making the Superior route a major artery of trade. Even Palliser, who did so much in other areas to reverse the image of the North West, remained sceptical of the feasibility of tying the North West to Canada via Lake Superior.[83] On the other hand, expansionists like William Dawson argued optimistically and somewhat unrealistically that even a crude wagon road 'would immediately transfer the trade from St. Paul's to Lake Superior.' It was not so much that they really believed that the Superior route was the natural one to the North West, but more that, as Draper said in 1857, 'unless you can succeed in making it so' the North West would never remain Canadian.[84]

The idea of the railroad as a national necessity thus worked from the beginning in tandem with the idea of the railroad as a developmental factor. As the North West increased in importance in the Canadian mind, so too did the railroad. By the time that annexation approached, the railroad, or at least some form of all-Canadian transportation to the North West, had ceased to be visionary or even to be a project for the remote future. In the minds of expansionists it had become, as the *Nor'Wester* argued on 26 June 1869, 'a necessity to this country, a necessity to the Dominion, and a necessity to the Empire.' Three years later George Grant found himself in agreement with the

Nor'Wester; the railway, he felt, was the key to national survival. The construction of such a transportation system, he argued, 'was wise, because it was necessary.' The railroad would proclaim to the world, and more particularly to the Americans, the intention of Canadians 'to work out their own future as an integral and important part of the grandest Empire in the world.'[85]

The new sense of urgency brought about a reversal in thought on the construction of the Canadian Pacific. Sandford Fleming, for instance, the man who took charge of the project in the 1870s, had initially viewed a transcontinental railway as the ultimate development of a transportation system that would increase in sophistication as the North West developed.[86] In other words, the railway would follow settlement. This was in keeping with the original expansionist idea of the North West as a hinterland to be exploited as Canadian requirements demanded. The Dawson route, as a basic and relatively cheap form of transportation, was an expression of this same train of thought. By the early 1870s, however, the railroad became to the expansionist not the ultimate stage of development but the initial prerequisite for it. Once again, Canadian fears of American ambitions played a role in formulating their demands. As early as 1868 Alfred Waddington warned that 'unless a counterline be built through British territory, this road [the Union Pacific] will furnish the only outlet for the Red River Settlement and Saskatchewan territory, and thus prepare the way for her separation from the Mother country.'[87] Thomas Spence saw the existence of the Great American Desert as increasing the necessity for a Canadian railroad. 'Upon the northern edge of the great Sahara,' he wrote, 'we have the valleys of the Red River and Saskatchewan, carrying their rich and grassy undulations to the gorges of the Rocky Mountains.' The temptation that such fertility presented to the land-starved Americans implied that 'the entire expansive movement of population on the North American continent will be concentrated in the direction of our fertile valleys.' Integration into the Canadian mainstream by means of an 'interoceanic railway' was essential if the region was to be preserved to Canada.[88]

Contributing to the sense of urgency surrounding the whole question of the railroad was the obvious failure of the Dawson route to act as a practical link between Ontario and Manitoba. Testimony was pretty much unanimous that, in spite of the capabilities of Simon Dawson, the route would never be a major artery for either goods or immigrants. In spite of all the efforts which had been made to improve it, the route was too rough and taxing for the average traveller. A young immigrant, travelling with her family to Manitoba, remembered the trip as 'six weeks of hardships such as they had never experienced before.'[89] George Grant commented that the route was 'all that tourists could desire,' but even he had to admit that as a transportation system for immigrants loaded with possessions 'the Dawson route is an absurdity.'[90] Such complaints were borne out by statistics: in the first three seasons of full operation the route carried only eight hundred 'emigrants' and the Minister of Public Works was forced to admit that the 'amount of travel has not kept pace with expectations.'[91] It was also an expensive failure: in 1872 the route carried only a hundred immigrants while the total cost of operation and improvements in the fiscal year 1872-73 was more than a quarter of a million dollars.[92] The rudimentary transportation system designed to meet economically the requirements of a developing hinterland had failed. Only a railway, it seemed, would ensure the firm connection of the North West with the rest of Canada.

The belief that the railway had to precede development encouraged the idea that the absence of a railway was sufficient to explain the problems of the North West in the 1870s. Without the railway the West would never achieve its full potential. This belief, combining as it did, faith in the West with faith in railways, served to make the railway the central symbol of western development. Only the all-powerful railway, 'the sceptre as well as the plough and the sword of the day,' could bring the desired growth and prosperity.[93] The implications of the railway were so vast that one writer termed it 'the magical wand which is destined to people the Great North West.' The idea became irresistible that 'as in the States let the railroad lead and then colonization and civilization will follow.'[94] Once build a railway and 'the imagination would almost fail to conceive of the great future of the Northwest.'[95]

The importance attached to the completion of the railway had significant implications. In the first place, support for the railway became equivalent to support for the North West. And, for those expansionists and settlers who saw the future of the North West as crucial to the future of Canada, the railway became a crucial part of national development. When the government of Alexander Mackenzie tried to slow down the construction of the railway in the face of depression and spiralling costs, it found itself disowned by the expansionists. 'I fear Canada raised up a Grit Frankenstein in this Mackenzie,' Charles Mair commented from his new home in Prince Albert. 'If Mackenzie is a reformer,' he concluded, 'then being a man of liberal mind, I confess myself a Tory.'[96] Even the memory of John A. Macdonald's behaviour during the Red River rebellion was overshadowed by the problem of immediate development. Mair, and those who equally felt the North West to be important, were not willing to return to the older concept of construction as traffic and population warranted.

The vigorous political and public debate of the 1870s was carried on not between those who favoured construction of the Canadian Pacific and those who did not. Rather it was a debate between those who insisted on immediate and transcontinental development and those who, like Mackenzie's cabinet minister, Edward Blake, favoured a more cautious approach but who, nevertheless, favoured eventual construction. In the end the expansionists were victorious. Aided by Macdonald's previous commitment to British Columbia, they were able to obtain the construction of the railway at as fast a pace as was possible.

The importance attached to the railway had a second and potentially disturbing implication. Expansionists, settlers, and the merchants of the North West had turned the railway into a panacea for their very real problems. The mystical powers which the railway had assumed in the Canadian imagination both explained the disappointments of the 1870s and promised the imminent arrival of the millennium. The region had originally been expected to fill with settlers as soon as Canada removed the iron-clad fist of the Hudson's Bay Company. In the 1870s, however, the railway became the new necessary prerequisite for development and the expectations were all the higher for the cost and magnitude of the project. The North West, in turn, was becoming increasingly seen by this group as the answer to the problems of Canada. Only this chain of logic could, in fact, justify the vast expenditures which were being made on the railway by a nation of only a few million people. The challenge of the 1870s with regard to the North West had been to translate visions into policy. In the process, however, the policy pursued had simply transferred and heightened the earlier visions. The question was whether expansionists and the growing number of settlers would find their expectations for both the railway and the North West met when the Canadian Pacific finally provided an outlet for what had come to be seen as the garden of North America.

6

The character of empire: the Britain of the West

From its beginnings, expansionism had social and moral overtones that imparted to the secular idea of potential wealth a sense of mission. The specific character of that mission had altered from time to time to adapt to the changing tempo of expectations for the West, but it was always present in some form. Alexander Isbister and the early critics of the Hudson's Bay Company had focused attention on the plight of the Indians under company rule. Canadian expansionists had made the Red River settler, supposedly longing for political liberty, the centre of their attention; that specific crusade had faltered in the face of the Red River resistance, however, and after 1870 the primary object of this sense of mission again shifted. The focus was no longer on the phenomena of the old order but on the new order that was to arise from the wilderness.

The resources of the North West offered Canada a great opportunity, but it was thought that full advantage could be taken of that opportunity only if a society of the proper moral character was developed in the new land. This concern for the nature of western society paralleled and to some extent qualified the materialism of the expansionists through the early settlement period. Growth alone was not sufficient to guarantee the future of the West; expansionists believed that an empire was being built in the West and that such an empire needed a strong moral as well as material foundation. George Grant, one of the most concerned with this question, felt it important enough to return to in one of the last speeches of his life. 'Let us always deprecate "raw haste" in its up-building,' said Grant of both the West and Canada; material development was not enough, he warned, for 'a country is great, not from the number but the quality of its people.'[1]

If the focus of the mission in the West changed over time it did possess one basic theme throughout. The Canadian sense of duty in the North West had as its initial determinant the sense of membership in the imperial community. From Isbister through Alexander Morris and Charles Mair, expansionists had always seen the development of the West not only within the national but within the imperial context; the North West was important to the role of Canada within the Empire and, possibly, the Empire within the world. Neither Confederation nor the annexation of the region changed this fact. Indeed, as the assessment of the value and potential of the West increased, so too did its importance to the Empire. In the 1870s George Grant lent his voice to the long string of expansionists who saw the North West as aiding Canada's mission to develop 'as an integral and important part of the grandest Empire in the world.'[2]

This sense of being a part of the imperial community provided the basic guidelines for the development of the new society in the North West. Canada, in developing and settling the region, wanted to 'build up a nation on the British plan.'[3] The British Empire was thought to represent man's highest achievement in the development of governmental and social institutions. The North West, promising great economic wealth, seemed to give Canada a unique opportunity to implant firmly these noble institutions in a rising world power. The North West offered 'an unequalled opportunity of developing British institutions on a grand scale,' and 'under such institutions, there is enjoyed civil liberty and social order, unequalled by that of any other system on the face of the earth.'[4] The vast territory of the West offered a canvas large enough to be appropriate for the moral grandeur of British institutions.

After 1870 the sense of mission contained within Canadian expansionism focused on this idea of developing a society worthy of the British Empire; it was also perceived to make the movement onto the western plains much more than an exercise in materialistic exploitation. American Secretary of State, William Seward, had once termed Canada a potential North American Russia, because of its size and northerly position. In physical terms the analogy made sense and was even flattering, but in moral terms the comparison to autocratic Russia was felt by Canadians to be inadequate. George Grant made a point of rejecting it, arguing that 'We shall be more than an American Russia' for the emerging Canadian nation would be enlightened to a degree not thought possible for the Tsarist dictatorship. Moreover, it was the continued connection with Britain that would give Canada the basis of its progressive institutions: 'Her traditions, her forms, her moral elevation, her historic grandeur shall be ours forever.'[5]

The continued connection with the British Empire also helped to differentiate Canada from the United States. In economic and physical terms Canada hoped to reproduce the historical experience of the United States. The character of the society which it was hoped would develop in the North West, however, had Britain as its model. Canada's mission in North America was as distinct from that of the United States in 1870 as it had been in 1783; the difference was that in 1870 Canadians believed this mission involved a potential world power. As one writer put it, 'to reproduce the British constitution, with its marvellous heritages of balanced power and liberty ... and to do this across the breadth of a whole continent, – these are objects which are worth some labour, some sacrifice to obtain.'[6]

This theme was not new. From at least the time of Morris's *Nova Britannia* expansionists had viewed the opening of the West as a part of the progress of British society and morality across the North American continent. By the 1870s, with Confederation accomplished and Canada 'a band of scattered homes and colonies no more,' the theme took on a new importance. It was Canada's 'noble task to fill the still untrodden plains' and eventually to assume the mantle of 'the Britain of the West.'[7] The North West was the means by which Canada could fulfil this role. As one individual wrote to George Grant, 'her vast area, her multiplicity of interests – in a word the internal questions of a country larger than all Europe afford sufficient scope for her public men and fosters a patriotic feeling that destroys provincialism.'[8] The old geography of British North America had cramped not only the physical but the mental outlook of Canadians; colonial subordination had suited such a spirit. The new transcontinental Dominion, however, would naturally find both its leaders and its goals uplifted until it could think of assuming a partnership with the mother country.

Closely related to this theme was the idea that Canada would not only become a partner with Britain but would some day replace it. Bishop Berkeley's image of the course of Empire westward had not disappeared from expansionist rhetoric. Britain, constrained by the compactness of its territory, overpopulation, and age would eventually decline in power; its successor, the argument went, was to be Canada. A British pamphleteer put the ultimate possibilities of the North West before his readers in 1872 when he suggested that the West 'might be the future of the Empire.' In case anyone missed the point, he emphasized it by quoting Berkeley's famous line, 'Westward the course of empire takes its way,' on the title page.[9] The continued intrusion of this theme made it seem even more important that Canada fulfil its mission in the North West. Canada might be the only means by which the great traditions of the Empire could continue to have an influence on the world. The civilization that grew up in the North West might determine whether British civilization would survive. Canada carried into the North West the whole moral weight involved in the role of guardian of the traditions of the British Empire:

> So long in the hereafter, our Canada shall be
> The worthy heir of British power and British liberty;
> Spreading the blessings of her sway to her remotest bounds,
> While, with the fame of her fair name, a continent resounds;
> True to the high traditions of Britain's ancient glory,
> Of patriots, saints, and martyrs, who live in deathless story;
> Strong, in their liberty and truth, to shed from shore to shore
> A light among nations, till nations are no more.[10]

It was an enormous responsibility and an enormous opportunity. The challenge was such that even the ebullient expansionist Charles Mair queried: 'do we faint at the portals of a realm so vast, or does the contemplation and possession of so much material grandeur lift our minds to the plane of more strenuous efforts and higher duties than have enriched our history in the past?'[11]

Themes such as this were not new to the North American experience. American writers had expressed them practically from the time of the first English colonies in North America. The Canadian version was, nevertheless, distinct from those that had gone before and exhibited particulars that distinguished it from its counterpart in the United States. The American frontier, once it ceased to be dominated by the idea of a route to Asia, became 'devoid of reference to the past, and indifferent to Europe except as a foil to make America seem more glorious by contrast.'[12] In so doing, the idea of the American frontier became introspective and somewhat narrow. The frontier was based in America and would contribute to America. Canada, in contrast, began its process of settling the West acutely conscious of the relation which the future of that region had to the history of the British Empire.

The contrast between the American and Canadian versions of this theme was revealed on a fairly immediate level by the attitude of the two nations towards the immigrant. In the United States the immigrant's contribution to the country was seen largely in material terms. He was the man who would, with native Americans, develop the frontier. In social and moral terms his duty was to adapt as quickly as possible to American traditions and to cast off his older and inferior European cultural baggage. Canadians, however, saw at least one class of immigrants in a significantly different context. Part of the role of the frontier might serve was the preservation of this immigrant's connection with the old world. The particular immigrant was, of course, the native of the British Isles and Canada had a duty to prevent this individual's estrangement from his mother country. 'In the opening of this, the last fertile region within reach of the Celtic and Anglo-Saxon races,' said one Canadian, the Dominion had a duty to 'reverse the former feeling' of disenchantment with Britain that had been a part of previous immigration. The material opportunities of the North West offered an opportunity to preserve among British emigrants 'a warm sense of gratitude which would bear practical fruit in later years.'[13]

Emigration from the British Isles to the North West could thus serve to strengthen the British Empire. In the process of sending men to Canada, the overcrowded mother country would benefit the entire Empire. 'For generations,' said George Grant, 'all this boundless extent of beauty and wealth had been here, owned by England; and yet statesmen had been puzzling their heads over the "Condition of England's poor, the Irish Famine, the Land and Labour Questions," without once turning their eyes to a land that offered a practical solution to them all.'[14] The mother country would be relieved of its surplus population and social unrest and at the same time the Empire would retain its loyal sons. The immigrant from Britain, the Department of Agriculture stated confidently, 'would have the satisfaction of feeling that he is assisting to build up a great British Empire, having for its seat the northern half of the continent of North America.'[15]

Canadians also felt that British institutions were the most reliable in terms of both social welfare and social stability. The development of such a society thus became a practical question. The stability of Canada and thus its ability to inherit the mantle of Great Britain depended to a large extent on its ability to develop and maintain a social fabric as strong as that of the mother country. The empty lands of the North West offered Canada a great opportunity to develop economically. The open land was, however, but a transient phenomenon. Ultimately Canada would find itself again without a frontier. If Canada was to achieve its destiny within the Empire it would have to seize the opportunity offered by the North West in such a way as to ensure that its benefits lasted beyond the frontier period. The very success of Canada's historical mission depended on it developing a society of sufficient strength and stability to survive the transition of the North West from frontier to mature community.

In the United States the official announcement of the end of free land in the census of 1890 would lead the American historian, Frederick Jackson Turner, to write down his thoughts on the significance of the frontier in American history. Turner was to argue that the American frontier did much more than simply provide an abundance of material wealth; it had also been a social factor allowing a continual recreation of democracy on the edges of civilization. 'Steadily the frontier of settlement advanced and carried with it individualism, democracy and nationalism and powerfully affected the East and the Old World.' Turner's theory was both complex and subtle but it made two major points. First, the frontier was a positive Americanizing force that fused the nation, regenerated the ideals of American life, and prevented the corruption that would have resulted had the nation become primarily urban. Second, in its openness and material potential the frontier offered 'a gate of escape from the bondage of the past,' in both a social and a material sense. The man from Europe, or from the eastern city, could refuse to remain an underpaid worker and could instead become an independent and even prosperous individual simply by removing to the frontier. Turner's theory of the frontier also had a disturbing side; he wrote his article in response to the end of that frontier and it thus inevitably posed a disturbing question concerning the future of the United States. 'And now, four centuries from the discovery of America, at the end of a hundred years of life under the constitution, the frontier has gone, and with its going has closed the first period of American history.'[16] The question was, of course, what was to be the second period of American history.

Many were satisfied that Turner's question had been answered long before it had even been posed. From early in the nineteenth century many British conservatives, including such eminent politicians as Robert Peel, Benjamin Disraeli, and Robert Lowe, had warned that the presence of an open frontier was the only reason that such an inherently unstable system as democracy had succeeded in the United States. Only when the frontier closed, they argued, would there be a real test of American political institutions.[17] These arguments had been common in Britain for some time and Canadians were probably aware of them. Certainly some seem to have picked up the theme and, with suitable variations, expanded it in an attempt to reconcile the problem of a transient frontier and the goal of permanent stability. The resultant Canadian version of the frontier thesis was both more pessimistic and more optimistic than Turner's. It was more pessimistic in that, like the British conservatives, it replaced Turner's open-ended, if disturbing, future with unqualified predictions of doom for the United States; it was more optimistic in that the nature of the theory implied that Canada, unlike the United States, could avoid the consequences implicit in the closing of a frontier of free land. At its basis was the assumption that American weakness and Canadian strength rested ultimately not on the land but on the character of society.

According to Turner the frontier democratized American life and acted as an agent of regeneration in the areas of political theory and social liberty. The Canadian variant equally placed the existence of land in an important position but, in contrast to Turner, saw these resources as allowing the United States to escape the disastrous implications inherent in a set of defective political and social institutions. 'The mighty resources of America,' Charles Mair cynically commented, 'would nurse the apathetic and brutalized civilization of the Turk into greatness; and had the carnal Chinese been the primary occupants of the land, they would long ago have converted it into a universal garden.' Material success under such conditions, Mair warned, said nothing about the underlying strength of society, and the American, for 'all his indomitable perseverance and material success,' was 'a living exemplification of the danger of wild assumptions and wild interpretations in politics and morals.'[18]

Nicholas Flood Davin, who developed the theory to its fullest, agreed with Mair but took it one step further. Despotism, he said, is out of the question for the present in the United States, 'not because of the nature of the government, or of the civilization, but because of the immense waste of unoccupied territory lying westward.' The frontier indeed acted as a safety valve but, according to Davin, that safety valve only served to 'absorb all the restless and adventurous elements of Society.' Had these people remained in civilized communities their influence would have increased social strife and further degraded political life. As it was they concentrated their energies on the relatively harmless business, to the nation as a whole, of 'dealing out a merciless policy to the poor Indian.' The American frontier would not last much longer, however, and the anarchic forces it contained would soon turn back on the nation as a whole. 'The time will come,' Davin warned, 'when all the conditions of old settled countries will be repeated on this continent.'[19] At that point in history, which Canadians tended to place in the very near future, the true weakness of America would be revealed.

Even though a frontier of open land had enabled the United States to avoid the worst consequences of its own moral defects, Canadians were able to find ample evidence of the failure of American civilization. The experience of the United States with the native Indian had been both violent and disreputable and Canadians turned to it as proof that, as Mair put it, 'there is extension which carries with it spiritual degradation and decay.'[20] By the 1870s a good many Canadians were convinced that the history of American Indian policy was, as the Toronto *Globe* once said, 'a dark record of broken pledges, undisguised oppression and triumphant cruelty.'[21] Canadians felt that the United States was practising a policy of extermination towards the Indian and that the government of the United States, rather than the Indian, must assume the major responsibility for the violence which had disfigured the frontier.[22]

In contrast, Canadians believed that their approach to the Indian, inherited from the British, was both just and practical. As such it gave them futher evidence that the British rather than the American model was best suited for the development of the frontier. No system could, it was true, avoid the basic trend towards the displacement of native society and culture and this did prompt a genuine sympathy from many who realized the changes being forced on that older culture. George Grant, passing through the Lake of the Woods area at the same time that the local tribes were signing away their rights to the land, expressed this sense of sympathy. 'Poor creatures!' he exclaimed, 'not much use have they made of their land; but yet in admitting the settler, they sign their own death warrants.'[23]

In the expansionist mind, however, this sense of sympathy in no way contradicted the right of European civilization to supplant the native. The certainty that their own civilization was superior and the ubiquitous doctrine of progress made them accept without question the idea that it was 'necessary that the Indian hunting-ground should in large measure be given up to the plough and the sickle of the white man.'[24] Even Grant, one of the most liberal men of his age in his view the Indian, ended his sympathetic comment with the cautionary note that 'these regions were surely meant to maintain more than a few thousand Ojibbeways [sic].'[25] The quarrel was thus not with the expansion of the American frontier but with the method of that expansion.

The American approach to the frontier was condemned in part because it had failed to act responsibly towards those whose civilization was being replaced. Canadian expansionists argued that while the displacement of the native was necessary and perhaps inevitable, there was nevertheless a duty on the part of the new civilization to aid the Indian. The ideal was assimilation and the policy was paternalistic in its approach, but those concerned with Indian affairs in these years saw assimilation as desirable and paternalism as necessary. With the Indian as the ward of the state, steps could be taken to protect him from the harmful effects of white culture while teaching him its benefits.

In the contemporary mind this mission to the Indian resolved the moral difficulty inherent in the removal of the native from his land. For years the Christian missionary had desired to take the Indian from a nomadic, hunting economy to an agricultural and Christian form of social organization. The settlement of the West, if the Canadian government and people fulfilled their duty, it could be argued, simply hastened the achievement of this desirable goal. Agriculture, education, and religion would, in time, provide the Indian with far more than he had lost. Eventually the settlement of the West would uplift the native from his state as 'a member of a barbarous, heathen horde, wandering aimlessly over this vast continent' and make him instead 'an enfranchised citizen of the first Christian nation in the world.'[26]

The contrast between Canada and the United States was seen as having a moral lesson with implications much broader than the subject of Indian policy. The failure of American Indian policy could be regarded as simply one symptom of the failure of American society. The fact that the American government had initiated a number of praiseworthy policies, many of which Canadians would soon imitate, and that these had seemingly failed, simply reinforced this belief. It was truly American societal will, not government understanding or policy, that was flawed. In contrast, Canadian fairness to the Indian became a test of the honour of the Canadian expansionist process and of the whole social and political morality of the Dominion: 'In this shocking contrast of the way in which the Governments of the two nations have acted towards the red man of the American continent we find an opposite illustration of the difference between an unlimited democracy like that of the United States, and a limited monarchy like that of Great Britain. In the former the national will too frequently rides rough shod over every check interposed by the national reason and the national conscience; justifying its worst deeds by pleading that it must work out its national destiny.'[27] Canada saw the success of its own Indian policy not only as proof of its own sense of fairness but as an indication that it had indeed followed in the footsteps of Great Britain. 'The Canadian Government is raising up in that vast country a monument to British authority that shall endure for all time, a monument in which strict justice forms a base, kindness the shaft, and the whole power of the British Empire the capital overlooking and adorning the rest.'[28]

There was also an important lesson to be taken from the results of the Indian policies in Canada and the United States. The pursuit of justice, Canadians could and did argue, had very practical consequences. In the United States the expansion of the frontier of settlement had been accompanied by continual warfare between Indian and settler. This warfare, argued Colonel J.F. MacLeod of the North West Mounted Police, was the natural result of a system where the Indian felt he could not rely on the American government for protection and justice. 'I think the principal cause of the difficulties which are continually embroiling the American Government in trouble with the Indians, is the manner in which they are treated by the swarms of adventurers who have scattered themselves all over the Indian country.'[29]

Acton Burrows, while more general in his assignment of the cause, agreed with the basic principle behind Macleod's comment. The difference between the two policies, he reiterated, was one of justice, for the Canadian policy 'stands in marked constrast to the systematic frauds perpetrated in the United States.' The results of the policies were as distinct as their approach.

In Canada the Indian 'knows that he is under the protection of the Great Mother, that her officers will protect him against harm and faithfully carry out the agreements made under the Treaties by which his title to the soil was surrendered to the Crown.' The American Indian had no such assurances and thus used force in a vain attempt to preserve his rights. In Canada, however, justice had triumphed and 'as a consequence, an Indian war in Canada is unknown.'[30] Even with a vast frontier of open land the United States had not completely escaped the fruits of its own moral failure.

Relations with the native tribes were thus seen to be a test of the general strength of the social and moral fabric of the two nations. The violence between whites and Indians on the American frontier was thought to be a prelude to the more widespread social problems that would become apparent only when the frontier closed. Canada, however, had escaped the initial stages of violence between whites and Indians by pursuing a policy of justice. It followed that the future cataclysm which was so readily predicted for the United States could be avoided in Canada. If the social and moral, as well as the political and economic, structure of the North West was made stable and resilient, then the passage from frontier to mature society could be accomplished with the same ease that Canada had handled the passages from a native to a white society on the plains. The moral and social aspect of western development thus took on increased importance. In a very real sense the character of the Canadian West might determine the future greatness of the Canadian nation.

In deciding the future of their own West Canadians throughout had two points of reference. As was the case in many aspects of Canadian life, Great Britain served as a positive model and the United States as a negative one. These models, needless to say, were not viewed completely objectively or realistically. Rather it was a somewhat stereotyped view of the long-term historical and social tendencies thought to be at work in both nations. Behind these stereotypes, nevertheless, were very real concerns that would have a direct influence on the way in which the Canadian West developed. The whole tendency implicit in the adherence to a British model was towards the preservation and extension of older cultural ideals. At the same time, however, Canadians were faced with a vast and largely empty land which was more closely comparable to the American frontier than to the mother country. The question, therefore, was how to direct the transformation from frontier to civilization in such a way as to allow the development of British society and British values in the New World context.

Given this challenge it is not surprising that after 1870 the Canadian sense of mission in the North West focused on the new order that was to arise from the wilderness. As a result, the region was seen almost exclusively in terms of the future and in the potential that the future contained. The old state, whether it was the wilderness or the social order of the wilderness, ceased not only to have any positive attraction but was not even considered. The efforts of Riel and the Métis to draw attention back to that old order failed to halt this tendency. To all intents and purposes the Canadian expansionist viewed the North West as a social *tabula rasa*, 'where the very rudiments of the social fabric have yet to be made and laid.'[31] In one sense this was a very exciting prospect: the physical opportunity for well-being and economic power was paralleled by the opportunity to build a society more closely approximating social ideals than any that had gone before. Canada had a chance to create a social order equal to the prospects of the vast land which it would dominate.

Such opportunities, however, equally presented the possibility of failure. The economic order rested on the enormous resources of the region and was thus thought to be secure. The social order, however, rested on man, and that was a much more fragile base. Moreover, failure in the formative stages of society could be much more disastrous than in a well-developed one. In an established civilization institutions and traditions gave the society a certain inertia and diluted the impact of change. This restricted the reformer seeking to better the social order but it also helped minimize the impact of corruption or other forms of negative social change. The North West, without that protective inertia, presented not only opportunity but also vulnerability. Each decision reached during the early stages of development could have a long range and ever-widening impact. The social fragility of the unformed society made it imperative that man act quickly to ensure that it developed along proper lines. 'We must help to mould these diverse elements,' the editor of the *Canadian Methodist Magazine* warned, 'or the powers of evil will mould them into a godless one.' It was imperative to keep the West 'from the vice of drunkenness and many grosser forms of evil, and to lay deep and strong the foundations of a noble Christian state.'[32] In the years of the fur trade the missionary's concern had been that the wilderness would swallow man's efforts to construct a moral and religious society. By the 1870s the concern had been reversed. Man, in his efforts to transform the wilderness too rapidly, might forget to lay the moral and spiritual foundations of the society that was to supplant that wilderness.

The creation of a proper moral order in the North West was thought to depend to a great degree on the development of a strong and permanent economic order. The whole rhetoric of expansionism by the 1870s was based on the assumption that the North West was to become an agricultural region and it thus followed that the social order had to be based on an agricultural economy and predominantly rural way of life. Such a society would provide the solid economic foundations thought necessary and thus encourage stability long after the region had been settled. In contrast, any social order that rested on the superficial and transient opportunities offered to the speculator and land promoter by the presence of an open frontier would ultimately prove far too shaky a foundation on which to build a world power. Charles Mair, who himself did not hesitate to speculate in land, outlined the two choices in a letter to Grant: 'It may be the home of a great, a comfortable and therefore a loyal and contented yeomanry with every other interest developing from its sturdy roots; or it may become the arena of unscrupulous and vulgar monopolies, of absentee landlordism and the whole train of proletarian and socialistic agitations which follows or attends such a state of things. In a word we may find the dreary miseries which are baffling statesmanship in Europe imported into this country.'[33] The basic economic strength of the North West lay in the fertility of the land and any social strength the region was to achieve had equally to be based on a class that would work that land.

The belief in a rural society and the benefits to be derived from the dominance of the agricultural class were clearly revealed in the ambiguity which writers on the North West displayed towards the growing towns and cities of the region. On the one hand the growth of such centres as Winnipeg were seen as evidence of the rapid material development of the North West and as such were pointed to with pride.[34] At the same time there was a strong feeling that, as Grant commented 'interesting, and after a fashion, phenomenal as Winnipeg is, it must not be supposed that we can find the true North West in its towns and cities.'[35]

In fact, the very things which had caused Winnipeg to grow so quickly disqualified it as a typical or desirable example of the development of the North West. It was, after all, a place where 'speculators congregate to get up "booms" and similar transactions, bogus or slightly otherwise.'[36] Such events indicated that the city and its society was being developed on a shaky and amoral foundation. The virtuous society could not be created in such surroundings. One strict Presbyterian even found the 'prevailing intemperance and lasciviousness' of the city so shocking that he felt impelled to warn that 'young men whose moral character is not already fully established should avoid Winnipeg as they would a den of rattlesnakes.'[37] Not everyone was so solicitous of the morals of Canada's youth, of course, or so harsh in their assessment of Manitoba's capital. Winnipeg, with its activity and boom psychology, was an exciting and potentially important part of the North West. At the same time there was a tendency to believe that it would be dangerous for the West to look to Winnipeg. An unformed society, as with an unformed individual, needed more solid roots.

Rather than being based on the possible riches of Winnipeg, the ideal society envisaged for the future was one based on the independent rural landowner. While he was unlikely ever to become rich, it was thought he could become comfortable by working the land. The North West was to be populated in accordance with the social needs of the multitudes rather than the opportunities of the few. 'We have also to remember,' wrote Alexander Russell shortly before annexation, 'that of the myriads of industrious poor and unemployed it is evidently the destiny of a few only to make money.' All the land in the world could not change that fact. It could, however, achieve an equally important end. 'The millions want independence and abundance of food and clothing; and to obtain them easily is much to them.'[38]

This idea persisted into the 1870s. Terms such as 'yeomanry' and 'industrious husbandman' were used to describe the type of man who, it was hoped, would form the basis of society in the North West. The future of most immigrants was, in Acton Burrow's words, to settle on the quarter section 'where, by moderate perseverance they may soon obtain a competency, and secure for their families a successful start in life.'[39] The condition of the ordinary farmer, economically and socially, would ultimately determine the strength of the nation as a whole. A superficial layer of wealth and speculation was, in comparison, unimportant. Immigration and agricultural settlement was the key to the development of the North West and it was believed that 'men of moderate means' were the basis of large-scale immigration.[40]

One particular group seemed to fulfil all the necessary prerequisites of the ideal immigrant. The British tenant farmer and farm labourer were constantly wooed in the years after 1870 as the type of settler who would be most valuable in the North West. There were several obvious reasons for this. First, these people were British and thus possessed a set of customs and sense of loyalty which Canadians felt coincided with their own. Secondly, as farmers they were more likely to succeed on the land rather than fail through inexperience and drift to the cities. Thirdly, and not the least important, this group seemed most likely to find satisfaction and contentment in the modest life of the independent farmer. The region seemed designed for them and they, it was assumed, would appreciate that fact. 'How many cottars, small farmers, and plough boys in Britain,' Grant asked, 'would rejoice to know that they could get a hundred acres of such land for one dollar an acre.'[41]

The concept of a society based on the British immigrant working the quarter section reflected the ideal of orderliness and stability in the Canadian view of the North West. The romantic image of Canada's new frontier became one of 'plains divided by hedges and fences, into regular fields, interspersed with groves of trees and dotted over with homesteads – the comfortable and substantial dwellings of a prosperous and numerous population.'[42] It was a conservative, even staid, concept. The frontier, in the Turnerian sense of an equalizer where man worked out anew the reconciliation of liberty and social harmony, was not a part of the Canadian ideal. Canadians felt that they had ample proof in the American frontier that such natural development would, at the very least, mean an unacceptable period of social chaos as the society progressed through its initial stages of formation. At the worst it could mean the development of an amoral and unsound social structure which would permanently poison even the most physically wealthy region. Only by actively directing the growth of the new society on the frontier, Canadians thought, could they be assured of achieving their goal.

The conservatism of the Canadian approach to the settlement of the North West was revealed in many ways. In the most general sense, it has been shown that the Canadian West was developed within the framework of metropolitan control rather than frontier autonomy.[43] Certainly the whole expansionist impulse exhibited this tendency. In the United States several instances of expansion can be traced largely to the efforts of Americans on the impending frontier of settlement. In Oregon, Texas, and California, American settlers pressured their nation to annex these new frontiers. The idea of annexation of the North West, in contrast, had its roots in Canada, not in the West. Even taking into account the efforts of the Canada party and the *Nor'Wester*, Toronto, not Red River, provided the main impulse for expansion.

This metropolitan interest in the West continued after 1870. In numerous ways the Dominion government tried to assert its control over the frontier. The Red River resistance and the consequent formation of Manitoba thwarted this design to some extent. Even in Manitoba, however, the government retained control of that most valuable of all western assets – land. Politically, although Manitoba was theoretically as autonomous as Ontario or Quebec, individuals like John A. Macdonald sought a strong position of influence for the central power. He revealed something of his attitude towards the West when, as late as 1883, he referred to the region as a 'Crown Colony.'[44]

Such attitudes reflected an eastern desire to retain control both of the direction of settlement and the opportunities to exploit the region. The West would in time resist such eastern domination and attempt to bring control into its own hands. Nevertheless these political and legal facets of metropolitanism were but the surface manifestations of a conception of the frontier that was expressed in the *Globe*'s maxim of a new Upper Canada in the North West or in Alexander Morris's idea of a *Nova Britannia*. The institutions and social practices of the East were to be as much as possible transplanted to the North West.

Crucial to the transplanting of eastern civilization to the frontier was the rapid institution of law in the North West. This involved not only a relative lack of violence, which had equally been a trait of Hudson's Bay Company rule, but also the establishment of the abstract idea of rule by law. The wilderness, though it might often remain peaceful, offered little security because there existed no clear means of determining the permissible or protecting the individual. As William Butler commented in a report to Governor Adams Archibald, in the wilderness 'the wrong-doer does not appear to violate any law, because there is no law to violate.'[45] All security thus became dependent on the capricious and temperamental nature of man. The consequences of such a situation were revealed by George Grant in relating in some detail the story of a Métis who, wishing to be rid of his Indian wife, simply murdered her. That he should resort to such a course, Grant felt, was a direct result of the absence of law on the plains. The only punishment extracted from him was the payment of two horses.[46] The idea of the North West as a particularly civilized frontier made either random lawlessness such as this or the establishment of lynch law as a means of security unacceptable. Law, as a concept and as a formal institution, had to accompany the settler in order to ensure the transformation of the wilderness. As Alexander Morris somewhat awkwardly phrased it, 'the most important matter of the future is the preservation of order in the North West and little as Canada may like it she has to stable her elephant.'[47]

The actual establishment of law in the North West has led to one of the most potent and enduring myths in Canadian history. In the first years after annexation the absence of a means to enforce the law led, in the words of one individual, to a situation where 'violence was in the saddle over Canada's West.' While, in fact, there is little indication that the North West was ever really violent, the myth created by the passage of time painted a picture of 'battle, murder and sudden death, a composite of evils which, from the Red River to the Rocky Mountains, exacted a grisly toll.'[48] Equally a part of the myth, however, was the idea that such violence was temporary. Disorder was simply the setting which led to the introduction of law and order in the North West under the banner of the North West Mounted Police.

While a mobile force had been suggested earlier by people like William Butler, it was 1873 before the North West Mounted Police came into being. The heroic, if slightly inept, march west, and the force's success in destroying the whisky trade, quickly made it a dominant symbol of the triumph of Canadian justice and British traditions on Canada's frontier: 'The Indians are tractable and amenable to law, and have, also, a pretty good idea of what the law is. Here, in the very heart of Blackfeet country, where formerly a man never ventured abroad without his Henry rifle, and that man, for the most part, one of the Montana desperadoes before mentioned, all is now quiet and orderly as in any civilized country, and the farmer and the stock raiser carry on their vocations without fear of molestation. And all this change has been wrought by a handful of red-coated constabulary.'[49]

The image of the force reflected the Canadian concern with the idea of law as an institution and in symbolic terms the North West Mounted Police were often depicted as the law itself. Sir Cecil Denny's memoirs on the police were entitled, significantly, *The Law Marches West*. Moreover, once the police came to symbolize the abstract concept of rule by law they were endowed with greater power and authority than could have been obtained through mere cunning or the crude use of force. In essence the individual policeman, though praised for his noble attributes, was subordinated to the much more powerful tradition of British law and British justice. The scarlet coat of the North West Mounted Police had been deliberately chosen in order to evoke this British tradition. Thus the myth of the police became in reality a part of the myth of the tradition of law in British society. When, for instance, the notorious American Sioux chief, Sitting Bull, was interviewed by a handful of police, tribute was given not so much to the men as to the tradition. 'Such an instance is surely, worthy tribute, if only from a savage, to the glorious colour which is the pride of every Englishman, and which has won respect in all quarters of the globe.'[50]

The myth has become a part of Canadian history. Countless stories have depicted a situation where the Mounted Policeman faced overwhelming odds. The policeman, however, aware of his position of authority under the law and the law as representative of British power, coolly handled the situation in such a way that it never resulted in conflict. The man and the abstract concept merged into a symbol that few dared to challenge. A passage from the popular novelist, Ralph Connor, clearly reveals this theme that arose in so much later writing on the police: 'Irresistible authority seemed to go with the word that sent him forth, and rightly so, for behind that word lay the full weight of Great Britain's mighty empire. It was Cameron's first experience of the North West Mounted Police, that famous corps of frontier riders who for more than a quarter of a century have ridden the marches of Great Britain's territories in the far northwest land, keeping intact the Pax Britannica amid the wild turmoil of pioneer days. To the North West Mounted Police and to the pioneer missionary it is due that Canada has never had within her borders what is known as a "wild and wicked west.""[51] From their very inception the North West Mounted Police have been depicted as deriving their authority from an 'intangible connection with the British empire,'[52] and, one might add, the civilization which it represented.

The rapidity with which the Mounted Police took on mythical connotations indicates the way in which the complex and subtle imagery of the force coincided with the Canadian ideal of North West expansion. The symbol of the Mounted Police allowed Canadians to feel that the rapid extension of civilization did not imply the collapse of either security or justice. On the contrary, the police brought that security and justice to the North West and in so doing transplanted some of the most important characteristics of civilization. 'Those engaged in trading and other pursuits,' commented the Department of the Interior in 1879, 'are able to do so with as much security as if they lived in the centre of civilization, instead of on the as yet sparsely peopled plains.'[53]

The security of the North West reinforced in the Canadian mind the contrast with the United States. Canadian settlements were 'distinguished by a good order and security so often wanting in outlying settlements across the border.'[54] This contrast served as further proof to Canadians that the justice and morality of their expansion had resulted in stability, whereas, across the border, the absence of social peace futher revealed the moral failure of the American frontier. The comment was general and applied to everything from lynching to gun fights, but, once again, it was most dramatic in the case of relations between the native Indians and white intruders. Where good relations with Indian tribes allowed Canadians to rest peacefully, 'their brethren across the border sleep with their rifles at their sides, prepared at any moment to hear the fearful war-whoops of the Indian.' The blame for such a deplorable situation lay squarely with the United States government, for the Indian could be expected to act in no other way when his 'most sacred rights have been trampled on by a government whose policy to them is injustice, and whose object is their utter extermination.'[55]

The desire for security and order in the North West extended beyond such matters as lack of violence and rule by law. The approach of the individual to the society around him was often as conservative as the society as a whole. Whatever the life of the homesteader may have been in fact, the ideal was to import the amenities and institutions of civilization to the North West as fast as possible. The romantic concept of the voyageur living off the land, never very strong in expansionist thought, had, by the 1870s, been completely submerged by the ideal of the settled community. Those who went west often sought to recreate as much as possible the habits and styles of living they had known in the East.

The experiences of Charles Mair after he moved to the West reflected this tendency to reject the anarchy implicit in the wilderness for the more structured life common in settled areas. Mair was an educated man with wide contacts in Canadian governmental and literary circles and as such his experience of the North West cannot be said to be typical. Nevertheless, in his efforts to seek out social groups that coincided with his own self-image he revealed much of the rejection of the frontier as a democratic experience. What is most interesting is that he was successful. In Manitoba, while living at Portage la Prairie, Mair became a member of the Manitoba Club where literate discussions and middle class membership insulated the individual from the frontier.[56] Moreover, the circle of friends he cultivated were for the most part educated Canadians recently arrived from the East and members of the newly forming élite of the province. Alexander Morris, John Schultz, and Alexander McLeod of the North West Mounted Police were among Mair's acquaintances in these years; they allowed him to travel in circles with pastimes and attitudes not all that different from those members of the Canada First party he had left behind in the East.

In 1877 Mair moved from the relatively settled area of Portage la Prairie to the more distant and wild banks of the North Saskatchewan to make his home in Prince Albert. Even here Mair was able to find a structured society. If suitable institutions did not exist when Mair arrived, they were soon coaxed into existence by himself and like-minded friends. Mair, Colonel Alexander Sproat, and others acted as the founding members of the Saskatchewan Club, an institution resembling Toronto's National Club. Other activities followed. There were St Andrew's day dinners and even a 'Young Men's Literary and Athletic Club' by 1883.[57] To this circle at least the frontier did not imply a rough, egalitarian existence. It was not an ideal of the Canadian West to throw all types and classes of men into close contact through the destruction of social institutions and thereby forge a new and more egalitarian society. The frontier was a place of opportunity where a man might rise in wealth and social status, but it was not, conversely, intended to pull others down by removing them from what were considered to be the necessary attributes of civilization. Both the institutions and the social structure were to parallel as much as possible those of the East.

The concept of a relatively stratified society with predetermined leadership was widely held as necessary to the creation of a strong social fabric. The 'seeding' of the North West with desirable individuals was, as has been mentioned, seen as part of the settlement process. The hope was that a loyal and intelligent élite would further stabilize and civilize the frontier. When, for instance, the North West Mounted Police were created in 1873, the act followed Butler's suggestion of some years earlier and provided for land grants to men who served in the force.[58]

Throughout the settlement period the federal government went out of its way to attract desirable leadership to the North West. When Major General T.B. Strange wrote to the Deputy Minister of the Interior, Lindsey Russell, on various matters in the North West, Russell thought it important enough to pass the letter on to Macdonald with a long series of comments. His attitude was both instructive and typical. Strange, he noted, was much more than just a rancher for 'he is trying to make a military "colony" of retired officers, their sons etc. and uses his grazing leases as the basis of the operation.' It was not the fact that these men would necessarily make the best settlers that made Strange's work important, for, as Russell admitted, such people 'do not always contribute most to the material advancement of the country.' Rather, what made the General worthy of attention was that such groups 'have a good influence for refinement' and 'tend by their contribution to the "breed" towards rounding off the coarser corners of the future western national type of Canadian.'[59]

Canadians were proud of the orderly fashion in which their frontier seemed to be developing and its stability was seen as a positive point which could be used to attract immigration. 'It is fancied,' said one pamphlet published by the Department of Agriculture, 'that because the country is young it must, of necessity, be wanting in many of the surroundings and characteristics of civilization.' In the case of the North West, however, 'a more mistaken idea could not possibly be entertained.'[60] Rather, Canada offered the immigrant new economic opportunity within a familiar social framework. Not only did the British immigrant 'not change his flag' but equally he did not have to, 'except to a very slight degree, change his mode of life or his companionship.'[61] A move from Yorkshire to Saskatchewan, it would seem, was hardly more disruptive than one to Dover or London.

This tendency was further emphasized in the rather limited fiction emerging from the North West in the later nineteenth century. It was often 'better suited to an English drawing room than a sod hut' in its emphasis on civilized manners and social structures.[62] Yet it was, in a way, appropriate in that as with much literature it reflected the aspirations of the men and women who wrote it. The romance of the West had been seen in terms of its potential for years, and that potential, at least in idealized form, was seen in terms of the drawing room of civilized society rather than in the rawness of the frontier.

The whole complex of ideas concerning society, man, and the mission behind Canadian expansion into the North West thus tended to minimize the impact of the wilderness on the man who went west. The arguments of immigration pamphlets and the depictions of romantic fiction were simply extreme and somewhat unrealistic applications of this ideal. Contained within this conservative approach to the frontier, however, was an undercurrent of thought which modified it. Civilized societies, even those of Canada and Britain, were recognized as being far from perfect; the openness of the North West seemingly provided an opportunity to remedy some of the defects that had become a part of older civilizations.

It is revealing, for instance, that at the same time that the prospective immigrant was being told of the similarities between the North West and Britain he was also pointedly reminded of some of the differences. In particular, immigration pamphlets stressed that Canada had adopted those institutions of the mother country it thought desirable while discarding those that derived from outmoded traditions. In the context of the immigrant farmer and the North West, this meant specifically the absence of feudal restrictions on land tenure. Nicholas Flood Davin stated it in somewhat melodramatic fashion when he noted that the immigrant to Canada need not fear 'being disturbed by the death rattle of feudalism in its last gasp.'[63] The Department of Agriculture expressed it more generally but with equal bluntness when it commented that the institutions developed in British colonies are better than those of the mother country because 'they copy all that is good and suitable in the Old World system, [and] avoid all that is bad and defective.'[64]

The expansionist sense of mission, in spite of the importance it attached to British traditions, thus looked to the empty land not only to replicate society but to improve it. Expansionists hoped that the institutions developed in the North West would be able to escape some of the crippling, traditional restrictions of older societies. While this strain of thought resembled the more purely frontier tradition, there were differences. According to the American myth of the frontier, society was improved because of the very freedom of the undeveloped frontier; the American frontiersman, freed of past restraints and with progressively less cultural baggage, created a society from within himself. And because it was held that the common man was inherently good, it was also believed that this new society would be freer of corruption and more in accord with liberal-democratic ideals than the civilization that had gone before. In contrast, in the Canadian mind the open land was thought to provide an opportunity to purify and improve old institutions. It was not believed, however, as Alexander Ross had not believed years before, that the wilderness itself – or, perhaps more accurately, man in that unstructured wilderness – was the means to a strong and improved social fabric. In the United States society was supposedly to be improved by putting man into a free environment; in Canada it was to be improved by putting institutions in a freer environment.

The duality of conservatism and reform in the Canadian approach to the North West was clearly revealed in the attitude towards education and religion. It was felt that such socially central institutions had to be established at an early stage in development; the failure of either to keep pace with an expanding population would prejudice the nation's chances of creating the strong and moral society in the North West. 'It is absolutely imperative,' wrote the editor of the *Canadian Methodist Magazine*, 'that our church follow with her ministrations those path-finders of empire, or multitudes may perish for lack of knowledge and the grandest opportunity for occupying the country in the name of the Lord may be lost.'[65] The impulse was as much social as it was religious; the church was thought to be a vital force in the shaping of society. As George Grant said, 'the presence of a church in a community is a guarantee of social order.'[66]

Education was thought to have the same dual purpose. It was valuable not only for the skills it taught but as well for the code of ethics it instilled in pupils. It was thus thought necessary to develop educational facilities at as early a stage as possible in the development of the North West. The efforts of a few dedicated individuals to develop first a college for the expanding region and then a religiously based university said much of the Canadian concern for the orderly development of society. Long before the North West had a significant population, steps were undertaken to ensure that its people would have access to higher instruction. At the same time, the evolution of such institutions as Manitoba College and later the University of Manitoba revealed the reformist side of a conservative process.

The roots of Manitoba College lay in the Kildonan School begun by the Presbyterian minister, John Black, in 1869. Its conversion to a college, however, and its development over the next several years, was largely the work of Black's successor, George Bryce. Bryce had been born and raised in Ontario. Educated at the University of Toronto, Bryce received his Bachelor of Arts degree in 1867 and his Masters a year later. In 1871 he was ordained and immediately after went to Winnipeg to join Black.[67] As with many others, Bryce was enthusiastic as to the possibilities of the North West and in his case this enthusiasm became centred on Manitoba College. As a minister Bryce was more sensitive than most to the social implications inherent in rapid expansion and felt that proper educational facilities were necessary to the creation of a new civilization. Years later he wrote with obvious pride that 'the progress of Manitoba College is an exact register of the advancement of Manitoba.'[68] Much of his life had been dedicated to ensuring that this would be the case.

It proved a difficult task to create an institution of advanced learning on the frontier. In its early years Manitoba College depended heavily on the support of the church in the East for its survival. This support was not always eagerly given. On more than one occasion the Presbyterian church appealed to its congregations in Ontario, Quebec, and the Maritime provinces for special donations in aid of Manitoba College only to meet with little response.[69] Manitoba College survived through the 1870s only because a few concerned individuals shared Bryce's belief that education on the frontier was too important to be left until the region had grown populous enough to support it.

Foremost among these allies of Bryce was George Grant. In 1875, with the college in a typically desperate position, Grant played a key role in finding the funds to pull it through the crisis. As he later recounted to Sandford Fleming, he had been at the general conference of the Presbyterian church: 'Our pioneer missionaries and professors sent a delegation to us pleading for aid, and cold weather was thrown on them plentifully, till I got up and urged their claim on us for sympathy and assistance.' Grant's appeal led to his election as chairman of a committee formed to study the whole matter.[70] The committee eventually concluded, no doubt with some help from Grant, that 'the College is in a hopeful state; and it should be maintained in efficiency in its various departments.'[71] Over the next years the efforts of Grant, assisted by Bryce and by other sympathetic individuals such as Daniel Gordon and Charles Pitblado, enabled the college to continue to pry money loose from a reluctant synod.

Increasing the importance of the college in the eyes of its supporters was its potential as a centre of religion in the new society. Here, once again, expansion apparently offered an opportunity to transplant eastern institutions and at the same time to improve them. In 1877 Manitoba College was federated with several other denominational colleges to form the University of Manitoba. The creation of a university seemed as premature in 1877 as had the creation of the college a few years earlier. Certainly neither the population of Manitoba nor, for that matter, the population of the whole North West justified the presence of a university. This early federation, however, was a conscious decision on the part of the people like Lieutenant-Governor Alexander Morris to assert a precedent in the still fluid society of the North West and thereby avoid the interdenominational rivalry which had so affected the history of education in the East.[72] Manitoba, it was hoped, by acting with an eye to the future, would provide an example of a better and purer approach to the problem of religion in education.

This spirit of interdenominational co-operation was far from unique in the early history of western Canada. In part the practical problems of dealing with a sparsely settled frontier forced such co-operation. This had been the case with Manitoba College where, due to a shortage of funds, the two factions of the Presbyterian church worked together to support the institution. Thus, said Bryce, 'it was the good fortune of Manitoba College to be an example of brotherly love years before the union of 1875.'[73] Such problems also forced churches to consider mutual support in the more general field of missionary work. The vast distances and thin population of the North West made it virtually impossible for each denomination to cover the whole of the region. In 1882, for instance, the *Canadian Methodist Magazine* pointed to the 'unprecedented deficiency of ministers' in the church. Nor was this likely to change in the future. The geography and economy of the North West seemed to indicate that even when the region was fully settled the population would be thinly spread on large farms. This would make the 'difficulty of supplying the settlers with the ordinances of religion much greater' than in Ontario 'with its numerous villages and hundred acre farms.'[74] Such problems and pressures encouraged often hesitant denominational groups to consider union. Eventually both the splintered Methodist church and the divided Presbyterian church would resolve their differences and reunite. As with Manitoba College, reunification in these cases was at least partly a matter of necessity brought about by the challenges of the Canadian frontier.

While co-operation was made more necessary by the requirements of the North West there were also those who saw in this an opportunity from which might develop the positive good of a united Christian church. The importance of the mission to the new frontier and the hopes for that frontier demanded a new spirit of Christian unity. 'Never did God give any nation such an opportunity.' In taking this opportunity, 'shall we perpetuate in the new Canada of the North-West, the denominational rivalries of the older provinces?'[75] For George Grant, who whole-heartedly supported co-operation between religious denominations, the answer was most definitely no. The successful unions of the Methodist factions on the one hand and the Presbyterian on the other led him to look forward to a time when the spirit apparent in the West would allow more significant reunions. 'Our environment,' he noted, allowed Canada to go 'in advance of the churches in the mother-land and even in the go-ahead United States.' Was it not possible that Canada would continue to take the lead in the revitalization and unification of the Christian church?[76]

There was a double theme in all of these discussions on the future of religion in the North West. In the first instance, the North West, through necessity and opportunity, would encourage religious unity. Eventually, however, as the churches and other social institutions in the West developed, they could be held up as examples to the nation as a whole, and perhaps the world. Implicit was the idea that in time the institutions and practices nurtured in the West would point the way to a new and better civilization for all of Canada. In its own way, then, the Canadian sense of mission in the North West had parallels to the American belief in the frontier as a place of renewal and improvement of national institutions. It is perhaps symbolic of the differences, however, that whereas the classic frontier thesis envisaged religious reform in terms of the ineffectuality of established churches and the consequent growth of sects, the Canadian North West was seen as a catalyst to the unification of previously disparate denominations.[77]

The sense of religious mission was an integral part of the more general desire to establish a moral and stable society in the best traditions of the British Empire. It has been argued that the Methodists 'never seemed to decide clearly whether they were spreading Christian civilization, moral respectability, or the blessings of the British civilization.'[78] The Methodists, however, as did the other major Protestant denominations, saw their purpose as involving all three goals. The end was the creation in the North West of both a moral and a stable society; for many religious leaders of the period, nationalism, religion, and loyalty to British traditions were the component elements that would ensure that this goal was successfully achieved. As George Grant clearly understood, if this set of premises was acted on, then Canada's duty in the North West would have been fulfilled: 'A great future beckons us as a people onward. To reach it, God grant to us purity and faith, deliverance from the lust of personal aggrandizement, unity, and invincible steadfastness of purpose. The battles we have to fight are those of peace, but they are not the less serious and they are surely nobler than those of war.'[79] The North West was already seen as a future centre of world power; if, as Canadians believed, they were able to implant in the West a set of just and progressive institutions, then it could also become a future centre of world enlightenment.

7

John Macoun's Eden: the final stage of expansionism, 1878-83

In the spring of 1879 a Canadian writer commented that 'of all things that have impressed us most in the history of Canada during the last twenty years, none has been so strange as the *apparent discovery* of new parts good for settlement.'[1] It was a perceptive statement for it summed up a great deal about the Canadian expansionist process. From the time that Palliser and Hind had reassessed the North West in the light of Canadian demands for expansion, geographical perceptions had altered not only according to scientific theory but also to meet the expectations of the nation. It was also a timely comment for in the later 1870s a number of forces came together to change once more the assessment of the North West. These forces raised the image of the West to new heights and shattered the last qualifications in the Canadian myth of the garden. Science and geography responded to the perceived needs of the Canadian nation and in so doing reflected the wider social, economic, and political currents that were affecting the nation at the time. The result was an image of the North West that was more idealistic and optimistic than anything that had gone before, or, for that matter, anything that has existed since.

Behind this reassessment was a growing challenge to the reservations implicit in the image of the West handed down from the time of Hind and Palliser. The expeditions of these two men had successfully dissociated the North West from the Arctic which had dominated the image of the region in the era of the fur trade. Equally, in the fertile belt they had carved out an area distinct from the Great American Desert which was supposed to exist in the south. The separation of the North West from the American desert, however, had not been complete; the continued existence of Palliser's triangle, it is worth emphasizing, retained a link between the image of the North West and the idea of aridity. The image of the garden thus had remained qualified through the years of expansionism and annexation.

Such a qualification had seemed largely irrelevant in the 1850s and 1860s. As the 1870s went on, however, and as expectations for the region rose and Canada become involved in competition for European immigrants, the presence of a desert in the midst of this supposedly fertile granary became increasingly unsatisfactory. Pamphleteers and promoters were especially reluctant to accept such qualifications and did their best to ignore the existence of the triangle completely. If they mentioned it at all, it was in terms such as those used by Thomas Spence, who in 1877 dismissed it as a 'narrow strip running parallel with the United States' northerly boundary line.'[2] Comments such as the one by Spence, though sporadic and hesitant, revealed the way in which Canadian hopes for the North West had outstripped geographical interpretations of the region.

If rising expectations for the West made re-evaluation desirable, the weather made it easier for that desire to be accomplished. Accurate statistics do not exist for the region in those years but there are indications that neither the 1850s nor 1860s were particularly good decades in terms of precipitation. Drought was a recurrent problem in various localities and the conclusions of Palliser and Hind most probably reflected the effects of these years on the drier parts of the prairies. In contrast, it would appear that the years from the mid-1870s through to the early 1880s were especially wet ones.[3] As Canadians sought to assess the land they now owned they were pleased to find evidence to indicate that earlier explorers had been unduly cautious in their conclusions. Caution was definitely not to be a dominant trait of those making the judgements in the 1870s and 1880s, and before long bold attempts to extend the area of good land within the region were to take shape.

The beginning of the second stage in the reappraisal of the North West dates from 28 February 1874 when the Dominion Lands Survey was given the authority to initiate a series of exploratory surveys.[4] It was intended that the survey teams working under this authority would range far beyond those lands ready to be subdivided into townships. They would concentrate instead on the delineation of base lines and meridians for future, more detailed work. In addition, these teams were authorized 'to obtain knowledge of the character and resources in the way of soil, timber and minerals, as also of flora and fauna, of the territories covered by the survey.'[5]

The outlook of the individuals connected with the survey made this latter term of reference especially significant. The Surveys Branch of the Department of the Interior was, in the 1870s, staffed with a number of men whose enthusiasm for the North West made it reminiscent of the Crown Lands Department in the 1850s. The Surveyor General was none other than J.S. Dennis whose affiliation with the Canada party in Red River in 1869 had

151 John Macoun's Eden

helped to precipitate the Red River rebellion. Head of the Special Survey was Lindsey Russell, son of the expansionist, A.J. Russell. The staff under Russell in the field, while serious professionals, showed an equal degree of enthusiasm that ensured that any assessment of the North West would be made in the light of the pre-judged estimate of its great importance to Canada.[6]

Over the next years the Special Survey consistently found, in the words of the Department of the Interior, 'that previously held estimates of quantities of first class arable land in any given part of the territory, have been within the mark. Districts hitherto roughly classified as inferior, prove to be but partly so, and those defined as fertile areas, have their limits more extended the fuller our information becomes.'[7] The process was a cumulative one. In the initial years the Special Survey worked largely within the confines of Hind's fertile belt. Thus the reports of good land did not alter the image of the North West or significantly extend the area of land thought to be suitable for agriculture. By 1877, however, the survey teams began to move out of the fertile belt and into more marginal areas on the edge of Palliser's triangle. In 1877 Lindsey Russell took a party west of the Assiniboine and north of the Qu'Appelle; he concluded that this region possessed an absolute minimum of 'two hundred townships of first class character for farming purposes.' The same year his first assistant, Alexander L. Russell, found land in the region of the Red Deer River good enough to include it within those areas designated as first class agricultural land.[8] Both areas had previously been seen as having generally poor soil with only isolated spots suitable for farming.

While both of these areas were outside of the fertile belt it was also true that neither were within the area known as Palliser's triangle. The next year, however, the latter region was explored by the surveyors and, at least on its fringes, was found not to be so useless as had been thought. Lindsey Russell concluded in that year that the Plains of the Souris, on the second prairie steppe between the border and the Assiniboine, were not desert. 'I am led,' he reported, 'to judge but a small portion of about 100 townships included between the 15th and 25th ranges, and south of the Assiniboine, will prove unsuitable for cultivation.'[9]

Equally important was the work of the respected geologist, George Mercer Dawson. While on the International Boundary Commission Dawson travelled through Palliser's triangle and made extensive notes on the geology, soil, and agricultural potential of the area. He did not really reduce the area of the triangle in his report; rather he redefined its nature. Except for a relatively small strip some fifty miles wide along the Milk River, he concluded that the area was not truly a desert; the character of the soil and the presence of regular rainfall, at least in minimal amounts, made such a definition unrealistic. In an assessment that was to become common in future years, Dawson decided that though the triangle was not good agricultural land much of its was 'well suited for pastoral occupation and stock farming.'[10]

By the later 1870s the image of the North West had thus already undergone considerable change. The concept of the fertile belt as a narrow and unique strip of land was replaced by a much more general definition of it as everything outside of Palliser's triangle. The marginal regions which had so concerned Palliser and Hind had definitely been incorporated into the area of first class agricultural land. Moreover, the idea that Palliser's triangle extended from the 100th to 114th meridian along the international border with an apex at the 52nd parallel had been considerably modified. Both its base and height had been diminished as a result of the work of the Dominion surveyors and others. Even the triangle itself had been seen by Dawson to be, if not good land, something better than desert. Nevertheless, there does not seem to have been any writer in the 1870s who dared to dismiss the concept of the triangle completely. The basic geographical configuration of the West set out by Palliser and Hind had been modified in some of its details, but, as of 1879, its general applicability to the region had not been challenged. One more step was necessary to do that and that step was to be the self-appointed task of botanist John Macoun.

John Macoun was no stranger to the North West or to the discussions as to the amount of available agricultural land. He had been one of the many who played a part in the gradual increase in the estimates of the worth of the prairies through the 1870s. In fact, his work in the area of the Assiniboine and Qu'Appelle rivers in the summer of 1879 had made him something of a celebrity. Returning east from these explorations he had found a large and enthusiastic audience awaiting him in Winnipeg. Macoun was not reticent about the publicity and enthusiastically told his audience that there was 'no finer region in the world.' This was what they had come to hear, but Macoun took the occasion to hint that, important though the conclusion was, it was but a prelude to more important work. He promised to return and after that, he said, 'I may be able to tell you of other and just as valuable tracts which I myself have explored.'[11] He more than lived up to his promise.

In the spring of 1880 Macoun was ordered by the Department of the Interior to return to the West in order to investigate further the lands of the southern prairies. His party followed an irregular course up the Assiniboine River to Fort Ellice; from there they went by land southwest across the Plains of the Souris, the Missouri Coteau, and south of the branch of the Saskatchewan until they reached the Cypress Hills and Fort Walsh towards

153 John Macoun's Eden

the end of July. Their explorations had taken them through hundreds of miles of territory which had been written off as wasteland by fur traders and early explorers alike. Camped in the shadow of the Cypress Hills, Macoun and his party dismissed these earlier opinions, concluding 'that none of the land was poor pasture and much of it had a good fertile soil well suited for agriculture.'[12]

The next stage of the journey took the party through the Cypress Hills and northward to the elbow of the Saskatchewan. The desolate heights of the Cypress Hills, the miserable location of Fort Walsh, and the large sand hills near the South Saskatchewan, all made Macoun more hesitant about the quality of the land in this country. Even in this case, however, he rejected the description of the region as a desert. Writing to Sandford Fleming from Fort Walsh, Macoun described crops he had seen growing at an Indian mission and stated that this sight encouraged him to 'take even higher flights than any I have taken before.' Fort Walsh was certainly not the most desirable spot in the North West but, he concluded, it was far from being a desert.[13]

The third and final stage of Macoun's journey took him eastward once again, though to the north of the route that the party had taken to Cypress Hills. Once again he found 'loamy soil and long rich grass' and any bad lands were concluded to be isolated exceptions in a generally fertile region.[14] By the time that the party reached Winnipeg in the autumn of 1880, Palliser's triangle, at least as far as John Macoun was concerned, no longer existed.

For all the earlier work by members of the survey and Macoun himself, the elimination of the triangle was still a remarkable and audacious conclusion. Dozens of reputable scientists, including George Mercer Dawson and the members of Palliser's highly qualified party, had travelled over the same ground as Macoun and had accepted the existence of a region unsuited for agriculture. Even if, as was the case, the mood of the age invited the abolition of the triangle, the man who undertook to do so put himself out on quite a limb. In his background, personality, and approach to scientific research, however, John Macoun was ideally suited for the role he adopted.

Macoun was born in 1831 in County Down, Ireland. His family seems to have been reasonably comfortable materially and thus he did not suffer the severe privation which was the fate of so many of his fellow countrymen during the potato famine of the 1840s. He was a witness to that famine, however, and it was a powerful example of the importance of agriculture to the happiness of man. In 1850 the Macoun family emigrated to Canada as part of the great tide of Irish that left their homeland in those years. They settled near Belleville, Canada West, and as a young man John Macoun tried various professions from farming through teaching and operating a general store. His real interests, however, soon became centred around the field of botany. At every opportunity he would take to the woods to collect new specimens or would spend his time categorizing and arranging his growing collection. In the late 1850s he had the opportunity to acquire some further formal education which allowed him to broaden the theoretical base of his botanical work. Over the next few years he maintained contact with several respected professors at Queen's University in Kingston. By the later 1860s John Macoun was beginning to acquire a reputation in eastern Ontario as a knowledgeable botanist and his hobby had become a full-time profession.[15]

Throughout his life the most notable feature of John Macoun's personality was a contagious enthusiasm. This enthusiasm was general and indiscriminate but came to the fore especially in those matters connected with botany. In 1872, while on a plant collecting expedition to Lake Superior, he accidentally met George Grant and Sandford Fleming as they embarked on their epic transcontinental journey. It was typical of Macoun that he became so excited by the possibilities of botanical research in the North West that he decided on the spur of the moment to join them. It wasn't long before he was a familiar and eccentric figure to the passengers of the *Frances Smith* as it steamed towards Thunder Bay: 'At whatever point the steamer touched, the first man on shore was the Botanist, scrambling over the rocks or diving into the woods, vasculum in hand, stuffing it full of mosses, ferns, lichens, liverworts, sedges, grasses, and flowers, till recalled by the whistle that the captain always obligingly sounded for him. Of course such an enthusiast became known to all on board, especially to the sailors, who designated him as "the man that gathers grass" or, more briefly, "the hay picker" or "haymaker." They regarded him, because of his scientific failing, with the respectful tolerance with which all fools in the East are regarded, and would wait an extra minute for him or help him on board, if the steamer were cast loose from the pier before he could scramble up the side.'

Later, after an arduous trip over the incomplete Dawson Road, the party stumbled into a way station at Oak Point late at night and immediately fell into bed. At eight the next morning they were awoken by Macoun shouting: 'thirty-two new species already; it's a perfect floral garden.'[16] Even the rigorous trip of the day before had failed to dampen his enthusiasm for this opportunity to collect new specimens. The prairie, with its botanical uniqueness and richness, made its mark on Macoun as it did on so many others. As he later wrote of that day: 'the impressions then made have never faded from my mind.'

Coupled with Macoun's enthusiasm was a romantic view of the natural world. His work as a botanist was as much an avocation as it was a livelihood and he seemed throughout his life happiest in the field, collecting his beloved specimens. While in British Columbia in 1875, for instance, he found the flowers and plants around him so compelling 'that I sat down in my loneliness – but not alone – and drank in the surpassing beauty of the scene.' Such a feeling for nature made Macoun accept readily the hardships associated with wilderness travel. 'While others cursed the road and the flies, I, in my simplicity saw nothing but Nature decked out in the springtime loveliness and, instead of grumbling at the difficulties of the way, I rejoiced in the activity of the animal and vegetable kingdoms.'[17]

This same romantic outlook was revealed again later in the same trip. While in the region of the Touchwood Hills Macoun remained in camp and wrote in his diary as the rest of the party set off across the plain. 'I am sitting on a gentle swell in the general level,' he began, 'and as the rays of the sun touch the grass as it waves in the wind it looks like waving gold. The prairie is as silent as the grave – my party are in a hollow and I am actually alone in an ocean of grass.' Any man with a touch of the romantic in him would have been affected by the scene, and John Macoun was no exception. 'There is something soul stirring,' he continued, 'in these great solitudes – truly this is a "lone land" yet it was not always so. There the buffalo ranged in millions – pursued by the wolf and the red man – now all are gone and the wind passes over the plain and brings no sound to the listening ear.'

With Macoun, however, as with Hind twenty years before, the romance of nature was inextricably part of a grander design. Nature existed in order to be utilized for the well-being of man. Even in the midst of his reverie at Touchwood Hills, Macoun's thoughts went naturally from the romance of the present emptiness to the romance of the future. 'But is this solitude to last – No! 200 miles eastward a low steady tramp is heard – it is the advance guard of the teeming millions who will yet possess this land from the Great Lakes to the Rocky Mountains and these plains will resound with the merry laughter of children and the 101 sounds of life.'[18] The man who had witnessed the Irish famine as a youth had a very real sense of the contrast between the potential of the North West and the famine and overcrowding that were a part of European history. 'A field of growing grain' and the 'untold wealth in the soil' of the North West were the real images of romance. A higher destiny demanded that the wilderness be transformed into a 'plain dotted with the cabins of settlers, and their cattle grazing peacefully in the little valleys or up the slopes.'[19]

The potential of the North West captured John Macoun's romantic enthusiasm from the time he first saw the region. In 1872 when he visited the North West with Grant and Fleming and in 1875 when he explored it on behalf of the Dominion government, he found himself increasingly excited by the possibilities of the region. In a word, John Macoun became an expansionist. Moreover, as a botanist and scientist he felt that he had a particular mission to fulfil. 'My duty becomes plainer,' he wrote during his 1875 trip. 'I shall not rest until the Canadian public knows the value of this immense country both as regarding [sic] its resources and its capability of development.'[20] The scientist now added a second and possibly conflicting role to his already active life, that of publicist and propagandist.

The enthusiasm which Macoun brought to his work was symptomatic of another less positive trait in his character. Once Macuon became entranced by the North West the worth of the region became for him, as Grant once said, a matter of faith.[21] Anyone who challenged that faith invariably aroused Macoun's anger. The result was an aggressiveness and combativeness unusual for the supposedly detached field of botanical research. Writing to Fleming in 1878, for instance, Macoun noted that he was in disagreement with Colonel G.A. French of the North West Mounted Police on the worth of the country. His approach to this difference of opinion revealed much about his approach to science. 'I think I see my way to annihilate French,' he wrote. 'I will touch him on his want of knowledge and also on his want of honesty.'[22] On another occasion while in the gallery of the House of Commons, Macoun was infuriated when Alexander Mackenzie, in a speech on the North West, failed to take into account one of Macoun's reports. Unable to restrain himself he leapt to his feet and shouted at Mackenzie until restrained by House officials.[23]

Macoun's emotional involvement derived as much from his sensitivity for his personal reputation as from a belief in the capabilities of the North West. Once, when a senior official in the civil service enquired how Macoun knew of the things about which he had recently spoken, Macoun replied by pulling out his notebook and showing the questioner his writings on the subject. Lest the individual challenge the worth of these notes, Macoun, as he later related, 'told my interlocuter that my statements were convincing to an intelligent man and that, if they did not convince him, I was sorry for his intelligence.'[24] For John Macoun, scientific conclusions were never very far removed from personal honour.

There is an interesting paradox in the recognition that Macoun received which may have accentuated his own personal sensitivity. On the one hand he was the toast of the political and scientific communities; on the other, however, his reputation as a scientist seems to have been under continual chal-

157 John Macoun's Eden

lenge. His superior, Lindsey Russell, termed him a 'superficial scientist, though a clever knave.'[25] Alexander Mackenzie was openly sceptical of much of Macoun's work and John A. Macdonald was less cynical only by comparison.[26] At the height of his fame he became involved, through no fault of his own, in a departmental squabble that did little to help him or his colleagues.[27] Throughout his career John Macoun found that being a man of prominence also had its costs, and this may have accentuated his already temperamental nature.

While John Macoun's background and temperament suited him for his role in the elimination of Palliser's triangle, it would be dangerous to divorce his work from the scientific age in which he worked. His dramatic reassessment of the southern prairie was possible only because of the questions he asked and the approach he took towards the problem of climate. By the later 1870s there existed a body of scientific literature which allowed a significant departure in the method of assessment from that used by Palliser and Hind. Macoun drew somewhat cavalierly on various sources in order to develop his own scientific approach, and in so doing was able to turn the presence of the Great American Desert into a positive, climatological influence on the North West.

One of the basic scientific weapons employed in the initial stages of expansionism had been the application of the isotherm to the North West by Lorin Blodgett. His use of this concept had freed the region from a geographical determinism that prejudged the area by latitudinal position. Ironically, one of the modifications of theory that was to influence Macoun reintroduced the idea of geographical determinism. Once the West had been successfully differentiated from the Arctic, it once again became useful to emphasize its northerly position in order to begin the dissociation from the desert which was thought to exist to the south.

In 1872 Jesse Hurlbert, a former professor of natural science at Victoria College, wrote a remarkable pamphlet entitled *The Climates, Productions and Resources of Canada*. In it he argued that, given a particular latitude and continental position, patterns of wind and rain were the same around the world. Once these patterns were deciphered, one need only look at a map to conclude that 'in general terms it may be stated that the Republic [the United States], in position on the globe, in climates and productions, is similar to China, Independent Tartary, Palestine and Northern Africa; and Canada to Central, Western, and North-Western Europe.' The implications of this fact were, to Hurlbert at least, quite obvious. The United States, faced with 'high temperatures and burning sun,' was at a strong disadvantage compared to Canada with its more northerly and cooler position. Moreover, 'the want of rain is another and even more grievous defect in the climate in those parts of the United States; for high summer temperatures, with heavy rains, are conditions of climate favouring tropical plants, but high temperatures, without rain, are destructive of all vegetation.' With the exception of the northeastern seaboard and a partial exception in the case of the areas bordering on the Great Lakes, the United States was useless as a crop growing region.

Hurlbert further argued that the implications of a disastrous climate, such as the United States seemed to possess, affected more than agricultural production. Climate, in North America as in the Old World, had its effect on man as well as on crops. And, although 'time has not yet been given in the New World to show the full effects' of this fact, signs were already becoming apparent: 'Throughout extended districts of the United States, and especially on the border of the desert areas, the lapse of a few generations has shown a marked change in the race from their European ancestors, in their thinner busts, smaller heads, slender and more elongated forms.' This changing physique pointed the direction of development for future generations. In time residents of the American West would become typical inhabitants of the desert, of which 'the Bedouin of Arabia' were a prime example. 'Their attenuated forms, their small and wiry limbs, seem rather to move with the drifting sands than to perform the labours of industry.'[28]

In contrast, Canada was suited over most of its surface for both man and crops. Grasses, barley, and oats, according to the map which Hurlbert included, could grow as far north as the Mackenzie Delta and across the largest part not only of the prairies but also of the Arctic. Only small regions in the northeast corner of Hudson's Bay, James Bay, and northern Quebec were excluded from the agricultural sections of Canada. Hurlbert was more conservative when it came to the cultivation of wheat, depicting it as growing only a little to the north of Great Slave Lake, Lake Winnipeg, and Lake Superior![29] He did exclude from his vast region a small version of Palliser's triangle, but, in a later work, distinguished between that triangle and the deserts of the United States.[30]

It is tempting to dismiss the work of Hurlbert as that of a crank and a charlatan. Certainly the ideas he espoused failed to achieve the dignity or respectability of accepted scientific theory. Hurlbert, however, was not just an isolated crank and his ideas did receive considerable attention and support in Canada in the 1870s and 1880s. His 1872 pamphlet, for instance, was given indirect government support in the shape of an introduction by the Surveyor General of Canada, J.S. Dennis. Dennis revealed his motives in writing such an introduction when he referred to the 'interesting knowledge it affords of the attractive and immense field for immigration now opening in Manitoba.'[31] As a work on climate Hurlbert's pamphlet was open to serious doubts, but as a

159 John Macoun's Eden

piece of immigration literature it was superb. This was further confirmed when the Department of Agriculture used large sections of the pamphlet in a widely circulated immigrant brochure.[32] A few years later, when Hurlbert developed an atlas to illustrate further his views, he found both Dennis and John A. Macdonald receptive to the idea of having it printed at government expense.[33]

Hurlbert's most important influence, however, may have been on John Macoun. The connection between the prevailing winds, the presence of the American desert, and climatological conditions in the North West which Macoun appropriated from people such as Hurlbert, and perhaps Henry James Coffin's *Winds of the Globe*, became a central feature of his arguments with regard to the climate of the North West.[34] By the time Macoun went west in 1879 he had access to climatological theory which facilitated the dissociation of the Canadian North West from the desert to the south. Basic to Macoun's reassessment was a modification in the measurement of aridity; he denied that it was a meaningful, or useful, to judge a region by looking at the precipitation for the whole year. 'Such a comparison,' said Macoun, 'is misleading.' What really mattered was the rainfall 'during the period of vegetation' and 'during the harvest months.' It may indeed be the case that on an annual basis Palliser's triangle had less rainfall than is normally associated with successful agriculture, but, if moisture was obtained for the plants during the crucial spring and summer months, then this annual measurement was irrelevant.[35] Using these more specific statistics, Macoun had no doubt that Palliser's triangle was a chimera.

One of the most interesting aspects of Macoun's dismissal of the triangle was his use of the American desert. In his writings the desert became a positive force in the formation of a beneficial and desirable Canadian climate. Turning, as did Hurlbert, to wind patterns, Macoun argued that the presence of a large area of aridity and high temperatures south of the 40th parallel shaped the direction of winds in North America. Eastern and western air currents were attracted towards this region but, in the shape they were bent, actually united over the North West. Once brought together they carried 'temperatures of latitudes extending almost to New Orleans over the North West, and confer on it the blessings of a climate, not only exceptional as regards character, but productive of results to the agriculturist, which, I believe, are unsurpassed in any other part of the world.'[36]

Unlike any theory that relied only on the isotherm, this use of wind patterns explained not only the exceptional temperatures of the North West but also separated it from the arid lands to the south. The winds bent towards the North West were originally from the oceans but the high temperatures in the

160 Promise of Eden

United States ensured that the crucial moisture would reach Canada. The heat prevented precipitation and only when the winds reached the North West their 'long borne and priceless load is given forth in the form of our summer rains.'[37] The Great American Desert ceased not only to have any existence in Canada but served as well as a positive force in ensuring that the North West remained both warm and moist. 'Were the American Desert an inland sea,' wrote Macoun, 'the summers of our plains would lose their exceptional character.'[38] In winter, of course, the prevailing winds shifted, ensuring Canada dry, if cold, weather.

The relation of the prevailing winds, the moisture they carried, and the temperature of the lands over which they passed, altered the placement of the American desert. The northerly position of Canada became an asset, drawing the moisture forth from the clouds. Moreover, as heat seemed to be the determining factor in the dryness of climate the desert was pushed southward and out of Canada. It may even have been, had someone pressed him sufficiently, that Macoun would have admitted that the border regions of the American West were not truly desert; certainly this would have fitted changing climatological opinions in the United States.[39] Generally, however, Canadians were interested only in the prospects of their own territory and thus placed the magic line between desert and fertile land pretty close to the 49th parallel.[40] Changes in scientific theory helped to move the American desert southward, but nationalism determined the exact placement of the desert's northern limit.

Expansionists had long wanted to dissociate the North West from the arid plains to the south and when Macoun offered them the opportunity they wasted little time. As soon as his reports from the North West reached the Department of the Interior they were incorporated into the annual report. Thus, as early as 1880, an official government body accepted Macoun's position, concluding with an almost audible sigh of relief that 'the portion of the so-called American Desert which extends northerly into Canadian territory, is proved to have no existence as such.'[41] When Lord Lorne visited Manitoba and the North West the next summer he reflected both the changing state of opinion and his exposure to Macoun at a lecture in Ottawa the year before. Heading south from Battleford, Lorne noted that his party traversed a region which had been thought of as an extension of the American desert. 'The newer maps,' he commented, 'especially those containing the explorations of Prof. Macoun, have corrected the wholly erroneous idea.' The Governor-General found not a desert but a region that could 'not be excelled for agricultural purposes.'[42]

The acceptance of Macoun's work in official circles was but a prelude for the rapid incorporation of his ideas into practically all the literature written on the North West. Thomas Spence, who, as an immigration promoter, had long wished to be rid of the triangle, found all the evidence necessary to do so in Macoun's work. George Grant and Sandford Fleming, travelling across the southern prairie in 1882, were also convinced. After the trip Fleming commented that 'generally it may be affirmed that in the five hundred and fifty miles of territory between Swift Current and Winnipeg the waste and worthless land is scarcely appreciable.' George Grant agreed and specifically praised Macoun's contribution. 'The experience of the settlers who have gone to both districts,' he noted of the Qu'Appelle and Souris regions, 'have proved that Mr. Macoun was right.' Daniel Gordon, on his own tour of the West, travelled only in the northern parts of the region. On the basis of Macoun's work, however, he felt able to assert the usefulness of the south. Previously, he said, the southern plains had been regarded 'as sterile, barren and useless,' but 'Professor Macoun traversed these plains from east to west, and although he found some parts unfit for settlement, he found many others rich in loamy soil and abundance of grass.'[43]

Suddenly it seemed that all those who had previously missed the fertility of the southern prairie had their eyes opened. The conclusions reached by John Macoun became a standard part of Canadian scientific and popular thought almost as quickly as had Hind's fertile belt. Even G.M. Dawson, who had personally undertaken more exhaustive investigations of the southern prairie than had Macoun, later accepted the latter's interpretation as scientific fact: 'These open plains never possess desert character within the limits of Canada, but are naturally clothed with nutritious grasses such as those named buffalograss and bunch-grass'; moreover, the area 'is adapted to agriculture, and already fields of grain are replacing the natural grasses.'[44]

Macoun's influence was as important in matters of policy as it was in matters of rhetoric. It is no exaggeration to conclude that he influenced decisions that shifted the whole axis of development in the North West. In 1880 the Conservative government had turned the construction of the Canadian Pacific Railway over to a syndicate. Less tied to previous plans and assumptions than had been such government engineers as Sandford Fleming, the leaders of 'the Syndicate' looked anew at all the problems related to the construction and operation of the railroad. One of the issues they examined was the route to be taken and at that point they asked John Macoun for his opinion. 'As we talked,' Macoun later recorded, 'I told them of my experiences of the year before and told them of the easy road that could be made from Moose Jaw, west to Seven Persons Creek, and I told them of looking up the Bow River Pass two years before and seeing a wide open valley.' The matter was discussed for a while longer and then the momentous decison was made to try and go by a southern route.[45] Of course the decision to change the route of the railway was not made simply as a result of the conversations with John Macoun. There were a good many reasons why the leaders of the syndicate wanted to make the change.[46] Had the original assumption still existed that the southern prairie was desert, however, the Canadian Pacific would not have been constructed through it.

The projected railway was a key factor in the direction of development in the North West, and before long the decision of the syndicate, coupled with Macoun's reassurances, led to other changes in development patterns. In 1881 the capital of the North West Territories was moved from Battleford to 'Pile of Bones,' rechristened Regina as a name more in keeping with its new station. Between the 50 and 51st parallels of latitude and at nearly the 105th meridian, the location of the new capital symbolized the rapid disappearance of the image of the southern prairie as wasteland. Edgar Dewdney, governor of the North West Territories and the man largely responsible for the choice of site, termed the location 'one of the most extensive and best Wheat districts in the North West.'[47] In the wake of the shift of the railway and government attention to the south, other changes naturally followed. Settlement, rather than swinging northwestward from Manitoba to the valley of the Saskatchewan, continued to progress directly westward, following the line of the Canadian Pacific on to the Plains of the Souris.[48] The Dominion Land Surveyors responded to the new thrust of settlement and also shifted their work to the south, concentrating on the area along the line of the railway.[49] Patronage, settlement, and, most importantly, the great transportation link, had all been affected by the work of John Macoun.

The result was nothing less than a new map of the North West. The most striking contrast between this and older maps was the lack of differentiation between regions. The fertile belt disappeared as a meaningful concept and, when used at all, meant only all those lands south of the sub-arctic. 'We have a continuous stretch of land,' noted the Department of the Interior, 'nearly a thousand miles in length, available for agriculture and stock-raising, which is not excelled in magnitude by any similar tract south of the 49th parallel and west of the 100th meridian.'[50] It really became clear how little the term 'fertile belt' meant after 1880, however, when a Canadian Pacific Railway pamphlet applied it specifically to the south: 'As the construction of the Railway has progressed through the Fertile Belt of the Canadian Northwest towns and villages have sprung up as if by magic.'[51]

While Hind's fertile belt became a meaningless term, Palliser's triangle, denoting a geographically distinct region, disappeared altogether. This allowed Canadians to claim a great deal more land as their agricultural heritage in the

North West. Hind had originally estimated that the fertile belt contained some 40 million acres of land suitable for crops.[52] Over the years this had gradually increased but as late as 1877 even John Macoun had dared not estimate more than 80 million acres as being the extent of cultivable land. By 1881, however, he had considerably revised his estimate to some 150 million acres.[53] He was not alone. The Grand Trunk Railway soon promised immigrants 184 million acres to choose from, and Alexander Begg, now writing for the Canadian Pacific, went so far as to proclaim 300 million acres of useful land in the North West.[54] When one considers that his estimate was more than seven times the figure originally given by Hind, the extent to which the assessment of the West had changed may be readily appreciated.

Until 1880 and John Macoun's explorations it had always been assumed that the northern part of the region would serve as the basis for development. The new evaluation of the southern prairies and the subsequent decison of the railway and the government to concentrate their attention on that region thus marked a relative shift between the prospects of sub-regions in western Canada. John Macoun, enthusiastic over his discoveries in the south, encouraged this; while he did not directly attack the accepted fertility of the North Saskatchewan Valley, he did refer to 'summer frosts and too much water and muskeg' in such a way as to leave the prospective farmer no doubt where his own preference lay.[55]

This shift of emphasis was not well received by those who had settled on the basis of older assumptions of western climate and soil. Not surprisingly, the strongest resistance to Macoun came from those who lived in the area of the North Saskatchewan. In the same issue of the annual report of the Department of the Interior that praised Macoun's work, Charles Mair inserted his own rather different views on the relative value of regions in the North West. Mair retained the use of the term 'fertile belt' in its original and more restrictive sense; he further concluded, hopefully, that Prince Albert would soon possess 'all the appliances and forces of modern civilization.'[56] If Mair wrote hopefully, newspaper editor William Laurie wrote with a tinge of bitterness from his home in Battleford, the former capital of the North West Territories. Battleford, he complained, had been the target for 'every variety of misrepresentation and falsification' and this led to the transfer of the capital to Regina.[57] Laurie, Mair, and the others who protested in a similar vein were unsuccessful. The removal of the railway from the valley was a more powerful force than any number of articles and pamphlets. The original assumption that the North Saskatchewan would form the nucleus for the settlement of the North West and that the south would be settled only afterwards had been reversed.

The resistance to Macoun from the North Saskatchewan had obvious motives. Not all the challenges came from that region, however, and one, from the unlikely place of Windsor, Nova Scotia, issued from a man with a long association with the North West. In 1883 Henry Youle Hind, then sixty years old, emerged from his quiet life to publish a set of letters he had written to various government officials. In these letters he had made an acerbic and strongly personal attack on Macoun's work, arguing that 'much of what he alleges he conceives to be the truth is manufactured falsehood and fraud.'[58] Hind warned that to enumerate all his charges against Macoun 'would require many folios,' but even the condensed list he gave left no doubt of the serious nature of his accusations: 'Those which relate to climate involve the selection and application of incompatible elements, and the drawing of broad generalizations from them. The *Falsification* and altering of recorded data and submitting conclusions therefrom. The description of enormous tracts of country he never saw. The ignoring of acknowledged, and the adoption of disproved data, on which to base his conclusions. The misquotation of responsible authors and the adaptation of those misquotations to prove his fallacious and misleading representations. With numerous minor frauds of a very disreputable character.'[59]

It was an exceptional attack on a series of scientific conclusions that, by 1883, seemed to be accepted without question. Hind made the accusations both because he believed Macoun had perverted science for his own advancement and because he disagreed with the way the government was portraying the North West to the public. Hind's own work had shown the way in which scientific research and nationalist aspirations could reinforce each other. The process could only go so far, however, before science suffered, and Hind felt that, in the years between his own work and that of Macoun, expansionism had degenerated into immigration promotion. 'All of these practices,' he wrote, 'have apparently one object, namely: to distort and magnify the physical features of Manitoba and the North West Territory for the purpose of inducing immigration.'[60]

Hind blamed the Department of the Interior and particularly the Geological Survey for this perversion of science. As the government body responsible for the assessment of the North West, Hind believed it had a duty to maintain the strictest scientific standards in the tradition set by its founder, William Logan. Logan's example seemed to have been forgotten, however, for 'the Geological survey does not sanction and promote these scientific and practical delusions for Truth's sake, or in the interests of science, or with the object of dispensing reliable knowledge.' Its real purpose was purely and simply the promotion of a favourable image of Canada in order to promote immigration. In Lindsey Russell, the deputy minister of the interior, and Ernest Deville, chief inspector of surveys, Hind concluded, one could 'furnish examples of the progressive depravity of a once proud department.'[61]

In their specifics Hind's charges were unduly suspicious. While there are instances, on the part of Macoun and others, of dubious use of evidence and obvious bias in conclusions, the indications are that what Hind saw as deliberate fraud was largely enthusiastic prejudgement. The Departmet of the Interior, the Geological Survey, and individuals like Macoun did not set out to promote immigration regardless of the facts. They were, however, so caught up in the rhetoric of North West development that they looked for, and readily found, evidence that the region was even more favourable for agriculture than had been thought. This predeliction for optimism indicated a dangerous lack of understanding among officials and enthusiasts of the difficulties facing the settler on the frontier. Moreover, in their lack of restraint they encouraged others who, with less understanding of the settlement process and less scruples, portrayed the West in dangerously excessive terms.

Once Macoun's work allowed the final qualifications in the myth of the garden to be removed, all restraints on the description of the North West collapsed. Increasingly in the early 1880s writers began to view the region as something approximating an utopia. As with most utopias the one created in the Canadian North West lacked certain elements of reality. The landscape became 'the largest flower garden on the continent' and the climate so tame that it could be said to be 'very much the same as it was in England 30 years ago.'[62]

The immigrant coming to the region not only had a chance to achieve material comfort but was practically guaranteed it. A Canadian Pacific Railway pamphlet set down in pounds and pence the costs and income of the new settler on the prairie with actuarial precison. In the first year the immigrant's efforts to establish himself would result in a deficit of £149. Thereafter, however, it would seem that neither the world price of grain, the cost of transport, nor the uncertainty of weather could prevent him from reaping a profit. The second year, it was true, that profit would amount to only £36, but henceforth the return would grow until by the sixth year he could expect to have amassed more than £1000.[63] It was an amount of money that most immigrants had never seen.

Nor did the achievement of such profits any longer imply a great deal of work. 'As in every other part of the world, labour is the condition of life and success,' one immigration pamphlet warned, but only enough, it would seem, to ensure the preservation of the work ethic. 'But we emphatically deny that the labour is arduous, or the privations to be endured excessive. In fact, compared to what hundreds of thousands of our countrymen have undergone in the older provinces of the Dominion, they are mere child's play.'[64] Another pamphleteer wrote that 'an extensive knowledge of British agricultural practices is not necessary to a farmer in the North West, where farming is of the simplest imaginable character in which ploughs are used at all.'[65] The most extreme simplification of the arduous process of earning a livelihood from the underdeveloped land of the North West, however, must be attributed to none other than John Macoun: 'Let a man settle where he may, between Winnipeg on the east and the Rocky Mountains on the west, and the International Boundary on the south and the parallel of 60 degrees north, and he will have no difficulty in procuring food. Should the soil give no returns the lakes and rivers teem with fish, and every marsh and pool swarms with water fowl. If he prefers the south he can raise fat cattle without an hour's labour, and if he tries the middle region a prolific soil will more than supply his wants. Here on an area of 350,000 square miles is everything to supply a vast population, and all that is needed is a mere scratching of the soil or the placing of a net in the water to supply a household with food. Want, either present or future, is not to be feared.'[66]

The initial stages of expansionism, though not without its own exaggerations, had had a certain respect for the size, emptiness, and challenge presented by the North West. There had always been enthusiasm and confidence, of course, but the emphasis on hard work and the admission that there was bad as well as good land, bad weather as well as good, had qualified Canadian enthusiasm. The triumph of John Macoun and the flood of increasingly utopian pamphlets in the 1880s reflected a growing lack of reality in dealing with the problem of settlement. The desire for immigration, the cumulative rhetoric of expansion, and the enthusiasm of people such as Macoun had turned the North West, in Hind's perceptive words, into a 'fictitious Garden of Eden.'[67]

It was this conversion of the land that, in the wider sense, brought Hind forth in 1883. Hind believed that the process involved in opening the West was much more complex than the literature of the 1880s indicated. 'It is known in properly informed circles,' he wrote, 'that Manitoba and the North West embrace a tolerably well decided and defined area of land fitted for present farming purposes by a *gradual process of cautious settlement*, consistent with the extreme character of the climate and the very scanty fuel and water resources of the prairie portion of the country suitable for that purpose.'[68]

Henry Youle Hind reflected the attitudes of an older generation of expansionist and it may have been that he was too conservative in his estimates of the North West. It is certain that he was too conservative for the mood of the nation. His protest went largely unnoticed by both the government and the

167 John Macoun's Eden

public. Nevertheless, Hind's call for restraint raises an interesting point at a time when government officials and immigration promoters tripped over each other in their efforts to extol the ease of settlement in the North West. The expansionist movement had never given much thought to the difficulties involved in carving a livelihood out of the quarter section farm. As the movement developed along increasingly utopian lines the promises made to the prospective settler became more and more divergent from the realities of life he would have to face. The real significance of Hind's protest was his attempt to introduce an element of caution into both the settlement process and the expectations of the immigrant. His failure meant that settlement would continue at as fast a pace as could be generated and the settler would be led to expect a relatively easy life in the new region. The commitment of thousands to a precarious livelihood without any real understanding of the difficulties involved practically guaranteed future discontent, if not disaster. Moreover, as the settler accepted this image of the North West, he focused his inevitable disillusionment not on the process of settlement itself but in other, external, directions.

8
Disillusionment: regional discontent in the 1880s

John Macoun's enthusiastic reappraisal of the North West coincided with a period of growth and prosperity. Practically every indicator of the economy in the West showed marked improvement in the years surrounding 1880. Land sales, homesteads, and pre-emptions rose from 132,918 acres in 1876 to over a million acres by 1879 and an astonishing 2,699,145 acres by 1882.[1] Grain exports, first begun in 1876, continued to increase in value with each succeeding crop. Settlers, encouraged by this prosperity, pushed westward from the fertile soil of the Red River Valley onto land that had only recently been declared suitable for agriculture. The long-awaited destiny of the North West seemed at last to be imminent.

In the centre of this prosperity was the city of Winnipeg and, as befitted the 'gateway to the West,' it experienced the most heady effects of growth. Its population doubled between 1875 and 1878 and by 1882 it was more than six times the 1875 figure.[2] The general prosperity of the West was magnified in the city until optimism and economic growth touched off a wave of activity that continually astonished visitors. J.S. Dennis, in Winnipeg in the summer of 1881, wrote in a tone of amazement that 'the excitement here as to lands is astonishing approaching nearly to a craze – that is in the matter of city, town and village lots.'[3] J.B. McLaren, recently arrived from the East, wrote his acquaintance, George Grant, that the city of Winnipeg was as much a unique feature of the West as was the prairie. He was fascinated by 'the craze that exists there for the West, for locating towns on the line of railway and selling town lots by auction before there is a settler within one or two score miles.'[4] Canadians had often looked with a combination of jealousy and derision upon American land booms. Now, it seemed, they were experiencing one of their own. *Grip*, the satirical Canadian version of *Punch*, was not about to ignore such an easy target simply because of its national origin:

169 Disillusionment

> Sing a song of millions,
> Spent like random shots,
> Up in Manitoba,
> Buying corner lots.
> Fancy paper city –
> Pretty Indian name –
> Is it very naughty,
> Playing such a game?[5]

While the years of good grain crops, growing shipments to the East, and a buoyant world economy all helped to create the speculation on lands in Winnipeg, the boom also fed upon itself. As with most other booms, much of the excitement was internally generated: speculators purchased property not because of the integral worth of the land but because they believed that the boom atmosphere would allow them to make a quick profit and sell out; each time the property changed hands the price was increased and each sale created stories of fast profits and easy money. The basic underpinning of the heady atmosphere that prevailed in Winnipeg in these months, however, was the arrival of that long-awaited symbol of development and progress, the railway.

In December 1878 Winnipeg was connected to the outside world by rail. It was true that the first link was not with the east but the south and that the facilities were so crude that a locomotive could not turn around at the Winnipeg end of the line. Nevertheless, the Pembina Branch heralded the long-awaited end of an era of isolation for the settlements on the banks of the Red River. As one contemporary put it, 'the "golden gate" to an immense country' seemed to have been opened 'and thousands, eager to participate in a share of the undeveloped treasure, poured into the land.'[6] The Pembina Branch was but the first of several railway-related developments in the later 1870s and early 1880s: a new railway, the Manitoba and South Western, was chartered in 1879, and in 1880 the greatest railway of all, the Canadian Pacific, decided to take its line through Winnipeg. Such events as these led westerners to feel that the time had come when potential would be translated into development.

There were those who expressed nagging doubts as to the direction that this development was taking. The heady speculation of the land boom was hardly the means to the sturdy agricultural economy and society thought essential. The whole speculative market was based on quick profits and rapid footwork rather than hard work, and men at the time recognized this fact. Dennis warned that 'some people will before long I fear come to unmitigated grief' and a visiting reporter from the Toronto *Globe* noted that he often heard the same prediction made in the streets of Winnipeg.[7] Not many people heeded these warnings, however, in the years of 1881 and 1882.

The desire to speculate in land seems to have been practically irresistible. Even Sandford Fleming, a man who had known the West for a long time and who was fairly cautious in financial matters, could not resist the temptation to make some investments while in Winnipeg in 1882. Nor was Fleming looking to the solid, long-range possibilities of such a purchase: he bought two lots in Rat Portage on 2 February and sold them six days later at a profit of $200.[8] Even the respectable and conservative Anglican bishop of Saskatchewan, John McLean, yielded to the worldly race after quick profits. Writing to Charles Mair in Prince Albert on almost the same day that Fleming purchased his lots, McLean asked on what terms he 'could secure a few lots for my own *private account*, not for church or school or any other Diocesan purpose.'[9] Unfortunately, McLean's choice of investments was not as sound as Fleming's; land prices in Prince Albert did not rise to nearly the same extent as they did in Manitoba.

The Winnipeg land boom was an aberration in the trends of western development. It was, nevertheless, a significant event in many ways. It reflected the optimism of the age and meant that the reality of development in the North West seemed to coincide with the increasingly utopian visions that had gained acceptance over the years. If the West was portrayed in extremely favourable terms it could also be said that the region was developing as rapidly as such images might suggest it should. Even in its most extreme phase, then, the expansionist image of the North West seemed only to be a reflection of the actual course of history. Such a pleasant state of affairs did not last for long.

As with most land booms, the one centred in Winnipeg collapsed suddenly. A good many people who held their property too long or who purchased at too high a price suffered as a result. The investment which had seemed so sound at the time suddenly proved practically worthless. In retrospect, there were many to be found who had condemned the boom and pointed to it as a well-learned lesson concerning the necessity of stable development. John Schultz, writing in 1884, could even take comfort from the fact that 'the bursting of the Boom has weeded out all the speculative and weakly ones and left a better element behind.'[10] 'W.F.C.,' writing in the Toronto periodical, *The Week*, in 1883, took the same position and interpreted the collapse of the boom as a swing of the economic pendulum now thankfully returning to an equilibrium.[11]

In spite of such hopeful statements, the end of the boom had a decidedly negative impact on the West. The collapse of land prices signalled the beginning of trouble in a number of economic areas. More significant than the price of land in Winnipeg was the decline of crop prices, commercial transactions, and, most central of all, the rate of settlement. Beginning in 1883 all of these key indicators fell. In 1883, 1,831,982 acres of land were alienated, down over 800,000 acres from the year before. Thereafter things got worse instead of better. In 1884 this figure dropped to 1,110,512 acres and in the troubled year of 1885, 481,814 acres.[12] The collapse of Winnipeg land prices marked the beginning of a serious and widespread depression that was to hang over the West for the next several years. Periodic recoveries proved to be only temporary and not until 1896 did the North West again really experience long-term prosperity.

The depression had a profound effect on those who had gone west on the premise that expansionist optimism was justified. For more than a generation Canadians had been led to believe that practically anyone who was willing to work would be able to live comfortably in Canada's illimitable granary. So long as it was thought that the West was moving towards the realization of its potential, this belief went unchallenged. The collapse of 1883, however, meant that reality and image no longer coincided. As Charles Mair wrote to George Denison, 'matters instead of improving in the North West are getting worse. To use an old phrase the bottom seems to have fallen out.'[13] The archetypal expansionist, the man involved in the West for nearly fifteen years, suddenly found himself wondering if the region was going to live up to the promises that had been made for it. Mair, as with many who had shaped their lives according to expansionist arguments, now faced bitter disillusionment.

Mair's disillusionment was with the economic conditions in the West and did not extend to the land itself. 'That matters will recover is certain,' he wrote on one occasion, for 'the country is there.'[14] This combination of faith in the land and disappointment with the actual state of things was widespread in the West in the 1880s. Those who had accepted the basic expansionist argument on the worth of the land never rejected it. George Patterson, writing in 1885 to explain the depression in the West and the discontent that existed, still maintained that the farmer in the region began with a great many advantages over farmers elsewhere.[15] More than a decade after the collapse of the land boom the faith still remained. In 1895 George Grant wrote to lament the continued lack of development in the North West. 'The most disheartening feature to the visitor,' he maintained, 'is the enormous quantity of land round the city which remains virgin prairie or is cultivated in a slovenly fashion.' It was especially discouraging because Grant felt that 'there is no such soil in the world for the production of cereals.'[16]

This mixture of faith and disappointment characterized the mood of the West in the 1880s and early 1890s. Those who had accepted the idea of expansionism were not willing to accept the qualifications that Henry Youle Hind had insisted were necessary. Even when westerners found that their actual lives had failed to live up to expectations, they retained their image of the North West as a fertile garden. Blame for the depression of the 1880s would not be directed towards the land itself. It would take another, much more severe, depression before there arose any serious challenge to the optimistic conclusions of John Macoun.

There were two possible explanations for the problems of the 1880s other than a stingy land. One was that those who had settled in the West had not applied themselves sufficiently to the task of building up a livelihood. Settlers who had undergone great discomfort and put in long hours carving a farm out of the quarter section they had been allotted, rejected this explanation out of hand. There was thus only one possible explanation left. The men who had gone west as part of a great national and even imperial project had been betrayed by those who had remained behind. While expansionism had always been metropolitan in tone it had also presumed that the relationship between the East and developing West would be beneficial to both regions and to the nation as a whole. As economic reality clashed with the expansionist image, however, many began to wonder whether the East, and particularly Ontario, was not concerned only with the exploitation of the West for its benefit.

In a speech given in honour of the Lieutenant-Governor of the North West, Charles Mair summed up this new attitude: 'To pass from the old state of things to the present is like going from warmth into chill air.' That this disillusionment was not with the land made the situation all the more intolerable: 'We find ourselves in the heart of a rich country, yet, through no fault of our own, confronted by a material outlook which bristles with difficulties.' Such a situation existed, he continued 'not through our own supineness, not through indolence or lack of industry, but through circumstances over which we have had no control and which we have fought in vain.' Mair's words revealed a sense of powerlessness and frustration that has since become a classic component of regional grievance.

The problem was not that there was no remedy but that only in the East could that remedy be found. We 'came here through public maps, through public declarations, and through public charters,' said Mair, 'every one of which we have lived to see cut down.' Expansionism, he felt, was a two-way contract. One party consisted of those who had responded to the call to settle the West. The other half of the agreement was made up of those in the East and the federal government who had depicted the development of the region as part of a great national campaign that would benefit all. These parties, however, had betrayed the contract by working against the prosperity of the

West. 'Like many others,' Mair 'was constrained to attribute the delay to eastern jealousy.'[17] The man who had dismissed the sectional and social concerns of Red River in 1869 found it necessary by the 1880s to assert western rights in the face of eastern indifference.

The particular thrust of the argument presented by Mair and others in these years was not against expansionism but against those who had failed to live up to its implications. They felt that the development of the West was being deliberately hindered by easterners who, in their short-sighted selfishness, failed to understand either the value of the West or the aspirations of the people. As the Edmonton *Bulletin* said on 19 January 1884: 'it is quite apparent that papers and politicians in the east have utterly false ideas as to the relationship of the North-West to Canada as a whole and the position to be taken in confederation by its people.' Even John Schultz wrote confidentially of his own party that 'if we had men in Ottawa instead of [?] like Daly and jackasses like some of the rest of them we might have an enormous aid in this development.'[18] The easterner was to blame for the failure of the West to live up to its promise. Nevertheless, many were discontented enough that they gave clear warning of their willingness to turn on expansionism itself if their grievances were ignored. In a significant resolution in 1884 the Farmers' Union attacked a basic tenet of expansionism when it recommended that until things improved in the West immigrants should not come to the region.[19]

The expansionist movement had always had regional overtones. Canada West had spawned it and provided it with its main personnel. In the 1880s, however, a new regionalism began to develop. Westerners, including many from Ontario, found a new focus for their interests in the land they had adopted. These interests, while still thought to be part of a plan to develop the nation as a whole, were not necessarily congruent with those of eastern Canada. Government agents and others still turned out enthusiastic pamphlets in praise of the North West, but it had become apparent that the expansionist movement had fragmented under the pressure of regional discontent. For westerners at least, the enthusiasm of earlier years had been replaced with a reserved scepticism.

Those who had gone west in the name of expansionism were not the only ones to suffer as a result of the depression of the 1880s. The Métis and the Indians, those remnants of the old order, had their own complaints. Over the last few years things had gone from bad to worse for both these groups. They had been seriously affected by the dwindling herds of the buffalo in the 1870s and, in some cases, had come close to actual starvation. Governor David Laird's lament to Mackenzie in 1879 that 'the disappearance of buffalo has suddenly brought thousands of Indians to the verge of starvation,' was all too typical of reports from the North West in the late 1870s and early 1880s.[20] In addition, incompetent and corrupt government officials, questions of land titles, surveys, and the advancement of an alien civilization itself, all contributed to the discontent of these two groups. In the early 1880s this discontent began to be expressed in increasingly vocal protests and isolated outbreaks of defiance to Canadian authority. As Ottawa continued to ignore these protests, the attitude of both Indians and Métis became more and more extreme.

Initially the Métis came close to forming an alliance not only with the Indians but with the white settlers as well. Several prominent farmers and political leaders in the North West attended joint protest meetings with the Métis; petitions to Ottawa often had as many signatures of white settlers as they did of Métis.[21] The return of Louis Riel in the summer of 1884 and the drift of the Métis towards violent resistance in early 1885, however, prevented the continuation of that alliance. Riel was already tainted with the aura of violence and most white settlers, even given their grievances, were not about to follow him in yet another attempt to defy Canadian governmental authority. Thus when, in March 1885, Métis protest flared into open rebellion, few white settlers were involved. Nevertheless, western analysis of the rebellion reflected a continued degree of sympathy for an end, if not the means, of the Métis.

'It is a mistake to suppose the rising is factious and sudden,' an anonymous correspondent to *The Week* wrote from Calgary in April 1885. 'It is the growth of years. In fact,' he continued, 'the whole country sympathizes with the rebels.'[22] Such a sweeping generalization required a certain alarmism or partisanship, but there was widespread sympathy for the position of the Métis. Frank Oliver, the thirty-two-year-old native of Peel County and editor of the *Edmonton Bulletin*, felt that while Riel could not be condoned for his actions neither could it be said he was the cause of the violence. 'A match will not fire a pile of greenwoood,' he wrote, 'but it will a pile of dry. Had the Saskatchewan country been in a satisfied condition a hundred such men as Riel might have come into it.' Given the treatment of the region in the past years, however, 'the pile was ready made for the fire-brand, and the fire-brand ready lighted came in the person of Riel.'[23] The *Manitoba Free Press*, its regional perspective reinforced by the partisan Liberal outlook of its editor, W.F. Luxton, came to a similar conclusion on 7 April. 'Wherever it is known that the half-breeds and Indians are in rebellion,' Luxton wrote, 'it is known that they were first deceived and wronged, then neglected, finally allowed to prepare openly for an appeal to arms without a step being taken to hinder them.'

175 Disillusionment

Major James Walsh, the well-known retired officer of the North West Mounted Police, warned that such attitudes were not uncommon in the West. In an interview for the Toronto *Globe* he urged the government to appoint a commission to treat with the Métis. 'Don't forget,' he commented, 'that these people have the hearty sympathy of all the white settlers in their district.' Even in the midst of violence Walsh maintained, as did many others, that 'these people are not rebels, they are but demanding justice.'[24] Even Charles Mair, whose personal antipathy to Riel went back to 1870 and who on hearing of violence regretted that Riel had not been hanged, directed his anger not at the half-breeds but at the government. 'I would not damage the Govt. openly,' he wrote George Denison, 'for the railway completion is of vast importance.' In his private correspondence, however, he had no such reservations: 'Had there been an energetic, patriotic fellow sent out as Lieut. Governor of the Territories instead of this lump of selfishness and greed – Dewdney – all this difficulty would have been avoided.' Later that day, after he saw the casualty lists from Duck Lake, Mair was even more explicit in his denunciation of the government: 'The Govt. and Dewdney are responsible for all this. Every species of warning was given and thrown aside.'[25]

While the western sense of discontent was strong and led to sympathy for the Métis, there were also emotions and forces at work which to some extent countered that sympathy. Faced with violence, many felt that challenge to Canada's authority outweighed all other matters. *Grip*, the satirical magazine that had so often criticized the government for its handling of the North West, dropped both its criticism and its satire as the first troops headed west. 'The departure of our gallant men for the scene of the rebellion in the Saskatchewan country,' it editorialized on 4 April, 'was perhaps the most stirring event which Toronto has ever witnessed.' There were doubts as to the government's handling of the situation but a time of crisis was not appropriate for their discussion: 'It will be time enough to debate the cause and affix the blame when the rebels have been subdued.'

Western Canadians were not exempt from this spirit of martial enthusiasm. The *Manitoba Free Press* took time out from its criticisms of the government to write enthusiastic editorials about Canada's 'citizen soldiers.'[26] Charles Mair, in spite of his harsh condemnation of the government, joined George Denison's force of the Governor General's Body Guards in order to fight for his country and, not incidentally, to continue the old quarrel with Riel. Nicholas Flood Davin, who represented the North West Territories in the federal Parliament and had often complained of the government's treatment of the West, was inspired to write a poem calling for national unity in the face of armed rebellion:

> Upon the field all rancour healed
> There's no discordant hue
> The Orange marches beneath the Green
> The Rouge beneath the Bleu
>
> One purpose now fires every eye
> Rebellion foul to slay
> Forward for Canada! 's the cry,
> and all are one to-day.[27]

Loyalty to country overcame regional protest and most westerners felt compelled to take their stand with the nation.

While the patriotism that prevailed in the spring of 1885 muted the sympathy that existed for the Métis position, it did not lead many westerners to assume that Riel was the real cause of the rebellion. Even as they marched to subdue the Métis they continued to point an accusing finger at the government in the East. Charles Pitblado, a Presbyterian minister in Winnipeg, volunteered to act as chaplain to the troops. On his return, however, he preached not of the evils of rebellion but of the evils that had caused that rebellion. The life of the Indian and half-breed 'has been paralyzed by our presence,' he charged. 'They have been robbed by our unprincipled traders. They have been corrupted by our vices. They have been pauperized by our charities. They have been demoralized and wasted by our neglect.' It was not surprising that violence should occur when 'on the vast prairies, where his fathers dwelt in ease, and lived in plenty, the aborigine of the western land roam an idle, naked, starving outcast.'[28] Daniel Gordon, who also acted as a chaplain, felt much the same, and later wrote to Grant that 'if I were an Indian I would take all the risks of an uprising and have done with it.'[29] The Anglican bishop of Saskatchewan, John McLean, found himself caught between national fervour and regional grievance: on the one hand he was noted in Prince Albert during the rebellion for 'the most deliciously jingo sermons';[30] on the other hand he saw the violence as an indication of the nation's failure to do its duty in the West.[31]

The pulls of national enthusiasm on the one hand and regional sympathy for the Métis on the other affected many westerners. In 1869 and 1870 Riel's actions were an attempt by the old order to protest the seeming intolerance of the new in Red River; as such, the new order, and those who supported its aims, had opposed the Métis. The 1885 rebellion has been interpreted as another, and final, attempt of the old order to halt the march of a foreign civilization.[32] It has also been seen, in an argument that focuses not on the rebellion but on the controversy surrounding Riel's execution, as a significant setback to the French-English co-operation implied by Confederation.[33] While both of these arguments have their place in any analysis of the rebellion, there is a third factor in the Métis and Indian resistance of 1885. Their discontent represented to some extent the discontent of the West in the face of eastern domination and eastern indifference. To this extent the settlers in the West were sympathetic to the Métis in a way that was not possible in 1870.

The Riel rebellion was simply a crisis that dramatically illustrated a longer-run trend towards regionalism. It was a movement that had begun before 1885 and would continue long after the Métis had been defeated. More and more people who had come west with a strong sense of association with Ontario would reject that background and identify with the West. Years after the rebellion Charles Mair found his sympathy for the Métis had not disappeared. 'It is monopoly has raised up any outcry there is here,' he wrote,'and well it might. I would have taken up the musket fast enough myself on that question.' Later he went further and implied in a letter to Denison that at some future time he might find himself on the rebel side, 'potting at you and Merritt and Dunn, not to say Baldwin from behind some coteau or bluff.'[34] It was a humorous remark, but the point was made none the less. By the time of the second Riel rebellion western complaints had gone beyond specifics to a general sense of grievance. This, easterners did not completely understand. Even those such as George Grant who were extremely sympathetic to the western position tended to blame matters on particular evils such as 'party' and 'Patronage.'[35] In contrast, those in the West were beginning to see a general eastern indifference and selfishness as being at the root of their problems.

By the summer of 1885 the editor of the Macleod *Gazette* so despaired of eastern understanding that on 13 June he called for a direct appeal to Great Britain and hinted that secession might prove the only real solution to 'an overbearing and unscrupulous federal authority.' The tone was not all that extreme in the troubled days surrounding the 1885 rebellion. Such discontent, even if exaggerated by the rhetorical flights of newspaper editors, indicated that the problems were perceived to have gone beyond questions of immediate policy and beyond the failures of the specific party in power. Rather a widespread feeling had developed that the West was being exploited by the East and those in the 'new Canada' being treated as less than full partners in Confederation. As the Edmonton *Bulletin* warned on 1 November 1884, even before the rebellion, 'the idea that the North-West is to eastern Canada as India is to Great Britain is one that will, if not abandoned, lead to the rupture of confederation at no distant date.'

In this context the attitude of any particular party was simply a manifestation of the larger problem, and thus there was no paradox in voting for the Conservatives in overwhelming numbers only two years after the Riel rebellion. The Liberal government, with its record of hesitancy and delay over the Canadian Pacific, had long ago lost any legitimacy as a vehicle for western interests; there was little reason to vote for it even though the Conservatives had proved themselves indifferent. Western grievances did not lead immediately to political shifts because, for many westerners, there seemed no place to go.[36] A disenchantment with the traditional party structure was growing, however, and this would contribute to both intra-party strife and, eventually, to the shattering of traditional party lines in the West.

The growing disillusionment implied a collapsing faith in the ability of current expansionist strategy to reconcile eastern, western, and national interests. It had originally been assumed that the immigration of a large number of English Canadians to the prairies would ensure a common sense of identity and interests between old and new English Canada. In the face of economic adversity and depression this had failed to materialize. By 1885 westerners were beginning to view their own region as distinct from the East. Conscious of their disagreements with Ontario, western Canadians began to look at national issues from a regional perspective. More and more it was argued that such issues could not be resolved without looking at them within the context of regional inequities in Canada. Some issues, such as imperial federation, took on different nuances. How, asked one writer, could Canada talk about joining a larger federation without first readjusting its own: 'It must be on a readjusted basis, having full consent of the loyal inhabitants of the Province [Manitoba] to cement the terms.'[37] Other issues, important in Central Canada, seemed less so from a western perspective. Even the great Canadian pastime of anti-Americanism suffered in this regard. When Denison wrote Mair excitedly in 1888 on the current fisheries crisis, the former Canada Firster replied that the main danger to Canada was internal not external. 'There is more danger in the North West to the Dominion from the reign of monopolies and Eastern self-seeking than in Yankee bluster, and unless the freest measures of development are applied in this country there will be antagonism roused of deeper note than Cleveland's message.'[38]

The collapsing sense of unity between eastern and western Canada in the achievement of the national destiny was two-sided. Throughout the 1870s Edward Blake had represented a stream of Ontario resistance to such costly schemes of western development as the Canadian Pacific Railway. As long as the West seemed about to offer Canada a glorious future, however, such protest was both qualified and limited. In the 1880s, however, as the West continued to prove to be an expensive and undeveloped burden, more and more easterners tended to criticize the cost of development. Western protests simply aggravated the situation and broadened eastern criticism to include comments on western selfishness and provincialism. In 1884 Goldwin Smith summed up, as he often did, the pessimistic side of Ontario's attitude when he asked: 'what will she gain by the Pacific Railway? Merely, as it would seem, the gratification of staring like a cow at the passing train.' *Grip* found itself in agreement with Smith's comment and set it in cartoon form.[39] The Riel rebellion accentuated these Ontario doubts over the great expansionist idea. Suddenly, it seemed, the annexation of half a continent presented more difficulties than had been thought: 'This affair brings home forcibly to us the remoteness of the North West from Old Canada and the magnitude of the natural barriers which lie in between. The same degree of military strength and compactness is perhaps not necessary to cohesion here which is necessary in Europe, but some degree is necessary even here. We have annexed a continent on the moon.'[40]

Moreover, it seemed as if Ontario was the only province with enough sense of loyalty to Canada to make a real effort to save the nation. In an editorial that unfairly reflected on the efforts of the rest of Canada, *The Week* complained that other provinces were showing a deplorable lack of enthusiasm for the suppression of the Métis rebellion. 'Alone, or with only the British quarter of Montreal to assist her, Ontario will have to do it; and some day she will grow tired of doing it alone.' The West, like French Canada and the Maritimes, seemed to draw on the strength of the nation without contributing to it. Though *The Week* represented only one segment of Ontario opinion, it, at least, was disenchanted enough by 1885 to adopt for some time thereafter an unenthusiastic and even hostile attitude towards the North West.[41] There was, then, disillusionment in Ontario as well.

While segments of Ontario opinion might grumble about the cost of the Canadian Pacific Railway, however, there was none of the deep-seated feeling of resentment that existed in the West. If nothing else, Ontarians still sensed that their province played a key role in government circles in Ottawa. The West, in contrast, had no such feeling and no assurance that the present state of economic depression might not continue permanently. It was thus in the West that the first concerted campaign began to readjust expansionist economic strategy in order, as the argument went, to put the West into a better position relative to the rest of the nation. The western sense of regionalism contained within this campaign made it contrast sharply with the centralist assumptions of earlier expansionist rhetoric.

Western discontent manifested itself in a number of ways through the 1880s. Questions of control of lands, Dominion-provincial rights, railway charters, and financial arrangements, all became issues as those in the West challenged the current relationship between their region and the rest of Canada. Of them all, however, perhaps none better summed up the mood and aspirations of westerners than the great vision of a railway to Hudson's Bay. Its place in the panoply of western grievances was given recognition when, in one of the last petitions to the government before the rebellion, Riel and his fellow petitioners had given a prominent place to the complaint that 'no effective measures have yet been taken to put the people of the North-West in direct communication with the European markets via Hudson's Bay.'[42] It was a matter of little importance to the Métis and Indians, but it was of the utmost significance to those settlers who they hoped to ally to their cause. As much as the rebellion itself, the demand for the railway was a product of western discontent.

The revival of interest in a transportation outlet via Hudson's Bay seemed to run contrary to the trends of the last quarter century. Even before annexation the Hudson's Bay Company ceased to employ the route as a major transportation link to the southern prairie, turning instead to the more economical land route via Minnesota. The growth of a Canadian presence in the West simply confirmed the abandonment of the route. Expansionist strategy made the use of an east-west route via Lake Superior essential. Initially by enlarging the canoe route of the North West Company in the shape of the Dawson Road and then by the projected all-land route of the Canadian Pacific Railway, Canada sought to compete with and eventually supplant the dominant southern route. Thereby, it was hoped, an integrated national trade pattern would emerge. In this contest the old route to the North West via Hudson's Bay was but a bystander. It seemed nothing more than the relic of an archaic economic and political era. Then, quite suddenly, interest revived in this traditional means of access to the North West.

Initially the revival of interest in the Hudson's Bay route reflected the optimism of the later 1870s about the prospects of the North West. Estimates of the region's potential had grown so great that even before the primary link had been completed men began to look for auxiliary means of transport to handle the future traffic of the region. The exports and imports of the North West, the argument ran, would be so great in the future that no single rail line could possibly handle them all. The answer, it seemed, was another railway running in this case to a port on Hudson's Bay; this rail line would then connect to ships running between the bay and the ports of Europe.

The original enthusiasm for the project was largely fostered by Robert Bell of the Geological Survey. In 1875 and 1877 Bell visited James Bay and in 1878 he explored the Nelson and Hayes rivers. Bell was a colleague of Macoun's and he possessed the same irrepressible sense of optimism when it came to the future of the North West. The Hudson's Bay route was his own particular contribution to the enthusiasm of the age. In reports, letters, pamphlets, and speeches this scientist argued the feasibility and practicality of a railway to Hudson's Bay.[43] By 1878 he had acquired two important allies. J.S. Dennis, seemingly willing to support any new project for the West, wrote Macdonald urging consideration of the route. Even more significantly, Henry Youle Hind testified, he later said reluctantly, that 'the establishment of a cheap and speedy means of communication between the North West and the open Atlantic via Hudson's Straits, would not only secure the rapid settlement of Manitoba, but open to successful immigration a fertile area twenty times as large as that Province.'[44]

In 1880 the connection of the bay and the prairie came a step closer to reality with the chartering of two companies with the avowed purpose of building a railway to Hudson's Bay. Each of these companies reflected different origins, different personnel, and, before long, different purposes. The first company was the Nelson Valley Railway and Transportation Company and was based on Montreal men and money; its founders included Montreal senator and businessman Thomas Ryan, George Drummond of the Canada Sugar Refining Company, and Alfred Brown, a director of the Bank of Montreal. The second company was based in Winnipeg which, for obvious reasons, had its own aspirations towards the bay. Hugh M. Sutherland, president of the Rainy Lake Lumber Company and future member of Parliament for Selkirk, was the moving spirit behind the organization but it also included a number of prominent Winnipeg figures such as John Schultz. Initially the two companies did not receive a great deal of encouragement. John A. Macdonald's Conservative government had gambled its future on the completion of the Canadian Pacific Railway and it did not welcome any scheme that would divert money and attention towards a second outlet. The Hudson's Bay railway would have to wait until the Canadian Pacific became a reality.[45]

The approaching completion of the Canadian Pacific did provide a new impetus for the Hudson's Bay railway but not in the way that had originally been thought. Rather, the same commitment which the government made to the completion of the railway by closing the deal with the syndicate signalled the beginning of doubts as to the boon the railway would confer on the North West. The long-awaited Pacific railway suddenly possessed an ominous degree of power and before long the great hope of the West would become its greatest source of complaint. These complaints provided new and compelling reasons for the construction of a railway to Hudson's Bay.

The control of the Canadian Pacific by a private company had in itself raised questions among those interested in the West. George Grant, admittedly biased because of his friendship with deposed chief engineer, Sandford Fleming, complained in 1880 of the contract that had been made with the syndicate. 'The Govt. is giving too much, and putting too much power in the hands of the Syndicate ... I have been doubtful all along. I am rather more than doubtful now.'[46] The sober-minded principal of Queen's University was joined in his concern by Jesse Beaufort Hurlbert who took time out from his optimistic writings on Canada's climate to protest to Macdonald that many Conservatives in the West opposed the syndicate bargain.[47]

Opposition was based not only on the specific details of the arrangement but also on a more general suspicion that the development of such a crucial national enterprise by a private company would raise up a dangerous power in the North West, and for that matter all of Canada. As Grant said, 'it looks as if now there would be no check on the plunderers.'[48] Not only was the syndicate a powerful company but, according to the agreement, it was given a monopoly of railway lines to the south of its own main line. Peter Imrie, in a long letter to the secretary of the Department of Agriculture, perhaps best summed up the range of fears which was shifting western opinion on the railway. 'The monopolist has the whole realm of the possible to work upon,' he wrote, 'and the few detailed arguments which precedent, or reason, or fancy, may enable anyone to adduce against monopolies can hardly represent anything but a mere tithe of the possible evils which may be put in operation.' The unknown as much as the known made the whole arrangement loathsome. 'It is to my mind, this very indefiniteness of the danger that makes if overwhelming, because otherwise – i.e. if we could imagine the precise manner in which the monopolist would use his opportunities – we could no doubt take some steps towards obstructing him. Probably enough your Railway Company will discover some quite new way of taking the cream off the country – some way that nobody even thought of before.'[49] By the time the railway was completed across the prairies many were convinced that Imrie's fears had been proven completely justified.

Many western interests felt themselves injured by the policy of the government towards the Canadian Pacific. The withdrawal of prime areas of land from settlement in order to allow the Canadian Pacific to choose its land grants was one of the first sources of complaint. It was also one of the most persistent. Even the North West Council, often accused of quietly accepting direction from Ottawa, felt constrained to pass a resolution condemning the 'Mile Belt.' It was, said the council 'detrimental to growth and prosperity – large blocks of land being held by the Government, and settlers being disbarred from locating on them.' By leaving large tracts in visible locations along the line of railway the immigrant was given 'a false idea of the North-West, and an inadequate and sometimes misleading impression of the character of the soil.'[50] The other major complaint against the railway was directed at the so-called monopoly clause. Even before the Canadian Pacific was complete, Manitoba had taken issue with the federal disallowance of provincial railway charters. The nature of the issue mixed economic policy with provincial rights and thus exacerbated the whole problem. Moreover, it seemed to many to prove that the Canadian Pacific had undue influence over the federal government. Immigration and development were still central to western growth and anything that might hinder these processes was bound to become a source of complaint. As soon as the Canadian Pacific appeared as an obstacle to western aspirations, it found itself with many opponents in western Canada.

If, at first, the term 'monopoly' related to a specific clause in the agreement between the government and the syndicate, it was not long before it took on a much more general meaning. The very dominance of the Canadian Pacific in the western Canadian economy, whether because of the monopoly clause or simply because it was the only means of transport, made the railway a symbol of eastern exploitation at western expense. The campaign against the monopolistic control of the Canadian Pacific became, in essence, a campaign against the general dominance of the western economy; as such, the railway became a scapegoat, and not completely without reason, for the ills of the West. Charles Mair summed it up tersely when he wrote in 1891 that 'the country is killed with C.P.R. extortion.'[51]

The growing antipathy towards the Canadian Pacific revolutionized the purpose behind the Hudson Bay railway. What had begun as an expression of western optimism became, by the mid-1880's, an almost desperate attempt to escape from dependence on the Canadian Pacific Railway. That railway, based on an east-west trade axis, served only itself and eastern Canada. The Hudson Bay railway, however, would challenge both the Canadian Pacific and the dominance of eastern Canada in the western economy. As Goldwin Smith pointed out, 'no point of commercial geography can be more certain than that nature has placed the commercial outlet of the prairie region to the south. But first, for political purposes, it was wrested round to the east; and now to break the monopoly thus established, an attempt is made to fix the outlet to the north.'[52] Far from denying this, proponents of the bay railway argued that the opportunity to break the power of the Canadian Pacific was one of the most compelling reasons behind the project. 'The Canadian Pacific Railway and its branches west, south and south-west of Winnipeg,' wrote bay supporter William Murdoch, 'are all tributary to the Hudson's Bay Railway, it being the shortest route to the sea; no corporation, however powerful, can coerce the channels of commerce, and the outlet is via Hudson's Bay.'[53]

The challenge to the Canadian Pacific was thus a challenge to the expansionist premise that an east-west flow of trade was essential for the sake of the nation. The whole idea of a major outlet via Hudson Bay implied a direct connection between the West and Europe, bypassing eastern points and, not incidentally, eastern control. Proponents of the bay scheme, while admitting their repudiation of past economic strategy, gave indications that they felt their idea to be a means of preserving the expansionist ideal – the rapid development of the West and thereby the nation. The bypassing of the east was, in terms of this principle, a minor readjustment. In fact, in the imagery, sense of zeal, and even in the personnel involved in the Hudson Bay railway scheme, one can sense an attempt to transport the expansionist idea to new, western, soil.

Two things stand out about the individuals involved in the Hudson Bay railway scheme in the 1880s. The first is that, not surprisingly, the majority of them had strong connections with Manitoba and the North West. The chairman of the federal select committee on the railway, for instance, was Joseph Royal of Manitoba. The secretary to the committee was Charles Tuttle, a transplanted Nova Scotian living in Winnipeg and founder of the Winnipeg *Daily Times*. Moreover, much of the strongest support for the idea came from Manitoba itself. A select committee of the Manitoba Legislature and the Winnipeg Board of Trade both reported favourably on the plan. Their efforts received the support of numerous individuals such as Charles Bell and Thomas Scoble of Winnipeg, Hugh Sutherland, Charles Mair and, in Edmonton, Frank Oliver. The Montreal-based group which had chartered a company in 1880 still existed, but by the middle of the decade played little part in what was essentially a regional discussion.

The second notable feature of the group was the number of members with expansionist affiliations. In some cases, such as Charles Mair and John Schultz, this affiliation was both immediate and strong. A good many others however, also revealed their expansionist leanings in less spectacular ways. Thomas Scott, for instance, member of Parliament for Winnipeg between 1880 and 1887, was a supporter of the railway. Born in Lanark County in 1841, Scott had edited the expansionist *Perth Expositor* in the 1860s. He had gone to Manitoba in 1870 with the Red River expedition and in 1873 had settled permanently in the province.[54] Charles Napier Bell had also been born in the expansionist Ottawa Valley town of Perth and went to Manitoba with the Red River expedition. Bell accepted the promises that had been made for

185 Disillusionment

the country and remained there permanently. By the latter 1880s he was both a supporter of the Hudson Bay railway and president of the Winnipeg Board of Trade.[55] Hugh Sutherland's background was in Prince Edward Island rather than in Ontario, but he too was an easterner who had chosen to cast his lot with the new West. In 1874 he had been sent west by the Department of Public Works as their superintendent for the North West Territories; he remained in that position until the change of government in 1878 left him out of work. It was then that he applied himself to a career in the West and to the Hudson Bay railway.

Those who did not live in the West but who did support the Hudson Bay railway almost invariably had expansionist backgrounds. Typical was S.J. Dawson who was on Royal's committee, as was Thomas White. Robert Bell's enthusiasm has already been mentioned. Even the elderly English writer, Joseph Nelson, who had turned out expansionist tracts in the 1860s, renewed his contact with the movement by compiling a collection of speeches and statements favourable to the bay route.[56] Western aspirations and expansionist enthusiasm thus came together in the 1880s to promote a new campaign, this one directed to the north.

The basic argument in favour of the Hudson Bay route rested on a straightforward geographical fact: Hudson Bay was the closest body of water to the wheat lands of the North West. Moreover, if one measured the distance from any port on the bay to England, it was found to be the shortest route to the interior of Canada. 'The fact of a seaport existing in the very heart of the continent more than 1500 miles nearer than Quebec to the centre of the North-West Territory, has scarcely begun to be noticed by the public,' lamented one writer. Unnoticed though it may be, however, 'its importance can hardly be over-stated. Churchill Harbour is only four hundred miles from the edge of the greatest wheat field in the world.'[57] If this route was developed, said Colonel Thomas Scoble, 'the centre of our vast fertile area would be as close to Liverpool as the present grain emporium of the United States – Chicago.'[58] Any map, as supporters of the bay constantly repeated, led one unavoidably to the conclusion that the potential of the route was immense.

In the same way that the expansionists had pointed to the prairie as a sign of destiny, the supporters of the bay turned the geographical situation of the bay into proof that nature intended it to be used. 'Should we not, as Canadians,' asked William Murdoch, 'anxious for the full development of the great national resources of our country, take what nature offers so freely, and make use of her bountiful gift?'[59] Canada had been given not only a vast west but also a 'great Mediterranean sea,' and destiny pointed to the future importance of it. Geography easily became converted into mythology as the myth of the north was given new application by the enthusiastic Charles Tuttle: 'The directive magnetic force that controls the mariner's needle is not a more attractive problem than is the not less unerring north-westerly trend of human progress. Westward and northward have the marching orders been, until the people of the present generation must look southward and eastward for the homes of their ancestors. The greatest deeds have always been accomplished in high latitudes, because the highest latitudes produce the greatest men.' Tuttle's enthusiastic statement was, however, qualified. 'Strange as it may seem,' he concluded, 'the north is always underrated.'[60] This tendency again revealed itself, promoters felt, in the case of the Hudson Bay route. The main obstacle to their scheme was the lack of knowledge concerning the ports on the bay and the route from these ports to the Atlantic Ocean. The general image of the entire region was that of an arctic wasteland and the effort to overcome this impression occupied a great deal of the time of those who supported the route.

In spite of its northerly position, promoters argued, the Hudson Bay route provided a feasible passage for ships. The history of the last two centuries had proven the bay to be one of the safest water systems in the world. Charles Napier Bell, in a report presented to the Winnipeg Board of Trade in 1884, pointed out that 'with the exception of one occasion (1779), Moose Factory has been visited by a ship in every year since 1735.'[61] Charles Tuttle concurred, recounted the history of the use of the bay, and concluded that 'Hudson's Bay and Strait has been utilized for more than two centuries, with a regularity that furnishes no insignificant recommendation of the route.'[62] If the men of the seventeenth century in their small sailing craft and with rudimentary navigational aids could regularly and successfully use the route, then there seemed no reason to doubt that the men of the nineteenth century could do so. E.P. Leacock, a member of the Manitoba Legislative Assembly, argued this point in 1888: 'If Cabot in 1498, Hudson in 1610, Gibbon in 1613, Baffin in 1614 and hundreds of others since...felt no fear and were able to venture through the Hudson's Bay, then the nineteenth century, with its steam, its iron ships, its thousand modern appliances, cannot be afraid to venture where men went fearlessly so many years ago.'[63]

Promoters of the route did not rest all their arguments on history. Once again scientists and popularizers reinterpreted geography and climate to support their own positions. In the case of Hudson Bay, it must be admitted, the task of dissociating the region from the Arctic was not so easy as it had been in the case of the North West. Nevertheless a valiant attempts was made to do so. 'In the popular mind,' said Robert Bell, 'Hudson's Bay is apt to be associated with the polar regions, yet no part of it comes within the Arctic circle, and the southern extremity is south of the latitude of London.' James Bay could be seen as practically temperate in its climate for it was 'in the latitude of Devonshire and Cornwall.'[64] Another former expansionist, William Kennedy, testified that 'we have the larger half of a continent teeming with animal, vegetable and mineral wealth, only awaiting the hand of labour to draw it forth and enhance its value a thousand fold; and nature opens the gateway by which this wealth may be sent to the remotest quarters of the globe, and the produce of other countries be brought into our midst.'[65] Charles Bell went even further and pictured the climate of the bay as both comfortable and attractive: 'Robson, Dobbs, Ellice, Hearne and other writers state that when Europeans have once lived in the country about the Bay, that they are never content to live out of it again.' In order to prove this, Bell cited some comparative statistics of dubious value to prove that the climate at York 'is but very little colder than at Winnipeg, and during the summer it is warmer there than in this Province.' Things seem to have changed a great deal since the 1840s when Robert M. Ballantyne had described York Factory as 'a monstrous blot on a swampy spot, with a partial view of the frozen sea!'[66]

The praise of the climate of Hudson Bay was part of the general attempt to make the idea of a railroad to that point seem attractive. Beyond the general image of the region, however, there was a very specific question that had to be answered. The Hudson's Bay Company, it was known, had sent only one or two ships a year to its ports on the bay; this could be done within the constraints of a relatively short navigation season. If a railway was to be worthwhile, however, the navigation season had to be long enough to allow a considerable carrying trade. Proponents of the route argued that this was no problem and that, as Robert Bell argued, only the freezing of the harbours would limit navigation.[67] Nevertheless, as even the most enthusiastic admitted, hard evidence was wanting, especially concerning the navigability of Hudson's Strait.

In order to provide information on this crucial question the Canadian government commissioned an exploring expedition under Lieutenant Andrew Gordon of the Royal Navy. Robert Bell accompanied the expedition as geologist and Charles Tuttle went along as an 'observer.'[68] He was also unofficially to act as a popular writer who could record the work of the expedition for public consumption. In the end the expedition did little to resolve the problems that existed. Unlike the Hind and Palliser expeditions, the efforts of science failed to provide the final proof needed by supporters of the route to convince those who took a more neutral position. If the uncommitted remained uncommitted, the supporters of the route found much in the conclusions of the expedition to support their case. In part this has to be attributed to the triumph of wishful thinking. Even Charles Tuttle found the bias of individuals such as Robert Bell somewhat amusing: 'He could not be persuaded it rained when it poured; or that there was any wind, when it blew at a gale of thirty miles an hour; or that there was any ice, when the Neptune was rearing and plunging in the midst of it like a mad bull; or that it was cold, when the mercury was down to 32 degrees above, and when he was pacing the deck, compelled to wear a good coat of reindeer; in fact he was prepared to believe that the propellor had hit a whale rather than ice.' Beside such enthusiasm John Macoun looked like a sceptic.

Tuttle's perceptive comments on Bell's attitude did not, however, stop him from himself adopting an extremely optimistic stance in his writings on the expedition. In the end the vision of the route dominated any untoward experiences of the voyage. Entry to the west via Hudson Bay, Tuttle argued, was not only feasible but also preferable and more comfortable than the regular route from the east. In fact, the immigrant coming in by the St. Lawrence River would gain an unfavourable impression of Canada, for he would see 'wretched shanties' and 'half-fed cattle gazing upon sterile fields.' In contrast, the immigrant who came via the bay would have the opportunity to see the 'glory and grandeur of Greenland's icy mountains' and perhaps even 'a sporting whale.'[69]

With such a long history of successful use and a pleasant, even, spectacular voyage before the person who undertook it, the sceptic might be prompted to ask why the route had not been developed before. In explaining the bay's lack of use, supporters of the route turned to the company that had been so long associated with it. Conspiratorial forces were seen to be at work in the propagation of the image of the bay as they had been in the image of the West. Charles Bell theorized that earlier in the century the Hudson's Bay Company had realized that 'it was highly desirable to keep any adventurous persons from trying to gain a foothold in the future, and the best means to be adopted were those of magnifying the dangers of navigation.'[70] The negative image of the route was thus of relatively recent origin and the product of a deliberate policy on the part of the monopolistic Hudson's Bay Company. 'Why,' asked one writer, 'has this route remained so long unused and ignored? The answer is: for the same reasons which untill [sic] now kept the fertile lands of the North-West unsettled and imperfectly known. The Hudson's Bay Company have until lately held the whole of the North-West as a hunting ground for its Indians, and the interests of the Company lay in discouraging settlement or intrusion on its domain.'[71]

Such charges were a direct extension of the expansionist rhetoric of the 1850s and 1860s. New conspirators were arising, however, to compete with the old. 'Is it not astonishing,' wrote Leacock, 'that the great corporations in eastern Canada, and the great corporation running through our midst should all unite with the Provinces and States in the East and oppose a scheme which will turn the channels of western trade away from them.' Not surprisingly it was the Canadian Pacific Railway, the 'great corporation running through our midst,' that became the focal point of the new conspiracy theory. 'It is no longer a secret,' Tuttle wrote the Premier of Manitoba in 1884, 'that the eastern Provinces generally and the Canadian Pacific Railway in particular are opposed to the Hudson's Bay Railway.'[72] Four years later, on 10 January 1888, the *Winnipeg Free Press* warned that 'the C.P.R. will bring its powerful influence to bear for the defeat of a more dangerous rival to its through traffic than even the abolition of monopoly would call into existence.' When Charles Mair was visited by some representatives of the giant railway, he noted with suspicion their dislike of the bay route: 'They pooh-pooh Sutherland's H.B. scheme and I think they mean to oppose it.'[73]

Given the purposes behind the bay route, the Canadian Pacific was much better suited to the role of conspirator than was the Hudson's Bay Company. The latter was, after all, but an obsolete monopoly which had unsuccessfully conspired against eastern expansion. The Canadian Pacific, on the contrary, represented those forces of eastern control and exploitation which westerners felt hampered their efforts to develop the region. At the same time, there was a depressing continuity in the whole process. As Charles Mair complained, government policy allowed a 'stall fed monopoly,' the 'Hudson's Bay Company in its new shape the C.P.R.,' to dominate the North West and frustrate its proper aspirations.[74] The bay route, however, would allow the West finally to break free of the powerful and exploitive corporations. By setting the bay against the transcontinental line the scheme became, on a symbolic level, the means of acting in a positive manner against all those remote forces that oppressed the West.

The Hudson Bay route thus became a method of assailing the unassailable and overcoming the helplessness that many westerners felt. By rendering the West independent of the East it would remove all those injustices of which the West complained. It was, to put it simply, seen as a panacea for all western problems. 'The hope of Manitoba,' wrote Tuttle, 'is in the Hudson's Bay route.'[75] Support for the railway was, in fact, a statement of faith in the West itself. The railway thus took on mythical qualities and, as one commentator noted, belief in it 'can be likened only to St. Paul's definition of faith: "It is the substance of things hoped for, the evidence of things not seen."'[76]

Given such an attitude it is not surprising that the railway took on a moral dimension; it was not simply an economic venture but a means to remedy the unjust exploitation of the West and as such its triumph would be the triumph of justice. 'The people of Manitoba are fully justified in their determination to secure free and untrammeled railway and water communication with all parts of the world,' wrote Tuttle. As the inhabitants of Red River had been thought to deserve the blessings of British freedom and as Canada had deserved the opportunity to develop the West, so the West now demanded the opportunity to alter the original expansionist strategy to ensure that they obtained their due. National destiny and human justice demanded the construction of the railroad. 'Let the walls of monopoly be broken down, and let us have competition in railway traffic.'[77] Destiny and justice displaced economics as Charles Mair warned angrily of the avarice that sought to block the opening of the bay:

Open the Bay! the myriad prairies call;
   Let homesteads rise and comforts multiply;
Let justice triumph though the heavens should fall!
   This is the voice of reason – manhood's cry.

Open the Bay! Who are they that say 'no'?
   Who locks the portals? Nature? She resigned
Her icy reign, her stubborn frost and snow,
Her sovereign sway and sceptre, long ago,
   To sturdy manhood and the master, Mind!

Not these the foe! Not Nature, who is fain
   When earnest hearts an earnest end pursue;
But man's old selfishness and greed of gain:
These ancient breeders of earth's sin and pain –
   These are the thieves who steal the Nation's due![78]

The Hudson Bay railway was not built within the lifetime of most of those who became its advocate in the 1880s. The concrete problems of navigation and the question of its economic viability could not be shunted aside as many would have wished. Nevertheless, many of the delays and broken promises concerning the route did reflect an eastern indifference and Canadian Pacific hostility that, in the extreme, nearly justified the conspiratorial images that circulated among the proponents of the bay. John A. Macdonald, for instance, was so sceptical of the worth of the bay route that he was willing to deal it a nearly fatal blow for the sake of political control within one Manitoba constituency.[79] Other eastern politicians showed an equal, if less spectacular, aversion to this particularly western scheme. Eventually the increased political power of the West, rather than any new interest in the scheme in the East or any new evidence of its viability, would lead to the construction of the railway. Only then did westerners find that the bay route would not magically free them from eastern control.

The indifference of the East simply deepened the western sense of alienation from the original expansionist idea. The call for the Hudson Bay route had been a demand for a major readjustment of east-west relations in order to revive and strengthen the national sense of unity while ensuring the achievement of the original expansionist goal of the rapid development of the West. When people in the West perceived that the East was ignoring their demands, whether on the railway or other issues, their earlier suspicions were deepened. The East seemed to have betrayed the original promises of the expansionist movement; in response, many in the West turned their back on the older perception of Canada and began to look for their identity in the land around them.

9

The West as past: the foundations of western history

The fascination for the West created by the expansionist campaign resulted in a widespread and rather uncritical interest in material on that region. Dozens of newspaper articles, pamphlets, and books brought information about the 'new Canada' to readers in the East and elsewhere. Given this atmosphere, Joseph James Hargrave might have felt hopeful that his history of Red River, published in 1871, would be received with interest.[1] If he had any such expectations, however, they were soon disappointed. His work received very little attention and such attention as it did get was far from encouraging. 'Voltaire,' wrote one of the few who bothered to review the work, 'makes a remark to the effect that ... men are apt to imagine that events of their own time and country, passing, as such events do, under their own immediate observation, are the most momentous that have befallen the human race since the creation of the world. It is only upon some principle of this kind, that such a phenomenon as the publication of a work like the present can be accounted for.'[2] In two sentences the reviewer dismissed not only Hargrave's efforts but the entire history of the region which had attracted so much attention in recent years.

The reaction to Hargrave's work was typical of the expansionist outlook. The image of the North West that had formed during the campaign for annexation had little room in it for history. As has been emphasized throughout this study, the North West of the expansionist was that of the future. The assessment of the region in terms of its potential rather than its current wilderness state had been one of the fundamental perceptual changes wrought by the movement. It had allowed the reappraisal of the land that was so necessary to the Canadian decision to expand. It had reduced the idea of the wilderness from a qualitative force to a matter of time and had, ultimately, left the Hudson's Bay Company with no defence of its fur trade empire. The emphasis on the potential of the region, however, and on its future utilization and settlement, had also reduced the history of the region to the level of propaganda.

Expansionists had looked on the years of rule over the North West by the Hudson's Bay Company as a sort of dark age. When Alexander Morris wrote in 1859 of the 'deep, thick veil of obscurity and darkness in which the territories were so closely enwrapped,' he summed up the prevailing image.[3] It was a comment both on the efforts of the company to prevent knowledge of the area from reaching the world and the perceived social and economic state of the region. In this sense the expansionist image of the past of the North West paralleled the missionary's attitude towards the wilderness. The land in its wild state was a region of secular and temporal darkness with little of value to redeem it. Similarly, the history of such a region contained little of interest to the man who looked to the future. When the expansionist movement triumphed over these forces of darkness, it turned to the future and forgot a seemingly worthless past. Once again Alexander Morris summed it up when he wrote to John A. Macdonald in 1869 that 'the history of the territory is yet to be made.'[4] The potential of the region had overwhelmed its present and past.

Even dark ages have histories, of course. The Canadian expansionist movement did, in the course of its campaign, develop an historical view of the North West. Written in bits and pieces and mixed in with articles attacking the Hudson's Bay Company, this history did attain a definite historiographical perspective. This perspective, however, reflected the purposes of Canadian expansionists as much as it did the trends of western history. The very fact that it developed as a part of the political literature surrounding expansion imposed on it a particular set of biases and conclusions. It developed not out of an interest in the past of the region but as part of the insistence that the 'dark ages' of the west be ended. In its assumptions, focus, and conclusions it was, above all else, a justification of Canadian demands for the North West.

The initial premise of this history concerned the role and character of the main obstacle to expansion, the Hudson's Bay Company. The company was believed to be engaged in an active and conspiratorial campaign to preserve the region as a wilderness in order to protect the profitable fur trade. Any historical interpretation of the West had to take this assumption into account. Moreover, the company was thought to be harsh to both Indians and whites throughout the territories. It had been common from the time of Isbister's protests to believe that all the residents of the region suffered from and resented the company's rule. The presence of a reactionary and oppressive taskmaster provided expansionists with the initial and essential basis for the creation of a dark age.

A second historical bias developed by the later 1850s. The myth of the North West Company as a symbol of Canadian interests and therefore as an intrepid and upright presence in the region had to be taken into account in any history of the region. 'The straight forward, unconcealed, humane, and patriotic merchant princes – alike honourable to themselves and beneficial to their country,' gave Canadians proof of their own past involvement in the region.[5] Given this myth, it became impossible for expansionists to attribute to the North West Company the evil purpose or reactionary views which were thought to be typical of the foreign Hudson's Bay Company.

In fact, the existence of the North West Company and its predecessors allowed the expansionists to divide the history of the West into three major eras. The first extended from the earliest penetrations of the region to the amalgamation of the two companies in 1821. In this period it was possible to emphasize the Canadian claims to the West through the efforts of New France and the North West Company. These Canadian firms, rather than the Hudson's Bay Company, were identified with the ambitious men who explored the vast North West and claimed it for the British Empire. The Hudson's Bay Company simply followed in the tracks of its rivals and made little contribution to either knowledge of the territory or natural claims upon it. Had these early companies been allowed to continue, it was argued, then the fur trade would have naturally given way to other forms of economic enterprise and, eventually, settlement. The absorption of the North West Company into the Hudson's Bay Company, however, marked the end of Canadian involvement in the West and the frustration of progress. In a betrayal of Canadian rights, the Hudson's Bay Company usurped the efforts of the North West Company. 'The Canadian people,' wrote John McLean, 'were deprived of all interest in the trade which owed its origin to the courage and enterprise of their forefathers.'[6]

The second era marked the triumph of obscurity. The Hudson's Bay Company ruled unchallenged in the North West and ensured that its lands remained closed to the outside world. Formed during the expansionist campaign, this image persisted even after the Hudson's Bay Company had capitulated and turned its lands over to Canada. 'After the coalition of the North-West Company with the Hudson's Bay Company,' wrote George Denison in 1873, 'the route (now the Dawson route) over which the North-west people had brought their goods, became disused, and reports were put into circulation that it was impracticable.'[7] Development and exploration ceased. The Hudson's Bay territory was cut off from civilization by a jealous and reactionary company.

The third era of western history was seen to have begun in 1856 and to have culminated in 1870 with Canada's acquisition of the land. If the period before was a 'dark age,' then this one can only be seen as a renaissance. Destiny, working through its Canadian agents, once again brought progress to the North West. 'The fullness of time arrived in 1857,' wrote John Macoun.[8] Under the guidance of men like Palliser, Hind, Buckingham, Coldwell, and Schultz, the idea of development was reintroduced into the Hudson's Bay territories. As Coldwell himself had said of the *Nor'Wester*, it was 'a ray of light' in a dark region.[9] 'Those were the palmy days of the Company,' said Denison of the years before 1857, 'but evil days were at hand. Canada sent Hind and Dawson to spy out the land, and from that moment the monopoly was doomed, and their deadly hostility to Canada and Canadians began.'[10] In the expansionist mind the real history of the North West began when Canada began to exert its influence in the region.

In general terms the expansionist view of western history was clear-cut, uncompromising, and in accord with their political aims and beliefs. There was, however, one period of western history that presented some difficulty. There had been settlement in the West long before annexation and it had not been on the initiative of Canada. In 1811 the Earl of Selkirk had founded a settlement on the banks of the Red River. Selkirk seemed to have done what Canadians were now trying to accomplish – plant a settlement in the North West. His efforts to establish a colony had to be explained by expansionists without sacrificing the assumption that the Hudson's Bay Company had consistently opposed colonization. The problem was further complicated by the fact that Selkirk had met active and violent opposition from the North West Company. This opposition had reached a tragic climax in 1816 at the battle of Seven Oaks when a band of Métis under the leadership of Cuthbert Grant had murdered several colonists, including the governor of the settlement.[11] The years 1811 to 1816 thus seemingly brought Canadian expansionists face to face with a time when the Hudson's Bay Company had acted as a force for settlement and progress while the Canadian North West Company had taken the role of the lawless opponent of civilization.

The only means by which the expansionists could get around this difficulty was to deny Selkirk's role as a colonist. Coincident with the opening of the campaign against the Hudson's Bay Company, writers began to discover evidence that Selkirk was simply acting to forward that company's position relative to the North West Company. As early as 1849 James Fitzgerald interpreted Selkirk's efforts as a scheme to block the normal supply routes of the North West Company.[12] The same year John McLean condemned Selkirk's visit to Montreal 'in the guise of a traveller' as a premeditated attempt to elicit information from the unsuspecting Nor'Westers.[13]

By the time the expansionist mood caught hold in Canada this interpretation had been fully developed. Selkirk's bold attempt at settlement was dismissed by a Canadian government report as a desperate attempt 'to assert the assumed privileges' of the Hudson's Bay Company and 'for this purpose a grant of country on the Red River was made to his Lordship.'[14] Once Selkirk's settlement became, as William Dawson termed it, a 'monstrous usurpation' of land for the sake of the fur trade, it became possible to interpret the violence of these years in a light favourable to the North West Company.[15]

As a conscious agent of the Hudson's Bay Company, Selkirk and those who followed him were seen as the aggressors. The North West Company was, in turn, forced into resistance by the provocative actions of this group. 'Resistance or extermination being the only alternative left to the Canada Company, civil war ensued.'[16] The violence was tragic and in the process a number of innocent people suffered, but there was no doubt that the fault lay with Selkirk and the Hudson's Bay Company. Selkirk's colonists, on arriving at Red River, attempted to expel the North West traders from the region. 'Their goods were seized and the channels of trade obstructed by the interception of their supplies.' Even the massacre of Seven Oaks, expansionists argued, was not the fault of the North West Company; the colonists, after all, had begun the battle. 'The Govenor was killed in leading an attack upon a party of the North-West Company who turned and gave battle.'[17]

One other difficulty in the expansionist interpretation of western history became apparent after 1870. It was common knowledge that the French half-breeds had been agents of the North West Company. In the 1850s and 1860s their inclusion in the myth of the company presented no problem. The Métis, as with the other settlers of Red River, were seen as British subjects seeking escape from the rule of the company. Their actions through history, from Seven Oaks to the Sayer trial, were interpreted in this light. Moreover, their ancestral connection with the voyageur of New France reinforced the contention that there was a Canadian claim on the West as a result of history. George Brown, for instance, emphasized this connection during the Confederation debates in order to encourage French-Canadian support for the idea of expansion.[18] Throughout the expansionist campaign to annex the West, the French presence in the North West Company did not affect that company's depicted qualities.

The Red River resistance changed all of this. The Métis, rather than acting as the allies of Canada, suddenly became its enemies. The violent rejection of expansion put them on the side of reaction. 'Averse to agriculture and to the slow tough steady gains of industry,' the Métis became the defenders of the wilderness.[19] This forced expansionists to reinterpret completely the significance of the Métis in the history of the region. Métis resistance in the past was now viewed as being directed not against tyranny but all authority; they became symbols of the lawlessness of the wilderness. 'During the year 1835,' noted John Macoun, 'the half-breeds, on account of their friends being ill-treated, made a demonstration against the Hudson's Bay Company, and so frightened the Officers that they yielded to most of their demands, and as a consequence, they became more over-bearing than ever.'[20] The Sayer trial and Seven Oaks could no longer be interpreted with any certainty as efforts to resist the tyranny of the company. Company weakness and Métis strength seemed to upset the image of the feudal taskmaster. In order to justify their own role in the 1870 rebellion, expansionists had to sacrifice the image of the Métis as part of the heroic North West tradition.

The inconsistencies in the role of Selkirk and the Métis could not be resolved within the framework of expansionist historiography. Such inconsistencies, however, while they revealed the problems of such an interpretation did not affect the general trend or significance of this eastern perception of the western past. More important than Selkirk's attempt at settlement was his supposedly cynical motivation and the opposition which it was felt the settlement faced from the company through the years. Without British institutions or liberty the colonists remained 'mere serfs of the officer in charge.'[21] More important than the politics of the Métis was their repeated resort to force to obtain their ends and the resultant disorder that plagued the colony. Under such conditions the Selkirk settlement could never become the basis for a great empire; it was shackled by a system 'which plants the civilised man amongst savages, not to illumine their darkness, but to be absorbed into their gloom.'[22]

The West as it was under the Hudson's Bay Company had no lessons of relevance to the future of the North West. According to the expansionist view of history, western development began not in 1811 but when Canada moved to open the region. The Selkirk settlement could develop from an oasis in the desert to the nucleus of an expanding civilization only because Canada had given it 'relief from the enervating thralldom' under which it had existed for so long.[23] And if the real development of civilization in the region was the result of Canadian intervention, it then followed that western society and the western identity had its real roots in the East which had provided the manpower, money, and direction for this development. Hargrave's careful chronicling of events in Red River was irrelevant because those events, in the expansionist mind, had nothing to do with the post-annexation West.

198 Promise of Eden

This assessment, or rather dismissal, of the western past continued to be reflected in Canadian histories in the years after 1870. In both organization and content the great majority of works written in the first years after Confederation revealed an ignorance of and disdain for the pre-1870 West. In most cases the history of the West under Hudson's Bay Company rule was brought into the work only in reference to growing Canadian interest in the region. W.H. Withrow's opening sentences on the West in his monumental 1886 *History of Canada* typified the approach of Canadian writers of history in the years after Confederation. Having taken over five hundred pages to trace the history of eastern British North America through to Confederation, he then mentions McDougall's negotiations with the Hudson's Bay Company in 1868: 'It will be convenient here to retrace briefly the history of that great monopoly that for two centuries had controlled the vast, and, in large part, fertile regions of this continent.'[24] Brevity was certainly the operative word, for Withrow managed to recapitulate two hundred years in less than eight pages. At least Withrow was accurate in his dates and facts, however, which was not the case with many other writers. Selkirk's De Meuron regiment was repeatedly turned into a regiment of Canadian soldiers sent by the Governor-General for the protection of the troubled colony, and many readers found that, according to the books they read, the North West had no history whatsoever between 1821 and 1858.[25] Compared to such sloppy treatments of western history, J.C. Dent's decision simply to ignore the western past completely was almost refreshing.[26]

The Canadian expansionist movement was successful in asserting a new social and political order on the North West of Selkirk and the fur trade. The development of western Canada was to be undertaken in the national and imperial context as interpreted by the self-appointed guardians of western destiny, eastern Canadians. Western history, it seemed, was to be interpreted in the same way.

Those living in the West in the years immediately after annexation seemed as little concerned with the history of their region as did easterners. It was a time when the expansionist orientation to the future was fully accepted and little thought was given to the society that was being supplanted. After Hargrave's effort the older settlers of Red River, perhaps concentrating on keeping pace with the changes around them, published nothing for several years. New westerners were even less concerned. The creation of a livelihood and the search for material gain fully occupied the attention of most of them. On the rare occasion when something was published, it tended to accept the expansionist view of western history.[27]

199 The West as past

The lack of interest on the part of westerners to the past of their region soon began to change. As in so many other instances in the development of the North West, the beginning of this change can be dated from 1879. That year saw the establishment of the Historical and Scientific Society of Manitoba in Winnipeg. The purposes of this society were well summed up several years later by Charles N. Bell as he accepted the post of its president. The society's object, he stated, was 'to collect and maintain a general library of books, pamphlets, maps, manuscripts, prints, papers, paintings ... and objects generally illustrative of the civil, religious, literary and natural histories of the lands and territories north and west of Lake Superior.'[28] The society more than lived up to its aims. Over the next two decades it was to develop a large library, hold regular and well-attended meetings, and develop a national reputation. More importantly, its members were to go a long way towards correcting the lack of knowledge and interest in the history of the West. By 1900 the society had published some fifty-six papers and its membership contained the great majority of early western historians.

The formation of the society was only one of the many occurrences that revealed a growing interest in the past. In 1880 the first history of Red River was published since the one by Hargrave a decade before. This one had also been written by an old Red River settler, Donald Gunn, though his untimely death meant that the latter part of the work was actually penned by the transplanted easterner, Charles Tuttle.[29] Equally significant was the beginning of work by a former Ontarian on the history of his new home province. George Bryce had never had trouble putting his thoughts into writing before, and his new concern for western history was to be a major impetus to that field. The publication of his *Manitoba: Its Infancy, Growth and Present Position* in 1882 was a landmark in western history for two reasons: it was the first of three major historical works Bryce would turn out before the end of the century and the second of at least twenty-five historically related publications that he would produce in the same period;[30] it was also the first history of the province written exclusively by a Canadian born in the East. When the energetic George Bryce turned his attention to the western past it marked the end of the casual indifference to that history that had prevailed to that time. As a mainstay of the Historical and Scientific Society of Manitoba and as a major historian in his own right, Bryce was to do more than any other single individual to record the history of the West.

Behind the increased interest in western history was a new awareness of the impact of change and the passage of time on the landscape of the West. Though it had been scarcely a decade from the time of annexation, the changes that had taken place in the West clearly indicated that the older era was rapidly disappearing. These changes were particularly noticeable in Manitoba and it was no coincidence that the initial impetus to the writing of western history was concentrated there. It is symbolic, for instance, that the creation of the Historical and Scientific Society should have come so closely on the heels of the arrival of the railway in Winnipeg. Together the two events indicated a newly developed level of sophistication but they also signified to contemporaries the passage of that older community which had seemed so much a part of the West when men like Bryce first arrived.

The indications that the older society was disappearing were to multiply rapidly over the next few years and to reinforce this newly found concern with the past. In 1882 one of the most famous landmarks of the fur trade was torn down. The destruction of historical Fort Garry in the name of progress was something that Bryce never forgot or ever quite forgave: 'It was sold by the Hudson's Bay Company in the inflation of 1882 for an enormous sum; and, shame to the vandalism of modern commerce, it has been partly removed to straighten Main Street; most of its buildings are unoccupied and, alas! all of those occupied are the headquarters of the Winnipeg street Car Company. The glory of the Winnipeg forts has departed!'[31]

The destruction of Fort Garry was but one symptom of a more general feeling that the past was rapidly disappearing. In the North West the buffalo, that staple of an earlier time, had become all but extinct. 'Tons of bones and skulls are piled awaiting shipment,' wrote John Schultz after a trip across the prairies, 'and soon not even these remains will be left of the mighty hosts which you once saw on the plains.'[32] By 1877 the last of the Plains Indians were under treaty and by the early 1880s most of them had settled on reserves. The famous Saskatchewan River was being navigated by steam boat and, with the completion of the Canadian Pacific Railway in 1885, a person could travel across the entire width of the prairies without ever setting foot on them. All of these events were, of course, objectives of the expansionist movement and Canadians extolled their achievements. None the less, there was a growing appreciation of the finality of these changes and their impact on the once seemingly endless wilderness.

The new awareness of the past was also a generational matter. As the years passed more and more of those who had taken an active part in the society of the fur trade had died. Those who remained began to be recognized and to see themselves as a unique group with a special understanding of the past of the West. The Historical and Scientific Society of Manitoba declared one of its primary objectives to be the desire 'to rescue from oblivion the memory of early missionaries, fur traders and settlers of aforesaid lands and territories.'[33] The society was far from unique in its interest in such matters and by the 1890s something of a cult had grown up around those who had lived in the West during the period of Hudson's Bay Company rule.

Those who lived or travelled in the North West in 'frontier times,' as the phrase went, were not at all reticent in setting down the record of their own experiences. In the latter part of the century memoirs became what travel accounts had been in earlier decades, the basic form of literature on the West.[34] Complementing the personal memoirs were biographies. Missionaries, those early bringers of civilization, were especially popular subjects for biography and such renowned individuals as James Evans and George McDougall had numerous works written on them.[35] A good many deserving men, and many not so deserving, found themselves the subject of study as fascination with the past continued to grow.

Whether one looks at the memoirs, the biographies, or the histories of the period, the degree of interest, if not fascination, with the past can be seen to reflect the growing belief that to lose the memory of events of the earlier era would be a tragedy. It was, in short, change that made the past seem more important. As William Dennis explained in a lecture before the Historical and Scientific Society of Manitoba: 'Here in the Northwest is just springing up what is destined to be one of the greatest and grandest nations in the world. Our history is already an intensely interesting one. We owe it to ourselves and to posterity to gather up all the fragments, and hand them down to the future. There are many old residents still alive who possess a vast amount of information of historical importance. I think we should make an effort to get at that information, get it in print and then it will be at our command for all time to come. If we allow the present opportunity to pass, it will, in a few years, be lost forever.'[36] The concern with the western past was thus initially historical rather than historiographical. In fact, the very importance that westerners attached to their past derived from the expansionist concept of rapid progress and change. Western history developed out of a concern for a disappearing past and was not, primarily, a challenge to the eastern perspective on that past.

This acceptance of expansionist historiography within the framework of western history was well illustrated by one of the first histories to develop out of the renewed interest in the past. In the 1880 work, *History of Manitoba* by Gunn and Tuttle, the cast of characters and the roles they assumed remained more or less the same as they had in earlier, eastern writings. Selkirk assumed the role of villain and the violence between the two companies was interpreted to be the direct result of his presence. There had been rivalry before but then differences had been 'speedily settled, generally in a very friendly and pleasant manner over a flowing bowl of Demera punch.'

Behind Selkirk was the Hudson's Bay Company, still seen as being opposed to settlement. The years under the rule of the Hudson's Bay Company remain for Red River a dark age without hope of British political or civil liberties. Fortunately for Red River and for the North West, Canada began to take an interest in the region. The publication of the *Nor'Wester* was termed 'the advent of an important era in the history of the settlement.' And, in an analysis that even many ardent eastern expansionists would have hesitated to make, the Dawson route was seen as evidence of the 'generous sympathy of the Canadian Government and people toward the residents of Red River.' Canadian self-interest and a sense of 'moral obligation' towards their fellow Britons in Red River led to the rescue of the settlers on the banks of the Red River from the stagnation and misery of the dark ages.[37]

While the initial western interest in history was not primarily historiographical, there was implicit in the very existence of that interest a rejection of the eastern interpretation of their past. Westerners were no longer willing to leave their history in the hands of those who would dismiss it in a few paragraphs at the end of what was essentially a history of the old Province of Canada. The importance of the West to Canada, in the minds of westerners, made it imperative to develop a balanced view of Canadian history.

This line of thought was one of the most notable features of George Bryce's 1887 work, *A Short History of the Canadian People*. 'The author aims,' he warned, 'at viewing Canada from a "Dominion" viewpoint.' There would not be 'whole chapters on the war of 1812-15; the rise and fall of administrations, whose single aim seemed to be to grasp power; and on petty discussions which have left no mark upon the country.' Bryce was as good as his word. Unlike the eastern historians of the period he did not bring the West in almost as an afterthought but in the proper chronological sequence. The founding of Red River takes place, in his text, before the War of 1812, and the period after 1821 is discussed in as much detail as was the Canadian political history of those years. The discontinuity in the narrative that resulted from such a juxtaposition of essentially unconnected events, Bryce obviously felt, was more than redressed by the removal of an odious bias.[38]

In its initial stages, then, the interest that developed in western history in the early 1880s was a reaction to the passing of an era. It was not an historiographical reaction against an expansionist interpretation of western history. Nevertheless, as westerners began to look at the past of the region in which they lived, it was perhaps inevitable that the perspective on that past would begin to change. That change began with questions of organization and chronology but would soon go far beyond that to problems of interpretation. This changing perspective on interpretation would be accelerated and accentuated as westerners became disillusioned with the expansionist schemes of social and economic development. A sense of alienation from the East would bring western historians to undertake a fundamental reorientation of their perspective on western development and western identity. These stresses led what had begun as an attempt to set down the history of the West to become an effort to develop a particular regional historiography. The result was the formation not only of histories of the West but a western school of history.

A change in historiographical perspective was implicit in the very interest in regional history. Even in the case of Gunn and Tuttle, with their emphasis on the importance of Canadian efforts to open the region and their condemnation of the Hudson's Bay Company, certain differences resulted from their western perspective. Most basically, whatever importance was attached to 1856 and the development of Canadian interest, it was impossible to overlook the long history of the Selkirk settlement. Unlike eastern Canadian histories this regional study could not pass quickly from 1821 to 1856; to have done so would have destroyed the very purpose for writing it. There was thus a new emphasis on the efforts of the Selkirk settlers to carve out a livelihood in the wilderness.[39] Once it was decided to follow the course of western history rather than the course of eastern involvement in the West, there followed a reorganization of the significant dates of western history. The year 1811 and the arrival of the Selkirk settlers overshadowed 1821 and the amalgamation of the two fur companies. As suited an age when the old timer was being eagerly sought out for his experiences, the Selkirk settlers began to assume an important place in the mind of western historians. It was not long before other changes in interpretation followed from this initial one.

Eastern historians, because they had had little interest in the Selkirk settlement, found it easier to sacrifice the reputation of Selkirk than that of the North West Company. George Bryce, writing in 1882 not as an expansionist but as a man interested in the history of Red River, found his priorities reversed. Rather than downgrade the story of the Selkirk settlers to a petty trade rivalry, Bryce reinterpreted the role of Selkirk. If, as was the case, he had to condemn the North West Company in order to make his interpretation consistent, then he was willing to do so.

This reinterpretation was also influenced by the research Bryce undertook in preparation for his history. His work brought him into contact with James Selkirk, grandson of the man who had founded Red River. While working on his history Bryce corresponded regularly with Selkirk and, while in Britain, visited both Selkirk and his sister. Bryce found the earl's knowledge and kindness to be both useful and stimulating and the earl, for his part, had a good many definite ideas on the place of his ancestor in history. The primary motive of the Earl of Selkirk, his descendant argued, was the aiding of displaced Highland crofters through a scheme of emigration. Previous efforts in Prince Edward Island and Upper Canada testified to the sincerity of his interest in colonization. Any association which he undertook with the Hudson's Bay Company came about only in order to further these emigration plans. 'He found on consulting the best legal authorities that the land belonged to the Hudson's Bay Company subject only to the rights of the Indian tribes; it was therefore necessary to acquire it from the Company, and this and nothing else was his object in joining them and buying shares.'[40] Thus it was Selkirk's altruistic concern for the poor people of Great Britain that prompted him to work with the Hudson's Bay Company, rather than, as had been argued previously, his association with the company that led him to develop a colonization scheme.

Bryce either agreed with or accepted James Selkirk's views on the founder of Red River. In fact, the vindication of the earl became one of the primary objectives of *Manitoba: Its Infancy, Growth and Present Position*. 'Why will men attribute sordid, impure, interested motives,' asked Bryce in his introduction, 'when pure patriotism or noble philanthropy are simple explanations, lying ready to hand.'[41] It was a pure and noble purpose, Bryce concluded, that led Selkirk to found his colony in the heart of North America. As one reviewer accurately commented, it was 'the best vindication of the character of Lord Selkirk that has yet appeared.'[42]

Bryce's reinterpretation of Selkirk in *Manitoba* was but the first of many which argued the case for Selkirk. Bryce, of course, continued to support Selkirk in later works. He was soon joined by individuals like Alexander Begg who, in his massive three-volume history of the West, also saw Selkirk's affiliation with the Hudson's Bay Company as less important than his interest in colonization. 'They were the masters of the situation,' he wrote, and therefore Selkirk cast his lot with them.[43]

These views found an even more ardent supporter in Roderick G. MacBeth. MacBeth had been born in Red River in 1858 and had grown up amidst the turmoil of the expansionist campaign and influx of immigration after the transfer to Canada. Moreover, he attended the University of Manitoba in the early 1880s and came under the influence of Bryce at the very time that Bryce was working out his own views on Selkirk. MacBeth accepted Bryce's interpretation and incorporated it into his own historical writings which began to appear in the 1890s. MacBeth had no doubt that the earlier charges against Selkirk were fraudulent and that the founder of the Red River settlement was 'actuated by higher than selfish motives.'[44] In one of the more dramatic reversals in Canadian history, George Bryce changed Selkirk from a cynical participant in a fur trade war to 'a man of thought and of deep sympathy for the sufferings of the civilized and the savage alike.'[45]

The reinterpretation of Selkirk's role inevitably forced a new assessment of the other factions involved in the history of Red River. The defence of the North West Company had always been premised on the assumption that Selkirk's motives were those of the fur trade rather than settlement. Once Selkirk was interpreted as a philanthropist the Nor'Westers assumed the role of villain for their opposition to his efforts. Their true character was revealed to the reader by Bryce long before Selkirk comes into direct conflict with them. When the Earl visited Montreal in 1803, Bryce stated, he noted 'their baronial hauteur and their lordly gatherings.' These were men with a contempt for society and a disdain for any law but their own. Their whole record of participation in the fur trade of the North West, illegal as it was, rested purely on force. 'The North-West Company in all its changes retained its special character of violence.' Violence and intimidation were, in fact, their basic strategy: 'The Canadian traders however, just in proportion to the weakness of their right, made up in strong reiteration of their claim, and from the first, as we shall see, resorted to violence as a means of gaining their ends ... The most daring and turbulent spirits were now attracted to the fur trade; indeed, the chief qualities sought in those sent out were a love of violence and a thorough hatred of the Hudson's Bay Company.'[46]

If the strategy was violence, the purpose was the preservation of the North West as a wilderness for the sake of the fur trade. 'The fact that an immense region existed fit to sustain them all in comfort was nothing to them. The empire of wolves and foxes was more congenial.' The images of the North West Company and Selkirk were reversed by Bryce; in his interpretation of events, the heroes of expansionism had been willing to undertake anything, even murder, to protect their economic position.

If the heroes of expansionist historiography found their reputation somewhat tarnished in this reversal of opinion, their arch-enemy, the Hudson's Bay Company, found itself somewhat redeemed. Western historians, at least in the 1880s, were not willing to attribute to the Hudson's Bay Company all the glory and purity which they gave to Selkirk. The company's attitude to the colony, at least after the death of Selkirk, was thought to have been that it was 'a difficulty to be dealt with as best could be done, but not to be increased.'[47] It was hardly a progressive view of events. Nevertheless, in the vindication of Selkirk and the condemnation of the North West Company, this historical interpretation admitted two points which expansionists had vociferously denied. First, the Hudson's Bay Company was seen as having a good claim to the North West under the terms of its 1670 charter and subsequent licences to trade. Second, Canadian pretensions to the North West were seen, at least by implication, to be fraudulent.

The changing historiographical perspective and the very importance attached to western history by Bryce and others suggested a great deal about the shifts in the western self-image in the 1880s. The writing of the history of the West was by its very nature a statement that there existed a western past and a western identity in that past. The West had its own history and one that stood comparison to the proud record of any eastern province. 'The career of the Hudson's Bay Company, which is in fact the history of Rupert's Land,' said Bryce in 1885, 'began 120 years before the history of Ontario, and there were forts of the two rival Fur Companies on the Saskatchewan and throughout the country, before the first U.E. Loyalist felled a forest tree in Upper Canada.'[48]

This new pride in the western past implied, in wider terms, the growing unwillingness of westerners to accept the subordination of their region to the East. The emphasis on a regional history demonstrated that, in 1870, when Canada annexed the North West, it was not taking an empty land to develop as its hinterland. It was, instead, joining itself to a people who had proven themselves in the wilderness. The western past gave westerners a right to determine, independent of the east, their own needs and goals. The recognition of the separate identity of western history was, at least indirectly, a part of the insistence that developed in the 1880s that western interests be recognized by the East: 'A strange picture has it been, indeed, to the traveller from Canada of the last few years to come to the new Province of Manitoba and find a people with a separate history, separate conditions, and a separate life, even from the native population around them. The feeling of the colony of being a different people from the natives of the country has never been lost; and though there are representatives of four generations of people living yet the people of Kildonan in 1870, were almost as thoroughly the pure Selkirk settlers in blood, as when they crossed the ocean to Hudson's Bay.'[49] Here was a group of Europeans who had entered the land for purposes both distinct from and more moral than the fur trade. They had retained their European traditions through the years and, having done so, deserved recognition of their place as colonizers every bit as much as did those who came from Canada after 1856.

The development of regional history under the leadership of Bryce resulted in a significant reversal of earlier views. Equally significant and perhaps even more dramatic was the course of western historiography as it developed over the two decades after Bryce wrote *Manitoba*. In these years the particular nature of the western historical perspective was further developed by continued disillusionment with economic, social, and political conditions. This disillusionment, as has been indicated, meant that those who came west after 1870 began to see themselves as separate from their native eastern Canada. The westerner, even if he was a transplanted easterner, was becoming less and less willing to define himself in terms of the province so associated with exploitation of the West. In this atmosphere the interpretation of western history became a means by which writers and intellectuals could search for a new definition of the westerner's place in society in the context of both the past and present. In addition, this continued disappointment with the present reinforced the attractiveness of that past. The people and events of the years before 1870 moved from obscurity to romantic idealization and, in the process, all events connected with the era took on a romantic colouring. The entire past became a part of the grand epic of western development, an epic that had previously been seen almost exclusively in terms of Canadian expansion.

Most suggestive of this tendency was the discovery by historians that for all its anti-progressive implications the fur trade was an adventurous activity which, in its own way, laid the foundations for future development. It had, after all, fostered the exploration of the interior of the continent and preserved that region from American or other encroachment. It was an interpretation that had existed before but which had not been seen for many years; during the debate of the 1850s over the future of the Hudson's Bay Company, many defenders of the fur trade had presented just such a thesis. Edward Ermatinger, for instance, had pointed out in 1858 that the officials of the Hudson's Bay Company were 'the custodians of the whole of that vast territory for the British Empire.'[50] Opinions such as Ermatinger's disappeared, however, in the face of the expansionist campaign, and not until the 1880s were they again presented with any conviction.

Once again it was George Bryce who took the lead in this reinterpretation. While admitting that the company had erected a 'Chinese wall' around the territories, Bryce concluded that 'the Hudson's Bay Company has done much to increase the geographical knowledge of Rupert's Land and the regions beyond.'[51] Alexander Begg, a man who had never accepted the expansionist view of western history, agreed, pointing out that 'it was in the fur trade that men were first induced to penetrate the wilds of the north-west, ascend its mighty rivers, and explore its mountains.' If for no other reason, this impetus to exploration made the fur traders 'the forerunners of civilization in North America.'[52] In contrast to the basic view of expansionism, this interpretation saw self-interest acting, indirectly, in the interests of the British Empire and civilization. By opening the territory and by laying claim to it for Britain, the fur trade companies undertook a patriotic and useful role. 'It never forgot the flag that floated over it,' said Bryce of the Hudson's Bay Company.[53]

While the North West Company was incorporated in a general way into this myth of the fur trade, the real effort at justification was reserved for the Hudson's Bay Company. In expansionist writings the North West Company had fared well because it had been seen as a Canadian company; conversely, the Hudson's Bay Company had been depicted not only as reactionary but as a foreign power ruling lands that rightly belonged to Canada. By the 1890s, however, historians writing from a western perspective tended to see the North West Company as a symbol of external, that is to say, eastern, interests and the Hudson's Bay Company as an integral part of their regional society and past.

The company may have had its faults but increasingly those historians writing in what could almost be termed a 'Manitoba School' of history saw these as outweighed by the strong and understanding involvement of the firm in the North West. Agnes C. Laut, another western historian influenced by Bryce, argued that there must be 'set over against its sins, this other fact, a record which no other organization may boast – the bloodless conquest of an empire from savagery.'[54] George Bryce concluded that the amazing thing was not that the company had made mistakes but that it 'bears, on the whole, after its long career over such an extended area of operations, among savage and border people unaccustomed to the restraints of law, so honourable a record.'[55]

This praise of the Hudson's Bay Company posed a question as to what had happened to the tyranny that had kept the people of Red River in miserable isolation and had eventually made them look to annexation with Canada for relief. In fact, the answer presented little in the way of an historical problem for the same tendencies which had romanticized the fur trade had, by the 1890s, converted the history of the Selkirk settlement into an idealized myth. The hardships and struggle which had been seen as a part of the history of the settlement by western writers in the early 1880s did not disappear entirely, but they were increasingly confined to the relatively short period between 1811 and 1821. After the latter date there was thought to have existed a unique and contented settlement on the banks of the Red River.

The major proponents of this increasingly romantic view of life in Red River were those older settlers who had actually experienced life in the settlement before 1870 and their descendants. Perhaps because they were uncomfortable within the new Ontario-dominated élites of Manitoba in the 1880s and 1890s, or perhaps because time had weeded out the negative memories of their past, these individuals moved to instil a new element into western historiography, a golden age. As early as 1884 Alexander Begg had written fondly of the pre-1870 settlement as a place where 'no nearer approach to perfect freedom have I ever seen or known.'[56] It was not until the 1890s, however, and largely through the Historical and Scientific Society of Manitoba, that this image of the past fully developed.

In 1893 Red River–born John MacBeth delivered a paper before the society on the social customs of Red River. The subject provided this 'old-timer' with an opportunity to develop his own ideas on the morality and pleasures of a vanished society. MacBeth granted that the Red River settlement was a small town with only the most simple of institutions and social pastimes. The activities that took place within this unsophisticated setting, however, MacBeth saw as 'particularly enjoyable.' It was an era of honest pleasure and friendly camaraderie that contrasted with the more sophisticated but more tainted activities of the present day. 'We used to play a game called "Bat,"' said MacBeth, 'which was practically the same as baseball, only we had no leagues, no professionals, and no gambling.' Even the famed horse races of Red River saw 'very little gambling.' It was a moral, upright, and thoroughly peaceful society and MacBeth, quoting a poem from another old-timer, ended his presentation with a clear expression of the romanticism that had run through his paper:

> O for the times that some despise,
> At least I liked them, me whatever,
> Before the Transfer made us wise
> Or politics had made us clever.
>
> Then faith and friendship, hand in hand,
> A kindly tale to all were telling,
> From east to west, throughout the land,
> Contentment reigned in every dwelling.[57]

A new and suggestive set of images had appeared in MacBeth's presentation. Not only was Red River praised as a contented and peaceful spot, it was also set up as a moral society in contrast to the jaded, complex city of Winnipeg.

MacBeth's depiction of an idealized Red River community was but the first of many such expressions over the next few years. R.G. MacBeth further developed the contrast between old and new societies, describing the history of Red River as 'an era of mutual helpfulness rather than opposition.'[58] Alexander Begg revealed in 1894 that his attraction to the old Red River community had strengthened with time: 'Socially there was much good feeling existing between all classes of the community, and a more hospitable or happier people could hardly be found on the face of the earth.'[59]

210 Promise of Eden

It was not until 1902, however, that the romanticism of Red River was expressed in its most extreme form. In that year Frank Larned Hunt presented his own thoughts on the settlement to the society. The title he chose for the paper summed up very neatly the thesis he developed. Red River was, he said 'Britain's One Utopia.' It was a land where the 'cursings and obscenities that taint the air and brutalize life elsewhere, were in the quaint old settlement unknown.' Even political parties were non-existent, for such things 'would be but throwing the apple of discord' into a peaceful and contented community. It was, all in all, a perfect land, 'a nomadic pastoral enwrought with Indian traits.' And where so many supposed utopias had proved delusory, the isolated settlement on the banks of the Red River succeeded:

Under conditions without precedent, and incapable of repetition, [there] evolved a community in the heart of the continent, shut away from intercourse with civilized mankind – that slowly crystalized into a form beyond the ideal of the dreamers, a community, in the past, known faintly to the outer world as the Red River Settlement, which is but the by-gone name for the One Utopia of Britain,

It was; brief as the few decades of its existence, still fate had caught away from time, the clear-cut impress of an exceptional people living under conditions of excellence unthought of by themselves until they had passed away.[60]

Extreme though Hunt's views may seem, they were widely accepted by western historians. Mrs George Bryce presented her own paper on Red River culture to the society. Details of education, music, and the arts were described to illustrate 'the efforts to promote the higher intellectual life in Red River.' It was a presentation that, whether intentional or not, was a direct refutation of those earlier missionaries who had pictured the North West as a place of gloom and barbarism. 'All honor,' concluded Marion Bryce, 'to the men and women who thus faithfully endeavored to make the wilderness rejoice and blossom as a rose.'[61] R.G. MacBeth restated the theme developed by Hunt when, in 1905, he argued that the people of Red River were 'contented and happy' under Hudson's Bay rule and entitled his chapter on the coming of annexation 'The Pathos of Change.'[62]

Perhaps the most important convert to this utopian picture of Red River was George Bryce. Bryce had, in fact, been working towards such a position long before Hunt enunciated it in 1902. Through the 1890s he had extended the admiration he felt for Selkirk to the settlement he founded in numerous articles.[63] His final adoption of utopian terminology, however, did not come until 1909. If it was late, however, it was also presented at an appropriate time. In order to mark the approaching centennial of the Red

River settlement, Bryce published his *Romantic Settlement of Lord Selkirk's Colonists*.

Bryce was so enraptured with the past by the time of this work that he quickly disposed of the unpleasant rivalries between the two fur trading companies and then portrayed Red River as having no internal or external enemies, except perhaps the grasshopper. Even Sir George Simpson, that arch-villain of expansionist history, found himself transformed into the 'Jolly Governor' working hard for the welfare of the people. Bryce had no hesitation in expressing his debt to Hunt and others who preceded him. In fact, so complete was his adoption of Hunt's imagery that he took his article, 'Britain's One Utopia,' and incorporated it completely in his own book. George Bryce had been captured by the idyllic visions of a past golden age, or as Bryce termed it, 'Apples of Gold.'[64]

The depiction of the Red River settlement in utopian terms and the location of a golden age somewhere between 1821 and 1870 signified a major shift in western Canadian thought. Until that time the golden age of the West had always been depicted as being in the future. Its placement in the past reversed both the basic expansionist presumption of the fur trade era as a dark age and the faith that Canadian expansion had begun an era of beneficial progress and development in the North West. It was still accepted that progress and development had been brought by annexation, but it was now being asked if that development did not have very real drawbacks. For the first time in a generation, writings on the West began to deal with the costs of progress.

In a limited way George Bryce had expressed a recognition of the costs of change as early as 1885. Describing the economy of Red River, Bryce was not yet ready to utopianize it and warned that 'the picture was hardly Arcadian.' In the same sentence, however, he also commented that 'the new order of things has borne pretty severely upon many, so that they feel as did the kindly old lady, the occupant of Colony Gardens till two years ago, that they were "shut in" by so many people coming up to the country.'[65] As the utopian view of Red River gathered strength in the 1890s, this feeling of loss developed to a much greater degree. The disruption of a utopia was hardly expected to be a completely happy event and Bryce, in his *Romantic Settlement*, followed this idea to its logical, if extreme, conclusion. His chapter on annexation was entitled 'Eden Invaded' and clearly reflected the negative side of progress. 'Certainly to the old people,' Bryce concluded, 'there was a feeling of freedom from care, as if it being a lotus-eaters land – an Utopia, an Eden, before sin entered and before man's disobedience brought death into the world and all our woe.' It was almost as if it took a conscious act of restraint for Bryce to add that 'we are not disposed to press Milton's metaphor any further in regard to the disturbers who came in.'[66] Bryce stopped just short of converting the expansionists from the bringers of light into a dark region into the agents of sin and greed in a previously idyllic world.

The writings of Bryce and the others of this period introduced into the image of the West what has aptly been termed the idea of 'the machine in the garden.'[67] The machine, in the symbolic sense, represented the forces and apparatus of civilization, disfiguring the natural and peaceful scene on which it intruded. It was not an image that derived from any pastoral ideal contained within the expansionist image of the West; such an image had never been a part of expansionist rhetoric. Rather, it was something new, developing from an increasingly powerful myth of Red River and the years before the transfer. The result was a new tension in the image of the West in which the forces of development contested with the desire to preserve and glorify an older order. It was perhaps symbolic that the last time this idea of tension had been clearly revealed, though from a different perspective, was in Alexander Ross's writings on the eve of the great expansionist campaign. Ross had been concerned lest the pervasive influence of the wilderness leave the settlement unprepared for the growing influence of civilization. In different circumstances the writers at the turn of the century feared that a triumphant civilization would overwhelm the traditions, values, and very land to which so many looked with fondness. For all their differences, however, both understood, in a way the expansionists never did, the problems inherent in rapid change. Moreover, both instinctively felt that if the desired goals were to be achieved, a means would have to be found to resolve this tension.

Alexander Ross failed in his quest, concluding only that the tension was destructive in that it prevented the colony from preparing for the new order and from living comfortably with the old. In contrast, the Manitoba historians of the late nineteenth and early twentieth centuries were successful, at least on the surface, in finding positive facets to this tension. From the beginning they had rejected the irrelevance of the western part to the present and future. The insistence on the importance of western history and its analysis as a continuing process from the fur trade to the present continued to be developed through the 1880s and 1890s. The result was an historiographical view that connected the events of the past to the character of the present and which allowed a resolution of the tension between an attraction for the past and an acceptance of change. Moreover, the same historiographical perspective pointed to the resolution of another problem. The sense of western consciousness reflected in this view indicated that these historians no longer looked on themselves or their society simply as something transplanted from Ontario. By tying the western past to the western present, new and regional roots were formed.

213 The West as past

By the turn of the century the year 1811 had become not only an important date in western history but the founding date. As George Bryce said of the first party of Selkirk settlers, 'there can be only one first party of those who laid the foundations of collective family life in what is now the Province of Manitoba – and what is wider – the great Western Canada of to-day.'[68] That distinction went not to the Canadians who had come west in 1870 but to the Selkirk settlers; they were the true founders of the province of Manitoba. Parallel to the process of romanticizing Red River was the development of the myth of the Selkirk settlers as the founding fathers of Manitoba.

The development of this cult of the founding fathers was suggestive. In eastern Canada the 1880s and 1890s saw a growing number of Loyalist enthusiasts.[69] Westerners, in developing their own myth of the Selkirk settlers, reflected the tendencies of the age but rejected the relevance of the founders of eastern Canada to their own land. Throughout the 1880s there thus grew up a parallel but quite separate historical myth in the West. As Bryce said, there could only be one founding party and that party came from neither the United States nor from eastern Canada but from Hudson's Bay.

If a date can be placed on the official ordination of the Selkirk settlers as founding fathers, it would have to be 19 June 1891. On that day a ceremony was held to mark the raising of a monument to the massacre of Seven Oaks which had been donated by the Countess of Selkirk. The battle itself, as Canon J.P. Matheson noted, had ceased to be a point of contention and had become instead the heroic testing of the blood which marked the triumph of the founding fathers: 'My feeling is one of thankfullness, and that thankfullness is of a three-fold nature. I am thankful, first of all, that we natives can claim such close kinship with the distant past of a country which is destined to have such a glorious future. I am thankful in the second place, that a wise Providence over-ruled the dissension of the past, and so soon welded the discordant and oppressing elements of those early days into a community of contented and self-reliant people. It was well, perhaps, that our colony was thus at its inception baptized in struggle. It tended to make these pioneer forefathers of ours staunch men, staunch and true to lay broad and deep the foundations of that God-fearing little community in which it was our privilege to be nurtured.' It was this group, added Charles Bell, 'who first proved to the world the fertility of the lands of the Red River valley.'[70] The elements of an heroic past had been set down. Struggle, sacrifice, bravery, purpose, and foresight marked the men who had laid the first elements of a future empire in the North West.

It was significant that westerners, including many from Ontario, should find the symbol of the United Empire Loyalist unsatisfactory for their own history. It was equally significant that westerners were very conscious of what they were doing. As early as 1887 George Bryce had described the founding of the Selkirk settlement and the founding of Canada by the Loyalists in terms designed to make the reader aware of the comparison. As the centennial of the founding of Red River approached, Bryce became even more explicit in his comparison. 'The U.E. Loyalists of Upper Canada and Nova Scotia draw upon our sympathies,' he wrote, 'but they afford no parallel to the discouragement, dangers, and dismay of the Selkirk colonists.'[71] When Bryce said they afforded no parallels, he of course meant the opposite. He was insisting, as were those who spoke at the commemoration of Seven Oaks, not only that the West had its own past but that it was a past as heroic and inspirational as was the myth of the United Empire Loyalists.

The elevation of the Selkirk settlers into a regional group of United Empire Loyalists provided a means of reconciling a belief in the importance and attractiveness of the past with the reality of rapid change and settlement. The lessons of the Selkirk settlers, as with the lessons of the Loyalists, were a vital part of present-day life. 'Our presence is a consequence of that past,' said Canon Matheson. 'We live to-day under the grateful shade of the tree which our forefathers planted. We reap in peace to-day the harvest, the seeds of which they sowed in toil and blood.'[72] The legacy of the founding fathers was not simply a material one. The Selkirk settlers and society of Red River were seen to have imparted a basic social and moral structure to the province of Manitoba. It was a legacy that had survived all the changes of recent years. 'If you seek their monument,' said R.G. MacBeth, 'look around you on the religious and educational as well as the material greatness of the North-West.'[73] The efforts of the early churches, concluded Bryce, 'laid the foundation for the general morality and advanced social life which prevailed in Red River and the regions beyond.'[74] In their concern for religion and especially in their continued efforts to bring a Presbyterian minister to the settlement, Bryce saw a religious spirit which lasted through the years: 'The sturdy stand for principle which the Selkirk Colonists made created an atmosphere which has remained until the present day ... In the Canadian West from the very day that old Verandrye [sic] took his priest with him, from the time when the first Colonists brought a devout layman as their religious teacher with them, from the hour when the stalwart Provencher came, from the era when the self-denying West visited the Indian camps and Selkirk's camp alike, from the time when the saintly Black came as the natural leader of the Selkirk Colonists, and during the forty years of the development of Manitoba, the foundations have been laid in that righteousness which exalteth a nation.'[75]

What was true of religion was also true of education. The basis for the University of Manitoba was to be found in the various schools and colleges of

Red River; their traditions had been preserved, expanded, and brought forward to meet the needs of the modern province. 'We of the present day owe much to the past regime,' said Marion Bryce. 'The educational ambitions and literary tastes of those early days have permeated our modern ideas and we can at least point to three of our prominent educational institutions as having had their roots in "Early Red River Culture."'[76] George Bryce substantiated this, pointing to the fact that the majority of the first Board of Management of Manitoba College consisted of men who had either been born in or emigrated to Red River before 1870; at least half of them had spent their entire adult lives in the Hudson's Bay territories.[77] The communal spirit and lack of dogmatism which was thought to characterize the University of Manitoba was now traced not only to the opportunities of an empty land but to those who had first settled there.

The myth of the Selkirk settlers was significantly strengthened and broadened by this direct linkage of past traditions and present practice. A founding myth is not very useful unless the majority of the population feels some connection to it. For that great majority of westerners who had not been born in Red River this connection was provided by the continued influence of the traditions of Red River in modern-day Manitoba. The uplifting spirit and high traditions of that colony affected newcomers as well as descendants of the original settlers. The myth of the Selkirk settlers could belong to all westerners.

Having opened the myth to all and having made a connection between past and present, it was then possible for the West to challenge the image of their region as a hinterland, subordinate to the East and under eastern tutelage. In the toil and sacrifice of the Selkirk settlers lay the rights of present-day westerners to full equality in the Dominion. For if the province of Manitoba owed a great deal to the Selkirk settlers, so too did the Canadian nation. 'We say,' argued Bryce, 'that had it not been for the Selkirk Colonists we would have stood to lose our Canadian West.' That West, as expansionists had argued for some time, was what enabled Canada to move towards greatness. 'We are beginning to see to-day,' Bryce continued, 'that Canada could not have become a powerful sister nation in the Empire had the West not been saved to her.' The region was essential to the nation for 'in territory, resources, and influence the West is making Canada complete. And if so, we owe it to Lord Selkirk and to the Selkirk Settlers, who stood true to their flag and their nationality.'[78]

This historical foundation also strengthened and made indigenous the sense of mission which had always been a part of expansionism. It was throught from the beginning that the West had opportunities to develop an improved set of social institutions. It had been assumed that this would occur through the selective transplanting of eastern institutions to a virgin land – taking the good while leaving the bad. As the comments on education and religion indicate, however, a new element had been added by the turn of the century. In addition to the freeing element of an empty land there was felt to exist the positive, if somewhat contradictory, influence of a set of western traditions and institutions derived from Red River. In education, religion, loyalty to the Empire, and rule by law, the Selkirk colonists had laid the foundations of western Canada. Contained within the image was a rejection of the eastern, and therefore derivative, nature of the contemporary western society. The sense of mission and morality of the Selkirk colonists, it is true, was reinforced and overlaid by the Canadian expansionists, but it could no longer be said that the Canadian sense of mission in the West had its roots solely in the East.

In fact, it could be argued that the westerner, with his unique blend of experience, opportunity, and history, best epitomized the spirit of the young Dominion of Canada. The West had lifted British North America from provincialism to nationalism and only the westerner could completely understand the new role Canada had assumed in the Empire and world. 'Canadians are at last conscious of a high destiny for their country,' wrote Charles Mair in 1889. 'The men of the North-West are perhaps more conscious of it than their brothers in the east, who have not yet got rid of their narrow provincialism.'[79] The trials and setbacks which Manitoba had faced, Bryce concluded, were but part of the struggle to establish a society which would reflect this new sense of Canadian nationalism: 'Next year Manitoba will have its fortieth year of history. Its people have seen pain, strife and defeat, they have gone through excitement and anxiety and patient waiting, and at times have almost given up the strife. But the province and its great city, Winnipeg, are the meeting place of East and West, the pivotal point of the Dominion. The national life of Canada beats here with a steadier beat and a more normal pulse than it does in any other part of Canada.'[80]

Resentful of their treatment at the hands of the East and Ottawa, westerners had rejected the eastern interpretation of their place within the nation and had looked to the land around them for a new definition of their role. In so doing they developed all the necessary prerequisites for a strong sense of regional identity. They had begun to define, for themselves, their place within the Canadian nation and to use the same perspective to define the role of the Canadian nation within the world. More importantly, that definition of Canada and the West was being put into western terms. The West was no longer merely an adjunct of the East or an annexed land; it was, westerners felt, something more than 'a new Upper Canada,' and something better.

Conclusion

Most of the political ends sought by the expansionists had been realized by the end of the nineteenth century. The North West had been annexed to Canada and preserved from the supposed expansionist designs of the United States. The once all-powerful Hudson's Bay Company had lost its control over the region and agriculture had become the basic activity over thousands of square miles of prairie and parkland. The Canadian Pacific Railway had been completed less than forty years after Synge and his contemporaries had first talked of a route to the Pacific. All these achievements seemed to give the men who had made up the expansionist movement good reason for self-congratulation.

Yet the prevailing mood in Canada in the 1890s was far from congratulatory. That decade brought instead a national sense of doubt and raised all the old questions of an uncertain future. The bustling confidence and youthful nationalism of the Confederation period had long since given way to doubts – most strongly expressed in Goldwin Smith's classic *Canada and the Canadian Question* – as to whether the nation had any future at all. Confederation, said Smith, had failed to create anything like a national identity or sense of purpose; Canada was nothing more than 'a number of fishing rods tied together by the ends.'[1] The most disturbing thing about Smith's pessimism was the number of events which seemed to bear him out. The Riel rebellion, the Jesuit Estates question, the bitter 1891 election, and the continued slow growth in the nation as a whole, all testified to the shortcomings of Canada in the years since Confederation.

Nowhere were these shortcomings felt more strongly than among those who had looked to the great North West as the answer to Canada's problems. The region which D'Arcy McGee had confidently predicted would be the home of ten million people within ten years had not even reached ten per cent of that figure a quarter of a century later. This relative failure was all the more discouraging because of the very success which the expansionists had attained in convincing the government to pursue a vigorous immigration policy. For nearly a generation the Old World had been subjected to a concentrated campaign promoting the region. Yet in 1895 Adam Shortt, a professor at Queen's University, asked with much reason why it should be that, 'in spite of the abnormal efforts put forth by the government and its immigration agents, not to mention the labours of the C.P.R., the colonization companies, and the Canadian school of patriots, – all setting forth the wonderful resources of the North-West Territories, – these regions fill up so slowly?'[2]

Shortt's comment was more an accusation than it was a question. From its beginning the expansionist movement had espoused extremely optimistic expectations for the future. The political ends which it had sought were really only the technical details in an essentially emotional appeal to a future destiny. It was a destiny predetermined by geography and providence, and such terms of reference had no place in them for economic depression or seemingly perverse behaviour on the part of the immigrant. From the time that Henry Youle Hind had depicted the West in terms of its agricultural potential rather than its actual state, the expansionist movement had rested on a myth of the future of the West. Shortt's question in 1895 simply pointed to the vast gap that existed between the promises entailed in this myth and the reality of a largely undeveloped and unsettled West.

It was a telling accusation, for if the great strength of the expansionists was their ability to evoke an image of the future, their great failure was their inability to maintain any sort of relationship between the myth and the much harsher and more prosaic reality of frontier life. The year 1870 marked the turning point. Thereafter the myth worked to distort an understanding of the West rather than to promote its development. The purpose of the myth had been served when the image of the West in the popular mind changed from that of an arctic wasteland to that of a rich agricultural hinterland. The image had been powerful enough to cause Canada to stake its future on the region. The challenge in the years ahead was to subordinate the myth of the future to the policies and problems of present development. This was not done. Success had become so important that it would not admit of any qualifications. The demand for an instant recreation of the American success story, combined with the need to justify the costs of the Canadian Pacific Railway, encouraged further embellishments upon the picture of the region as a utopia simply awaiting the presence of settlers to blossom into a rich agricultural paradise. The problem was that, as with most utopias, this paradise was unattainable; inevitably those who believed in it were disillusioned.

Disillusionment with the myth of the West set in even as John Macoun and others seemed to be confirming its truth. The collapse of the Winnipeg land boom and the general depression that followed brought home to many the illusory nature of expansionist promises. The completion of the Canadian Pacific in 1885 failed to translate potential into actual prosperity and growth. Finally, expansionism itself lost its vitality. The image of the West had been purged of all its imperfections and the promises had all been made; the movement had little new to offer after that, and the literature that continued to flow forth began to sound increasingly hollow to anyone who knew the real state of affairs.

By this time a good many people had already taken up new lives in the West on the basis of expansionist promises. For years men had been told that if they moved west they could not help but succeed. Such promises only served to obscure the very real difficulties involved in carving a livelihood out of a quarter section of land. The discrepancy between the reality and the myth was nowhere more evident than at this individual level. The inevitable result was disillusionment and an attempt to explain why the glorious promises had yielded such a stingy reality. 'The farmer's grievances against the grain traders, the elevator companies, the railways, the banks and the federal government that maintained what was to him an iniquitous tariff structure were real grievances but behind them lay the fact that he had been permitted and indeed encouraged to place himself in an impossible situation.'[3]

Disillusionment with the West affected national hopes as well as regional protest. After 1856 the West had assumed ever greater importance to Canada as a whole. From a necessary hinterland in the 1850s it became by 1880 the answer to practically all of Canada's problems and the means of realizing all its hopes. The development of the West, expansionists had promised, would ensure Canada's economic prosperity, enhance its political power, and even allow moral improvement. The West would promote the development of a strong and unified Canadian nationality on the northern half of the American continent. Eventually it would even mean that the colony could make the transition within the Empire and assume equal partnership with Great Britain. This new British Empire would have purged itself of former petty religious, racial, and political divisions and ensure the continuation of the best of the British social and political spirit.

Once again the expansionists had promised too much. The problems of the late 1880s and 1890s made a mockery of earlier confident statements. Canada had not achieved anything like equality with either the United States or Great Britain. In fact, as the debates over the implications of reciprocity in the 1891 election revealed, there was still some doubt as to whether the nation could even survive in the face of its powerful neighbour to the south. The disillusionment was so strong and came so quickly because expansionists had not only developed a set of expectations for the future but had given their achievement a definite schedule. Although no exact date had ever been given for the establishment of a fully developed western community, the implication had been repeatedly made that if Canada acted to annex the West it would feel the beneficient results almost immediately. 'All that Illinois, Wisconsin, Iowa, Nebraska, Kansas, and Minnesota are now combined, our own North-West may be within the lifetime of many amongst us,' the editor of the *New Dominion Monthly* had promised in 1874.[4] Yet a generation later the whole of the North West still had less population than many single mid-western states. The United States, as George Grant noted in 1893, still attracted the majority of immigrants and was even able to create a land race for the marginal farming regions of Oklahoma when that region was expropriated from its Indian owners.[5] The expansionist assumptions about the rate of development as well as the promises of its ultimate effects led to disillusionment when those expectations were not met: 'We have repeated boom estimates and quoted boomsters' figures about everything until we have created in our minds the vision of a region which does not exist anywhere on earth; and now that it has been shattered by the prosaic revelations of the census, we are weak enough to feel sorry at being undeceived.'[6]

In the face of delay and disillusionment the expansionist movement split apart. In the latter half of the 1880s the enthusiastic writings began to dwindle. Of course there were still those paid by the government or private corporations who produced pamphlets on the wonders of the North West, but they were no longer an extension of any significant spirit within the nation. The East – or rather Ontario – lost much of its enthusiasm for the West in the 1890s. There were still hopes of a growing trade with the region but the expectations as to what the West meant to the nation had decreased. The expansionist movement originated in Ontario and expressed that province's interests; an Ontario-based economy and Ontario ideas, it had been hoped, would spread westward to become the major forces in British North America. Instead Ontario found itself disowned by the West which it had done so much to shape. The great partnership which was supposed to develop between the metropolitan centre and the hinterland was rejected by the hinterland even before it had been fully formed.

There was one exception in the 1890s, one issue in which Ontario forces took the lead in determining the shape of western society. In August 1889 an Ontario member of Parliament, Dalton McCarthy, went west and launched an attack upon the use of the French language in the western school system.[7] In doing so he asserted one of the original, if less laudatory, ideals of expansionism. The Manitoba schools question finally gave English-Canadian expansionists their revenge for the Red River resistance of 1870.

The favourable response that McCarthy received in the West was an indication both of demographic trends and intellectual convictions. The West was overwhelmingly English-speaking and to that extent the desire for a unilingual school system was simply a practical matter. At the same time, however, the emotions aroused in Manitoba by McCarthy revealed a deep-seated conviction that there was no room in the West for a recognized minority. The developing sense of identity had excluded the Métis Catholic traditions of Red River in favour of English Protestant traditions.

Given the one-sided nature of the Canadian expansionist movement, this was perhaps inevitable. French Quebec had not felt the early enthusiasm for the West, and when the region became a part of Canada it was from English Canada that the largest immigration came. Even after annexation French Quebec was never able to overcome its reservations about sending its sons to the distant and increasingly English North West. Without such immigration the religious and linguistic guarantees of the Manitoba Act became increasingly meaningless; they corresponded to no significant conviction within the western community. French Canadians wanted and desired recognition within the new society as the controversy over the Manitoba schools makes clear. They failed, however, for by the time Dalton McCarthy arrived in Manitoba there was no strong indigenous voice to urge protection of traditional rights. That tradition had been swept aside by a tide of English immigration and by the myth of the Selkirk settlers, Seven Oaks, and Métis lawlessness.[8]

In spite of the specific alliance between McCarthy and the Equal Rights Association and western interests, the whole debate over language in the West further illustrated the failure of expansionist ideals. The new Canada, it seemed, had not provided an answer to the questions that had plagued the older Canada. On the contrary, the new Canada was to be dragged into these old, eastern controversies. Rather than establish a society above racial and religious jealousy, the development of the west perpetuated animosities rooted in the colonial era.

The schools question and the controversy surrounding it was a pointed indication that the moral goals of expansionism had not been achieved any more than the material goals. A great deal had been hoped for in social terms from this 'new Canada.' The region would, it was hoped, provide the seed bed for a further evolution of British institutions. The sturdy yeoman farmer and the twin pillars of education and religion would provide a stable basis for Canadian morality not only for the West but for the nation as a whole.

Such expectations had always rested on the assumption that a high rate of material growth and a degree of economic success were more or less assured. When it became apparent by the 1890s that such was far from the case, many began to wonder whether it was possible to create a new social order until some degree of material stability had been achieved. Canada would not benefit by attracting those who were bound to fail. One of the greatest dangers facing the West, Shortt warned, was the immigration agent 'who estimates national greatness by the census lists.'[9] The cynical propaganda campaign the government waged, George Grant warned, drew 'the weak, the credulous, the unfortunate and the deadbeats.'[10] In its increasingly desperate attempts to meet its own expectations the nation had sacrificed meaningful and stable development for sheer population growth. This was hardly the means by which the social order of the future could be developed.

Ironically, if any of the utopianism of expansionism survived it was among those westerners who led the way in the formation of a regional rejection of the East. Western alienation challenged many of the expansionist planks, but it also appropriated much of the expansionist spirit and rhetoric. Supporters of the Hudson Bay railway, for instance, simply modified ideas and terms that had their roots in expansionism and tailored them to fit a new, regional context. The image of a fertile land and the whole myth of a utopian future remained intact in the work of western writers and promoters.

The 'boom or bust' psychology of the western farmer further sustained elements of the old expansionist outlook. Prosperity one year gives no guarantee that an early frost, a fall in wheat prices in Europe, or a drought may not occur in the next to bring ruin. Equally, disaster one year does not preclude hope for the next. Faith in the future is an essential part of the farmer's character if he is to persevere in his precarious livelihood. In its outlook such an attitude is strikingly similar to the tendency of the expansionists to look not at the actual state of things but at the potential of the land for the future.

The survival of utopianism in western writings was also a direct legacy of expansionism. Any myth of the future, if it is to be indeterminately delayed, must provide explanations for that delay. Expansionists used transportation problems to explain the disappointments of the 1870s. With the completion of the Canadian Pacific, however, there were no more probable excuses to be offered and the movement began to fall apart. As westerners began to develop a regional outlook, however, they found many reasons to explain why the land should have so much potential and yet remain undeveloped. The Canadian Pacific, eastern politicians and manufacturers, it was argued, used every possible means to thwart the true destiny of the West within the Canadian and world economy. Western distrust of the East was based on real problems.

Nevertheless this distrust also provided westerners with an essential demonology for their faith. By developing a new set of evil and malignant forces, western writers could explain the failures of the West without challenging its potential in the same way that expansionists in earlier years could point an accusing finger at the Hudson's Bay Company in order to explain the reason for the region's undeveloped state. 'I confess to a feeling of hopelessness,' wrote Mair in 1888, 'when I think of the insanity which permits a stall fed monopoly to lord it over the North West people as if they had no rights such as are vouchsafed to them by *our old friend the Hudson's Bay Company in its new shape [,] the C.P.R.*'[11] Western alienation, as it developed in the late nineteenth century, allowed something of the spirit of expansionism to survive – albeit in almost inverted form.

W.L. Morton, in attempting to understand the 'bias' of prairie politics, has argued that three stages can be distinguished in prairie political activities. 'The first may be called the colonial period, from 1870 to 1905. The second is the agrarian period from 1905 to 1925, and the third the utopian from 1925 to the present.'[12] He further argues that the first instance in a long tradition of western protest may be seen in the Red River rebellion of 1870. It is an astute and perceptive explanation of the nature of western politics. It may be argued, however, that the original bias of prairie throught was expressed not so much by the conservative Métis in 1870 as by the optimism of the expansionists in the same period. It may perhaps also be argued that expansionism initiated a utopian tradition that, with suitable modifications, has continued to be expressed in western writing through much of the twentieth century.

It is tempting to conclude that the spirit of expansionism survived, or was reborn, in a more direct way after 1896. The upturn in the world economy, good climatic conditions, and generally favourable prices for grain helped encourage a new 'wheat boom' on the Canadian prairies in the years of Wilfrid Laurier's administration. Population and wheat cultivation grew dramatically in this period and, at long last, many of the hopes of early years seemed to be realized. Certainly there are striking similarities between these years and those of the original expansionist movement. 'The Last Best West' of the early twentieth century has the same 'sunny slopes and fertile valleys,' the same 'clear healthful atmosphere,' as did the 'Great North West' of the 1870s and 1880s.[13] Equally, expectations for Canada as a whole revived, and as the West of the Confederation era was to assure Canadian greatness so the West of this period was to make the twentieth century Canada's.

While there are similarities, however, there are also differences. Time could not be reversed and the sense of regional grievance, once implanted by disappointments, could not be erased by prosperity. Paralleling the growth of the

West in the first years of the twentieth century was the formation of economic and political movements based on the assumption that large-scale enterprises prevented the farmers from reaping the main benefits of prosperity.[14] The conception of the West as a vast hinterland continued to be resisted by that hinterland, no matter how prosperous it might be.

Moreover, new forces were present during the Laurier wheat boom and they too gave that period its own mood and concerns. Under the direction of Laurier's Minister of the Interior, Clifford Sifton, new attention was paid to potential immigrants in southern and eastern Europe. The thousands of 'Galicians,' as Canadians indiscriminately termed these peoples, who responded to Sifton's appeal did much to create the growth and economic stability which expansionists had sought. At the same time, they seemed to many to challenge another basic expansionist assumption, that the West would be British in character. The settlement of the West in large numbers by people 'without knowledge of British institutions and principles of life'[15] created new concerns and, all too often, brought forward racist fears. The West, it appeared to many, might be prosperous at the price of not being British.

The mood and concerns of the West in the first years of the twentieth century were thus not simply an extension, or revival, of those of the expansionist years. New forces and continued grievances meant that even in a period of considerable prosperity it was in many ways a time of social tension. The power of these tensions would be fully revealed in the troubled years after the First World War and in the anger and frustration of the One Big Union movement and the Progressive party. The Laurier years in the West thus have their own configuration, and any conclusions on them must await further study. In some ways the successes and failures of expansionism helped to shape these years, but as a movement expansionism was long dead. It had died because its own expectations had been too high to face the test of time and because it had never been able to reconcile its national goals with the regional perspective, whether eastern or western, inherent in the very process of expansion.

Notes

INTRODUCTION

1 A.I. Silver, 'French-Canadian Attitudes toward the North-West and North-West Settlement, 1870-1890,' unpublished MA thesis, McGill University, 1966, and 'Quebec and the French-speaking Minorities, 1864-1917,' unpublished PHD thesis, University of Toronto, 1973; Robert Painchaud, 'French-Canadian Historiography and Franco-Catholic Settlement in Western Canada, 1870-1915,' *Canadian Historical Review*, LIX, 4 (Dec. 1978), 447-66, 455-61

CHAPTER 1: A far and distant corner of the Empire

1 Earl of Selkirk, 'Prospectus,' in John Strachan, *A Letter to the Right Honourable the Earl of Selkirk on His Settlement at Red River* (London 1816), 69
2 *Ibid.*, 10, 17-18
3 *Ibid.*, 41, 54
4 W.S. Wallace, 'The Literature Relating to the Selkirk Controversy,' *Canadian Historical Review*, XIII, 1 (March 1932), 45-50
5 Harold Innis, *The Fur Trade in Canada* (Toronto 1956), and A.S. Morton, *A History of the Canadian West to 1870-71* (Toronto 1939), give two of the most detailed accounts of the history and economics of the fur trade.
6 Estimates of population varied a great deal but generally ranged from 40,000 to 60,000. See Eric Ross, *Beyond the River and the Bay* (Toronto 1970), 'Appendix,' for figures by Alexander Henry and Duncan McGillivray in 1805 and 1809. See Great Britain, House of Commons, *Report from the Select Committee on the Hudson's Bay Company*, 1857, p. 57, for Sir George Simpson's estimate.

7 On church missions, see Grace Lee Nute, ed., *Documents Relating to Northwest Missions, 1815-1827* (St Paul 1942); W.H. Brooks, 'Methodism in the Canadian West in the Nineteenth Century,' unpublished PHD thesis, University of Manitoba, 1972; Frits Pannekoek, 'Protestant Agricultural Missions in the Canadian West to 1870,' unpublished MA thesis, University of Alberta, 1970.
8 Innis's *Fur Trade in Canada* is the classic work on this subject.
9 Morton, *History of the Canadian West*, 514-26
10 *British Parliamentary Papers*, Colonies, Canada (Shannon, Ireland 1969), vol. 18, 1849 Session, 406, Griffiths to Earl Grey, 18 Jan. 1849
11 J. Wreford Watson, 'The Role of Illusion in North American Geography,' *Canadian Geographer*, XIII, 1 (Spring 1969), 10-27, 10
12 Dobbs, *An Account of the Countries Adjoining to Hudson's Bay in the North-West Part of America* (London 1749), 2, 54-5; see also Joseph Robson, *An Account of Six Years Residence in Hudson's Bay* (London 1752).
13 Umfreville, *The Present State of Hudson's Bay, Containing a Full Description of that Settlement, and the Adjacent Country* (London 1790)
14 W. Kaye Lambe, ed., *The Journals and Letters of Sir Alexander Mackenzie* (Cambridge 1970), 411; J.B. Tyrell, ed., *David Thompson's Narrative* (Toronto 1916), 241
15 Donald Creighton, *The Empire of the St. Lawrence* (Toronto 1956)
16 *St. Catharine's Journal*, 4 Nov. 1852
17 John Warkentin and Richard Ruggles, *Historical Atlas of Manitoba* (Winnipeg 1970), 105
18 Sir George Simpson, *Narrative of a Journey round the World During the Years 1841 and 1842* (London 1847), I, 80
19 (London 1823); also Franklin, *Narrative of a Second Expedition to the Shores of the Polar Sea* (London 1828)
20 Richardson, *Arctic Searching Expedition* (New York 1852), 1-60
21 *Ibid.*, 389
22 John Warkentin, 'Steppe, Desert and Empire,' in A.W. Rasporich and H.C. Klassen, eds., *Prairie Perspectives 2* (Toronto 1973), 102-36, 106-8, discusses the terminology of these years and the impact of the American image on British Americans.
23 Simpson, *Narrative of Discoveries on the North Coast of America* (London 1843), 45
24 Henry Nash Smith, *Virgin Land: The American West as Symbol and Myth* (New York 1950), 202-3
25 Richardson, *Arctic Searching Expedition*, 339
26 *Anglo-American Magazine*, Sept. 1852, p. 198

27 Warre, *Sketches in North America and the Oregon Territory* (Barre, Mass. 1970), 15; first published 1848
28 Anderson, *A Charge Delivered to the Clergy of the Diocese of Rupert's Land at his Primary Visitation* (London 1851), 27
29 R.M. Ballantyne, *Hudson's Bay* (Edinburgh 1848), 28
30 Tytler, *Northern Coasts of America and the Hudson's Bay Territories* (London 1854), iv
31 Kane, *Wanderings of an Artist among the Indians of North America* (London 1859), 49
32 Alexander Ross, *The Fur Hunters of the Far West* (London 1855)
33 Sévère Dumoulin to Bishop Plessis, 10 Sept. 1818, cited in Nute, *Documents Relating to Northwest Missions*, 157; G.J. Mountain, *The Journal of the Bishop of Montreal* (London 1845), 98-9
34 Simpson, *Journey round the World*, I, 56
35 Tucker, *Rainbow in the North: A Short Account of the First Establishment of Christianity in Rupert's Land* (London 1851), 35
36 R.M. Ballantyne, *The Young Fur Trader* (London 1856), 4
37 Simpson, *Narrative of Discoveries*, 15-16
38 Warre, *Sketches in North America*, 16
39 J. Russell Harper, *Paul Kane's Frontier* (Toronto 1971), plate XX, fig. 92
40 Eric Quayle, *Ballantyne the Brave* (London 1967), 106
41 Ballantyne, *Young Fur Trader*, 5, 291-2, 428
42 Ross, *Fur Hunters of the Far West*, I, 21
43 Alexander Ross, *The Red River Settlement: Its Rise, Progress and Present State* (London 1856), 22
44 Ross, *Fur Hunters of the Far West*, I, 142-3
45 *Ibid.*, 285, 170, 290, 292
46 Alexander Ross, *Adventures of the First Settlers on the Oregon or Columbia River* (London 1849), 337
47 Ross, *Fur Hunters of the Far West*, II, 233
48 *Ibid.*, I, 94
49 Ross, *Red River Settlement*, 1, 210, 124-5
50 *Ibid.*, 94, 169, 60, 335. It should be noted that Ross tended to divide the colony by language; the Scottish half-breeds were seen as part of the 'European party' and the French Canadians as Métis.
51 *Ibid.*, 143, 337
52 *Ibid.*, 221, 408
53 T.C.B. Boon, *The Anglican Church from the Bay to the Rockies* (Toronto 1962), and Brooks, 'Methodism in the Canadian West'

228 Notes to pages 23-31

54 John West, *The Substance of a Journal during a Residence at the Red River Colony, British North America* (London 1824), 4
55 *Church Missionary Record*, XII, 1 (Jan. 1841), 11
56 Tucker, *Rainbow in the North*, 63; Mountain, *Journal of the Bishop of Montreal*, 48
57 West, *Substance of a Journal*, 42-3
58 Mountain, *Journal*, 34
59 *Church Missionary Record*, 11
60 Tucker, *Rainbow in the North*, 5
61 Frits Pannekoek, 'The Churches and the Social Structure in Red River,' unpublished PHD thesis, Queen's University, 1973, pp. 22, 55. He also argues, pp. 44-6, that the Catholic clergy were not so hostile to the wilderness.
62 John Ryerson, *Hudson's Bay or, A Missionary Tour in the Territory of the Hon. Hudson's Bay Company* (Toronto 1855), 125
63 Boon, *Anglican Church*, 8
64 Anderson, *Primary Visitation*, 24-5
65 Pannekoek, 'Churches and the Social Structure in Red River,' has the most detailed discussion of the relations between the missionaries and the company.
66 Brooks, 'Methodism in the Canadian West,' 64
67 E.E. Rich, *The Hudson's Bay Company, 1670-1870* (Toronto 1960), III, 254
68 W.L. Morton, *Manitoba: A History* (Toronto 1957), 74-5
69 A.K. Isbister, *A Few Words on the Hudson's Bay Company* (London 1847), 1, 24, 2, 4
70 *Ibid.*, 24
71 Rich, *Hudson's Bay Company*, III, 546
72 *British Parliamentary Papers*, Colonies, Canada, vol. 18, p. 302, Elgin to Grey, 6 June 1848
73 Cited in the *Globe*, Toronto, 7 Oct. 1848
74 McLean, *Twenty-Five Years Service in the Hudson's Bay Territory* (London 1849)
75 *British Parliamentary Papers*, vol. 18, p. 409, B. Hawes to Isbister, 23 Jan. 1849
76 Rich, *Hudson's Bay Company*, III, 755
77 Synge, *Canada in 1848* (London 1849), 3; Carmichael-Smyth, *A Letter to His Friend the Author of the Clockmaker* (London 1849), 6
78 Synge, *Great Britain, One Empire* (London 1852), 56
79 Wilson and Richards, *Britain Redeemed and Canada Preserved* (London 1850), 19
80 Carmichael-Smyth, *Letter*, 5

Notes to pages 32-40

81 Carmichael-Smyth, *The Employment of the People and Capital of Great Britain in Her Own Colonies* (London 1849), vii, 4
82 Keefer, *Philosophy of Railroads* (Toronto 1849); Whitney, *A Project for a Railroad to the Pacific* (New York 1850)
83 Wilson and Richards, *Britain Redeemed*, 76
84 Synge, *Canada in 1848*, 3; Wilson and Richards, *ibid.*, 18-19
85 Carmichael-Smyth, *Letter*, 15
86 Wilson and Richards, *Britain Redeemed*, 274
87 Carmichael-Smyth, *Employment of the People*, 4
88 Wilson and Richards, *Britain Redeemed*, 215
89 *Ibid.*, 124, and passim; Synge, *Great Britain, One Empire*, 91-3
90 Alexander K. Isbister, *A Proposal for a New Penal Settlement* (London 1850)
91 Martin, *The Hudson's Bay Territories and Vancouver's Island* (London 1849), 6, 13, 95
92 Fitzgerald, *An Examination of the Charter and Proceedings of the Hudson's Bay Company* (London 1849), 237, 10-11
93 Aborigines Protection Society, *Canada West and the Hudson's Bay Company* (London 1856), 1
94 *Globe*, 12 Nov. 1850
95 Province of Canada, *Journals of the Legislative Assembly*, 1851, app. UU
96 *Ibid.*, Macdonnell, 'Observations upon the Construction of a Railroad from Lake Superior to the Pacific'
97 Public Archives of Canada, George Brown Papers, vol. 1, McLean to Brown, 17 Nov. 1850

CHAPTER 2: New worlds to conquer

1 Public Archives of Canada (PAC), Charles Bell Papers, Simpson to Ross, 17 Dec. 1850
2 Great Britain, House of Commons, *Report from the Select Committee on the Hudson's Bay Company*, 1857, iii-iv
3 Donald Swainson, 'The North-West Transportation Company: Personnel and Attitudes,' Historical and Scientific Society of Manitoba, *Transactions*, series III, no 26 (1969-70), 59-77, 66-7
4 *Ibid.*, 66
5 A.C. Gluek, Jr, *Minnesota and the Manifest Destiny of the Canadian Northwest* (Toronto 1965), 225
6 J.M.S. Careless, *Brown of the Globe: The Voice of Upper Canada, 1818-1859* (Toronto 1959), I, 235

230 Notes to pages 40-6

7 *Gazette*, Montreal, 9 Sept. 1856
8 Roche, 'A View of Russian America, in connection with the present war,' Literary and Historical Society of Quebec, *Transactions*, vol. IV, part IV (Feb. 1856), 263-328
9 PAC, John A. Macdonald Papers, vol. 209, Draper to Macdonald, 25 Jan. 1857
10 *Ibid.*, Draper to Macdonald, 8, 19, 21 Feb. 1857
11 On Russell and Dennis, see *Canadian Almanac and Repository of Useful Knowledge*, 1857, p. 35; Alexander Morris, *Nova Britannia* (Montreal 1858)
12 Keefer, *Philosophy of Railroads* (Toronto 1849), 32
13 J.M.S. Careless, *The Union of the Canadas: The Growth of Canadian Institutions* (Toronto 1967), 144-5
14 'Preliminary Address,' Jan. 1856, p. 1
15 Cited in *Gazette*, 4 Sept. 1856
16 'Excerpts from an Essay by Alexander Morris,' *Canadian Journal of Science, Literature and History*, Sept. 1855, p. 353
17 *Annual Report of the Commissioner of Crown Lands*, 1856, pp. 44-5
18 *Ibid.*, 1856, p. 6; 1857, p. 7; 1863, p. 7
19 *Ibid.*, 1856, p. 43
20 Province of Canada, *Journals of the Legislative Assembly*, 1857, app. 2; see also S. McKee, Jr, 'The Traffic of the Middle West,' *Canadian Historical Association Annual Report*, 1940, pp. 26-35, 34.
21 Population figures are from Peter Goheen, *Victorian Toronto, 1850 to 1900* (Chicago 1970), 49, and D.C. Masters, *The Rise of Toronto, 1850-1890* (Toronto 1947), 53.
22 *Globe*, Toronto, 28 Aug. 1856
23 Chester Martin, *'Dominion Lands' Policy* (Toronto 1973), xx; F.H. Underhill, 'Some Aspects of Upper Canadian Radical Opinion in the Decade before Confederation,' *Canadian Historical Association Annual Report*, 1927; George W. Brown, 'The Grit Party and the Great Reform Convention of 1859,' *Canadian Historical Review*, XVI, 3 (Sept. 1935), 245-65
24 *Globe*, 13 Dec. 1856. See, on Brown's metropolitanism, J.M.S. Careless, 'The Toronto *Globe* and Agrarian Radicalism, 1850-67,' *Canadian Historical Review*, XXIX, 1 (March 1948), 14-39.
25 Morris Zaslow, *Reading the Rocks: The Story of the Geological Survey of Canada* (Toronto 1975), 50-2
26 Keefer, *Montreal and the Ottawa* (1854), in *Philosophy of Railroads and Other Essays*, ed. H.V. Nelles (Toronto 1972), 76
27 The *Annual Report of the Department of Public Works*, 1859, contains Shanly's report.
28 *Gazette*, 9 Sept. 1856

Notes to pages 47-54

29 PAC, Records of the Governor General, G20, vol. 383, 'Petition of the Inhabitants of Lanark and Renfrew,' 17 March 1857
30 *Globe*, 4 Dec. 1856
31 *Ibid.*, 19 Dec. 1856
32 *Annual Report of the Commissioner of Crown Lands*, 1856, p. 43
33 Allan Macdonell, *The North-West Transportation, Navigation and Railway Company: Its Objects* (Toronto 1858), 7, 10
34 Henry Nash Smith, *Virgin Land* (New York 1950), and Leo Marx, *The Machine in the Garden* (New York 1964), both discuss this theme at some length.
35 Great Britain, *Select Committee*, 'Minutes of Evidence,' 218
36 Macdonell, *North-West Transportation ... Company*, app.
37 *Globe*, 10 Dec. 1856
38 *Select Committee*, 'Minutes of Evidence,' 7
39 *Journals of the Legislative Assembly*, 1857, app. 17, 'General Remarks'
40 McLean, *Twenty-Five Years Service in the Hudson's Bay Territory* (London 1849), 321
41 Macdonald Papers, vol. 209, Draper to Macdonald, 8 Feb. 1857
42 *Journals of the Legislative Assembly*, 1857, app. 17
43 *Select Committee*, 'Minutes of Evidence,' 212
44 Alexander Begg, *History of the North-West* (Toronto 1894), I, 309
45 *Select Committee*, app. 8; comment by William Dawson
46 *Globe*, 13 Dec. 1856
47 Aborigines Protection Society, *Canada West and the Hudson's Bay Company* (London 1856), 6
48 *Globe*, 2 Sept. 1856; letter from 'Huron'
49 *Select Committee*, 'Minutes of Evidence,' 123
50 *Gazette*, 6 June 1857
51 *Globe*, 4 Dec. 1856
52 Alexander Morris, *The Hudson's Bay and Pacific Territories* (Montreal 1859), 7
53 *Globe*, 2 Sept. 1856
54 24 March 1857
55 *Select Committee*, 'Minutes of Evidence,' 339
56 PAC, Sir Edward Watkin Papers, vol. 2, Watkin to Head, 24 July 1863
57 *Globe*, 19 Aug. 1856; letter from 'Huron'
58 *Ibid.*, 26 Aug. 1857
59 Morris, *Hudson's Bay*, 13
60 *Select Committee*, 'Minutes of Evidence,' 249
61 Macdonnell, *North-West Transportation ... Company*, 8

62 *Globe*, 6 May 1857
63 *Journals of the Legislative Assembly*, 1857, app. 17
64 *Select Committee*, app. 8, pp. 388, 402
65 Morris, *Hudson's Bay*, 13
66 Instructions to Draper cited in Begg, *History of the North-West*, I, 310-12
67 *Gazette*, 23 June 1857
68 *Globe*, 30 Sept. 1856; letter from 'Huron'
69 Charles Bass, *Lectures on Canada* (Hamilton 1863), 14
70 Morris, *Hudson's Bay*, 39
71 Morris, *Nova Britannia*, 45-6
72 Bass, *Lectures on Canada*, 45
73 Morris, *Hudson's Bay*, 56
74 Roche, 'A View of Russian America,' 310. Note that this quotation is used by Morris in *Nova Britannia*, 55.

CHAPTER 3: A means to empire

1 Great Britain, House of Commons, *Report from the Select Committee on the Hudson's Bay Company*, app. 8, pp. 399-400
2 See comments by William Kennedy in the *Globe*, Toronto, 21 Aug. 1857; and report of meeting in Hamilton, *ibid.*, 25 Sept. 1857. See also Province of Canada, *Journals of the Legislative Assembly*, 1857, app. 17.
3 Public Archives of Canada (PAC), Devine, 'North West Part of Canada,' VI-1100-57, Toronto, March 1857
4 *Select Committee*, 'Minutes of Evidence,' 13, 152, 124-5
5 *Gazette*, 8 Jan. 1856
6 *Select Committee*, 'Minutes of Evidence,' 212
7 *Ibid.*, app. 8, contains Gladman's testimony.
8 Henry Youle Hind, *Narrative of the Canadian Red River Exploring Expedition of 1857 and of the Assiniboine and Saskatchewan Exploring Expedition of 1858* (London 1860), I, 267
9 Morris Zaslow, *Reading the Rocks* (Toronto 1975), 78, and as yet unpublished biography of Hind by W.L. Morton
10 *Ibid.*, 96
11 J.K. Johnson, ed., *The Canadian Directory of Parliament* (Ottawa 1968), 155-6
12 Palliser, *Solitary Rambles and Adventures of a Hunter in the Prairies* (London 1853)
13 Irene Spry, ed., *The Papers of the Palliser Expedition, 1857-1860* (Toronto 1968), 'Introductions,' xxiii, xxi
14 *Ibid.*, xxi

15 Earl of Southesk, *Saskatchewan and the Rocky Mountains* (London 1875), xxxii
16 Public Archives of Manitoba, Winnipeg, Schultz Papers, vol. 16, Henry McKenney to Schultz, 22 March 1859
17 The relative youthfulness of this group is easy to demonstrate: William Buckingham was 26 when he moved to Red River; William Coldwell, 24; Alexander Begg, 30; Thomas Spence, 34; Charles Mair, 31.
18 United Kingdom, *Further Papers Relative to the Exploration of British North America* (London 1860), 5
19 See Schultz Papers, vol. 16, Mair to Schultz, 14 May 1866, for an indication of his earlier interest in the West.
20 *Globe*, 4 Jan. 1869; letter from Mair
21 Hind, *Narrative*, contains the route map; PAC, 'Route of the Exploring Expedition under Command of Captain Palliser,' VI/701, 1857-58, shows the route taken by that expedition.
22 T.J.J. Loranger to Hind, 27 April 1858; cited in Henry Youle Hind, *North-West Territory, Report on the Assiniboine and Saskatchewan Exploring Expedition* (Toronto 1859), 2
23 G.S. Dunbar, 'Isotherms and Politics,' in A.W. Rasporich and H.C. Klassen, eds., *Prairie Perspectives 2* (Toronto 1973), 89
24 Blodgett, *Climatology* (Philadelphia 1857), 533, 529
25 *Ibid*., 'Introduction'
26 Dawson cites Blodgett in his 1859 report; *Journals of the Legislative Assembly*, 1859, app. 36. 'The Great North-West,' The *Canadian Almanac and Repository of Useful Knowledge*, 1858, also cites Blodgett and is attributed to Hind in John Warkentin, 'Steppe, Desert and Empire,' Rasporich and Klassen, *Prairie Perspectives 2*, 132-3, n 40.
27 Blodgett, *Climatology*, 529
28 Warkentin, 'Steppe, Desert and Empire,' 116-21
29 United Kingdom, *The Journals, Detailed Reports and Observations Relative to the Exploration by Captain Palliser*, 1859, 'The General Report,' 7, 10-11
30 Hind, *North-West Territory*, 31
31 *Journals ... by Captain Palliser*, 'General Report,' 7; Hind, *ibid*., 123
32 Hind, *Narrative*, I, 'Map of the Country from Lake Superior to the Pacific Ocean'
33 Hind, *North-West Territory*, 124
34 *Journals ... by Captain Palliser*, 86; Palliser, *Papers Relative to the Exploration of British North America* (London 1859), 30; Hind, *ibid*., 53
35 Hind, *Narrative*, II, 234
36 [Hind], 'North-West British America,' *British American Magazine*, May 1863, p. 3

37 *Nor'Wester*, 'Prospectus,' 1859
38 'Report of the Committee of the Executive Council,' approved 11 Nov. 1864; *Documents Relating to the Opening up of the North West Territories to Settlement and Colonisation* (np 1865), 4
39 *Canadian Journal*, March 1861, p. 175
40 Charles Mair, 'The New Canada: Its Natural Features and Climate [Part 1],' *Canadian Monthly and National Review*, VIII (July 1875), 1-8, 1
41 Southesk, *Saskatchewan and the Rocky Mountains*, 13; Viscount Milton and W.B. Cheadle, *The North-West Passage by Land* (London 1865), 98
42 Hind, *Narrative*, I, 70-2
43 Hind, T.C. Keefer, J.G. Hodgins, Charles Robb, M.H. Perley, Rev. W. Murray, *Eighty Years' Progress of British North America* (Toronto 1863), 88
44 Hind, *North-West Territory*, 52, 44
45 Hind, *Narrative*, I, 124, 134
46 *Ibid.*, 373
47 Milton and Cheadle, *North-West Passage by Land*, 72
48 *Journals of the Legislative Assembly*, 1859, app. 36
49 *Globe*, 20 Jan. 1869; letter from Mair
50 George V. Le Vaux, 'The Great North West – No. II,' *New Dominion Monthly*, Jan. 1869, p. 226
51 Alexander Morris, *The Hudson's Bay and Pacific Territories* (Montreal 1859), 7-10
52 Province of Canada, *Parliamentary Debates on the Subject of the Confederation of the British North American Provinces* (Quebec 1865), 86
53 Hind, *Narrative*, I, 191
54 *Globe*, 28 May 1869; letter from Mair
55 Milton and Cheadle, *North-West Passage by Land*, 160; David Anderson, *A Charge Delivered to the Clergy of the Diocese of Rupert's land at his Triennial Visitation, January 6, 1860* (London 1860), 8
56 *Nor'Wester*, 14 Feb. 1860
57 Hind, *North-West Territory*, 68
58 *Nor'Wester*, 'Prospectus'
59 *Globe*, 14 and 27 Dec. 1868; letters from Mair
60 *Nor'Wester*, 5 March, 16 April 1862; Wilson, 'Science in Rupert's Land,' *Canadian Journal*, July 1862, pp. 336-47
61 Wilson, *ibid.*, 336; *Nor'Wester*, 16 April 1862
62 *Journals of the Legislative Assembly*, 1859, app. 62 36
63 Le Vaux, 'The Great North West – No. II,' 222
64 *Confederation Debates*, 86
65 Hind et al., *Eighty Years' Progress*, 80

Notes to pages 76-83

66 'W.H.W.,' 'The Red River Settlement,' *New Dominion Monthly*, May 1868, p. 101
67 *Nor'Wester*, 'Prospectus'
68 Alexander Russell, *The Red River Country, Hudson's Bay and the North-West Territories Considered in Relation to Canada* (Ottawa 1869), 5
69 *The Interests of the British Empire in North America* (Ottawa 1868), 5
70 Queen's University Library, Kingston, Mair Papers, vol. 1, Denison to Mair, 10 March 1869
71 Carl Berger, *The Sense of Power: Studies in the Ideas of Canadian Imperialism, 1867-1914* (Toronto 1970), 49-51
72 Speech read before the Montreal Mechanics' Institute; cited in *Nor'Wester*, 15 April 1868
73 *Globe*, 28 May 1869; letter from Mair

CHAPTER 4: Conspiracy and rebellion

1 E.E. Rich, *The Hudson's Bay Company, 1670-1870* (Toronto 1960), III, 891-8, has a detailed account of the transfer negotiations. See also 'Report of the Delegates Appointed to Negotiate for the Transfer of Rupert's Land,' Dominion of Canada, *Sessional Papers*, 1869, no 25.
2 Public Archives of Canada (PAC), Macdonald Papers, vol. 252, Morris to Macdonald, 15 July 1869
3 *Ibid.*, vol. 102, McDougall to Macdonald, 31 Oct. 1869
4 W.L. Morton, *Manitoba: A History* (Toronto 1957), 118
5 W.L. Morton, ed., *Alexander Begg's Red River Journal and Other Papers Relative to the Red River Resistance* (Toronto 1956), 'Introduction,' 23
6 G.F.G. Stanley, *The Birth of Western Canada* (Toronto 1960) 63-4; see also J.S. Dennis to McDougall, Aug. 1869, in Canada, *Sessional Papers*, 1870, no 12, pp. 5-6.
7 *Globe*, Toronto, 5 March 1857; letter from Isbister
8 Great Britain, *Report from the Select Committee on the Hudson's Bay Company*, app. 12, p. 439
9 *British Parliamentary Papers*, Colonies, Canada, vol. 27, p. 485, 'Resolution Adopted at a Public Meeting of the Inhabitants of the Red River Settlement,' dated 17 Jan. 1867
10 *Nor'Wester*, 12 Jan. 1869
11 Begg, *Dot-It-Down* (Toronto 1871), 108
12 *Nor'Wester*, 28 Nov. 1864
13 Public Archives of Manitoba, Schultz Papers, vol. 16, Mair to Schultz, 14 May 1866; B. Chewitt and Co. to Schultz, 30 Dec. 1867 (for a subscription for S.J. Dawson)

236 Notes to pages 83-9

14 *Nor'Wester*, 22 Sept. 1865, 1 Dec. 1866, 13 July 1867, 4 Aug. 1868
15 Fleming, *Memorial of the People of Red River to the British and Canadian Governments* (Quebec 1863); *Nor'Wester*, 24 Jan. 1863
16 *Dot-It-Down*, 107
17 *Nor'Wester*, 14 Dec. 1862
18 *Globe*, 28 May 1869; letter from Mair
19 Macdonald Papers, vol. 102, McDougall to Macdonald, 13 Nov. 1869
20 Begg, *Dot-It-Down*, 47-8
21 P.F. Tytler, *Northern Coasts of America and the Hudson's Bay Territories* (London 1854), 313
22 Kane, *Wanderings of an Artist among the Indians of North America* (London 1859), 51
23 Province of Canada, *Sessional Papers*, 1859, no 36
24 *Ibid*.
25 Glenbow Institute, Calgary, William Fitzwilliam, Viscount Milton Papers, undated manuscript, 'Plains Crees and Half-breeds'
26 Simpson, *Narrative of Discoveries on the North Coast of America* (London 1843), 14; Kane, *Wanderings of an Artist*, 51
27 Exploration, British North America, *The Journals, Detailed Reports and Observations Relative to the Exploration by Captain Palliser*, 61
28 Ross, *The Red River Settlement: Its Rise, Progress and Present State* (London 1856), 194
29 *Journals ... by Captain Palliser*, 61
30 Milton Papers, 'Plain Crees and Half-breeds'
31 A.I. Silver, 'French-Canadian Attitudes toward the North-West and North-West Settlement, 1870-1890,' unpublished MA thesis, McGill University, 1966, p. 106
32 Wilson, 'Displacement and Extinction among the Primeval Races of Man,' *Canadian Journal*, Jan. 1856, p. 12
33 *Globe*, 4 Dec. 1868, 16 Feb. 1869; letters from Mair
34 Queen's University Library, Mair Papers, Denison to Mair, 29 March 1869
35 Macdonald Papers, vol. 102, McDougall to Macdonald, 13 Nov. 1869
36 *Ibid*., McDougall to Macdonald, 31 Oct. 1869
37 *Ibid*.
38 Canada, *Sessional Papers*, 1870, no 12, McDougall to Howe, 5 Nov. 1869
39 *Nor'Wester*, 5 Feb. 1862; see also 28 July and 28 Sept. 1860, 28 May 1862, 13 July 1867, 12 Jan. 1869.
40 A.C. Gluek, Jr, *Minnesota and the Manifest Destiny of the Canadian Northwest* (Toronto 1965), 263-94, outlines the American involvement in the Red River resistance.

237 Notes to pages 90-8

41 Macdonald Papers, vol. 102, McDougall to McTavish, 2 Nov. 1869
42 Canada, *Sessional Papers*, 1870, no 12, Schultz to McDougall, Nov. 1869; see also Mair to McDougall, 8 Nov. 1869.
43 *Ibid.*, McDougall to Howe, 13 Nov. 1869, pp. 37-8
44 Macdonald Papers, vol. 102, Brown to Macdonald, 26 Nov. 1869
45 Schultz Papers, vol. 16, John Garrioch to Schultz, 12 March 1871
46 Macdonald Papers, vol. 516, Macdonald to McDougall, 8 Dec. 1869; vol. 102, McDougall to Macdonald, 31 Oct. 1869
47 *Globe*, 9 Dec. 1869, 4 Jan. 1870
48 (Montreal 1869)
49 15 April 1870
50 William McDougall, *The Red River Rebellion: Eight Letters to the Hon. Joseph Howe* (Toronto 1870), 44
51 G.F.G. Stanley, *Louis Riel* (Toronto 1963), 56-9, 87-8
52 G.T. Denison, *Reminiscences of the Red River Rebellion of 1869* (Toronto 1873), 'Letter by Charles Mair,' 6
53 D.G. Creighton, *John A. Macdonald: The Old Chieftan* (Toronto 1955), II, 47
54 Macdonald Papers, vol. 516, Macdonald to McDougall, 20 Nov. 1869
55 G.T. Denison, *The Struggle for Imperial Unity* (Toronto 1909), 37-8
56 *Globe*, 7 April 1870
57 Macdonald Papers, vol. 516, Macdonald to McDougall, 8 Dec. 1869
58 *Globe*, 31 Dec. 1869
59 *Debates*, 1st Parliament, 3rd Session, 21 Feb. 1870, pp. 111-16; also, McDougall, *Red River Rebellion*, 5-6
60 W.A. Foster, *Canada First, or, Our New Nationality* (Toronto 1871), 33
61 G.L. Huyshe, *The Red River Expedition* (London 1871), 23
62 Canada, *Sessional Papers*, 1870, no 12, 'Proclamation by J.S. Dennis, December 9, 1869,' 101
63 *Globe*, 7 April 1870
64 Macdonald Papers, vol. 102, McDougall to Macdonald, 31 Oct. 1869
65 Denison, *Struggle for Imperial Unity*, 42; see also Norman Shrive, *Charles Mair: Literary Nationalist* (Toronto 1965), 112-15.
66 *Carleton Place Herald*, 9 Feb. 1870
67 *Ibid.*, speech by McDougall
68 *Debates*, 2 May 1870, p. 1302
69 Huyshe, *Red River Expedition*, 212
70 McDougall, *Red River Rebellion*, 46
71 Stanley, *Birth of Western Canada*, 157
72 *Globe*, 7 April 1870
73 Morton, *Manitoba*, 146-50

238 Notes to pages 99-105

74 Glenbow Institute, Calgary, William Laurie Papers, 'Gleanings from My Memory of Fifty Odd Years Ago' (1924), 11
75 Schultz Papers, vol. 16, Denison to Schultz, 28 Jan. 1871
76 Macdonald Papers, vol. 342, Haliburton to Macdonald, 7 Oct. 1870. See also Haliburton to Macdonald, 6 Oct. 1870, and Haliburton, 'The Queen and a United Empire,' *St. James Magazine and United Empire Review*, Jan. 1874.
77 *Ontario and Manitoba* (Toronto 1872), 14
78 'Current Events,' *Canadian Monthly and National Review*, VI, Sept. 1874, p. 250
79 Morton, *Manitoba*, 159
80 Macdonald Papers, vol. 252, Morris to Macdonald, 1 Oct. 1872
81 *Ibid.*, Morris to Macdonald, 25 Jan. 1873

CHAPTER 5: The geography of empire

1 PAC, Macdonell Papers, vol. 40, undated manuscript on the subject of Confederation
2 *Globe*, Toronto, 27 Dec. 1868; letter from Mair
3 Sproat, *Canada and the Empire* (London 1873), 11
4 'Review of the Times,' *New Dominion Monthly*, Feb. 1874, p. 128
5 White, 'The Immigrant in Canada,' *Canada Monthly and National Review*, II (July 1872), 6
6 Spence, *The Saskatchewan Country* (Montreal 1877), 27
7 Grant, *Ocean to Ocean: Sandford Fleming's Expedition through Canada in 1872* (Toronto 1873), 6
8 Patterson, *Some Plain Statements About Immigration and Its Results* (Ottawa 1872), 1
9 Chester Martin, *'Dominion Lands' Policy* (Toronto 1973), xxi, 15-16
10 PAC, McDougall Papers, vol. 1, Thomas Barrie to Macdonald, 3 Sept. 1869; marginal comment by Macdonald
11 Butler, *The Great Lone Land* (London 1872), app., 381
12 PAC, Edward Watkin Papers, vol. 1, Fleming to Watkin, 30 July 1863
13 W.L. Morton, *Manitoba* (Toronto 1957), 113-14
14 Canada, *Journals of the House of Commons*, 1874, app. 7, 'Second Report of the Select Committee on Immigration and Colonization,' 1
15 Department of Agriculture, *Province of Manitoba: Information for Intending Emigrants* (Ottawa 1873); Spence, *Saskatchewan Country*
16 *Journals of the House of Commons*, 1874, app. 7, 'Report of the Select Committee on Immigration and Colonization,' 1

17 Waddington, *Overland Route through British North America* (London 1868)
18 *Journals of the House of Commons*, 1877, app. 6, 'Report of the Select Committee on Immigration and Colonization,' 92
19 'Rustic Jottings from the Bush,' *New Dominion Monthly*, Sept. 1871, p. 130
20 Watkin Papers, vol. 2, draft of a speech on the Red River rebellion
21 Horetzky, *The North-West of Canada* (Ottawa 1873), 3
22 John Cameron, 'Experiences of the Great North-West,' *Canadian Monthly and National Review*, VIII, (Nov. 1875), 378
23 Gates, *The Dominion of Canada: Its Interests, Prospects and Policy* (Montreal 1872), 7
24 *Province of Manitoba: Information for Intending Emigrants*, 9
25 Spence, *Saskatchewan Country*, 7
26 Acton Burrows, *North-Western Canada: A Practical Guide to the Habitable Regions of Manitoba and the North West Territories* (Winnipeg 1880), 13
27 *Information for Intending Emigrants*, 37
28 Grant, *Ocean to Ocean*, 76, 83
29 Bryce, 'Our New Provinces: Manitoba,' *Canadian Monthly and National Review*, III, (May 1873), 377; Trow, *A Trip to Manitoba* (Quebec 1875), 55; Horetzky, *North-West of Canada*, 10
30 PAC, Grant Papers, vol. 4, J.B. McLaren to Grant, 9 June 1881
31 Mair, 'The New Canada [Part 1],' *Canadian Monthly and National Review*, VIII, (July 1875), 5
32 *Journals of the House of Commons*, 1877, app. 6, 'Report of the Select Committee on Immigration and Colonization,' 96
33 Mair, 'The New Canada [Part 1],' 5. Mair was not unique; see Grant, *Ocean to Ocean*, 112-13.
34 Charles Lindsey, *The Prairies of the United States: Their Advantages and Drawbacks* (Toronto 1860)
35 A.J. Russell, *The Red River Country, Hudson's Bay and the North-West Territories Considered in Relation to Canada* (Ottawa 1869), 31
36 G.V. Le Vaux, 'The Great North West – No. II,' *New Dominion Monthly*, Jan. 1869, p. 343
37 Rupland, *Our Northern Empire* (St Catharines, 1874), 6
38 PAC, George Denison papers, vol. 18, brochure, 'The North West Emigration Aid Society'
39 [David Currie], *The Letters of Rusticus. Investigations in Manitoba and the North-West for the Benefit of Intending Emigrants* (Montreal 1880), 76
40 Grant, *Ocean to Ocean*, 82
41 *A Plea for the Development of Our Resources* (Winnipeg 1873), 4

42 Trow, *Trip to Manitoba*, 74; Burrows, *North-Western Canada*, 16
43 Henry Youle Hind, *Narrative of the Canadian Red River Exploring Expedition of 1857* ... (London 1860), I, 143-4
44 Grant, *Ocean to Ocean*, 195
45 Gates, *Dominion of Canada*, 17
46 *Annual Report of the Department of Agriculture*, 1872, p. 8
47 Department of Agriculture, *Canada: A Handbook of Information for Intending Emigrants* (Ottawa 1877), 51
48 Spence, *Saskatchewan Country*, 16
49 *Journals of the House of Commons*, 1877, app. 6, 'Report of the Select Committee on Immigration and Colonization,' 162
50 Thomas Spence, *Manitoba and the North-West of the Dominion* (Toronto 1871), 24-5
51 James Whitman, 'The Confederation of Canada with Britain in Relation to the Canadian Pacific Railway,' *Rose-Belford's Canadian Monthly and National Review*, II, (March 1879), 324
52 Queen's University Library, Mair Papers, vol. 9, undated manuscript, 'Wheat is Empire'
53 *Annual Report of the North West Mounted Police for the Year 1874*, 41
54 Butler, *Great Lone Land*, 273
55 Dawson, *Report on the Geology and Resources of the Region in the Vicinity of the Forty-Ninth Parallel* (Montreal 1875), 301, 299
56 *Annual Report of the Department of the Interior*, 1877, part III, 3
57 J.S. Dennis, 'A Short History of the Surveys Performed under the Dominion Lands System,' Canada, *Sessional Papers*, 1892, no 13; *Annual Report of the Department of the Interior*, 1877, 'A Map of the North West Territory,' and *ibid.*, 1879
58 'Map of the Country to be Traversed by the Canada Pacific Railway,' 1876; reprinted in Don Thomson, *Men and Meridians* (Ottawa 1967), II, 86
59 Hind, *A Sketch of an Overland Route to British Columbia* (Toronto 1862), vi
60 Horetzky, *North-West of Canada*, 15
61 Mair, 'The New Canada [Part 2],' *Canadian Monthly and National Review*, VIII (Aug. 1875), p. 157
62 Grant, *Ocean to Ocean*, 350. See also G.M. Dawson, *Report on the Geology*, 283-4; Sproat, *Canada and the Empire*, 12-13.
63 Spence, *Saskatchewan Country*, 22
64 Burrows, *North-Western Canada*, 12
65 Department of Agriculture, *Canada: A Handbook of Information*, 47
66 Shantz, *Narrative of a Journey to Manitoba* (Ottawa 1873), 10

241 Notes to pages 117-23

67 PAC, Fleming Papers, vol. 17, Gordon to Fleming, 7 March 1883
68 Trow, *Trip to Manitoba*, 61; Begg, *A Practical Hand-Book and Guide to Manitoba and the North-West* (Toronto 1877), 44
69 Mair, 'The New Canada [Part 1],' 5
70 Carl Berger, 'The True North Strong and Free,' in P. Russell, ed., *Nationalism in Canada* (Toronto 1966), 3-26
71 Haliburton, *The Men of the North and Their Place in History* (Montreal 1869), 16
72 Mair Papers, vol. 1, Denison to Mair, 10 Nov. 1870
73 PAC, Records of the Department of Public Works, series III, vol. 121, 19 Aug. 1871
74 *Ibid.*, 6 March 1872
75 *Journals of the House of Commons*, 1877, app. 6, 'Report of the Select Committee on Immigration and Colonization,' 12
76 Public Archives of Manitoba, James D. Gemmel Papers, Schultz to Garrioch, 12 Jan. 1877
77 *Annual Report of the Department of the Interior*, 1877, p. 4
78 Hind, *Overland Route*, 46
79 E.A. Mitchell, 'Edward Watkin and the Buying-Out of the Hudson's Bay Company,' *Canadian Historical Review*, XXXIV, 3 (Sept. 1953), 219-44
80 Watkin Papers, vol. 2, Hind to Watkin, 24 March 1863
81 Fleming, *Memorial of the People of Red River*, app.; Watkin Papers, vol. 2, S.J. Dawson to Watkin, 21 Aug. 1863
82 Province of Canada, *Journals of the Legislative Assembly*, 1859, app. 36
83 United Kingdom, *The Journals, Detailed Reports and Observations Relative to the Exploration by Captain Palliser*, 1859, 'The General Report,' 6
84 Great Britain, House of Commons, *Report from the Select Committee on the Hudson's Bay Company*, 399, 230
85 Grant, *Ocean to Ocean*, 7-8
86 Fleming Papers, vol. 23, Fleming to W. Howland, Feb. 1864
87 Waddington, *Overland Route through British North America*, 14
88 Spence, *Manitoba*, 9-10
89 PAC, Mary Brown Memoirs, 1
90 Grant Papers, vol. 14, diary entry for 31 July 1872
91 *Annual Report of the Department of Public Works for 1873* (Ottawa 1874), 51. It should be noted that the figures cited exclude troop movements to and from Manitoba over the Dawson route.
92 Canada, *Sessional Papers*, 1875, no 37
93 M. McLeod, *Pacific Railway Canada* (Ottawa 1875), 7

242 Notes to pages 123-32

94 Le Vaux, 'The Great North West,' 226
95 Whitman, 'The Confederation of Canada,' 326
96 Denison Papers, Mair to Denison, 16 March 1876

CHAPTER 6: The character of empire

1 PAC, Grant Papers, vol. 24, Grant, 'Thanksgiving and Retrospect,' 227
2 Grant, *Ocean to Ocean: Sandford Fleming's Expedition through Canada in 1872* (Toronto 1873), 8
3 Thomas Cross, 'Canada and the Empire,' *Rose-Belford's Canadian Monthly*, VII, (Sept. 1881), 302
4 Wilkes, 'Britain's Future Corn Supply,' *ibid.*, V (Aug. 1880), 113-24, 120
5 Grant, *Ocean to Ocean*, 358
6 'Review of the Times,' *New Dominion Monthly*, 1874, p. 252
7 'Fidelis,' 'Dominion Day, 1879,' *Rose-Belford's Canadian Monthly*, III, (July 1879), 8
8 Grant Papers, vol. 3, G. Johnson to Grant, 3 Nov. 1880
9 Alex Rivington, *In the Track of Our Emigrants: The New Dominion as a Home for Englishmen* (London 1872), viii
10 'Fidelis,' 'Dominion Day, 1879,' 8
11 Mair, 'The New Canada [Part 2],' *Canadian Monthly and National Review*, VIII, (Aug. 1875), 160
12 H.N. Smith, *Virgin Land* (New York 1950), 217
13 Wilkes, 'Britain's Future Corn Supply,' 120
14 Grant, *Ocean to Ocean*, 114
15 *Annual Report of the Department of Agriculture*, 1879, 'Reports of the Tenant Farmers' Delegates,' iv
16 Turner, 'The Significance of the Frontier in American History,' *Annual Report of the American Historical Association*, 1893, pp. 199-227, 225, 227
17 William M. Tuttle, Jr, 'Forerunners of Frederick Jackson Turner: Nineteenth Century British Conservatives and the Frontier Thesis,' *Agricultural History*, XLI (July 1967), 219-28
18 Mair, 'The New Canada [Part 2],' 162
19 Davin, *British versus American Civilization* (Toronto 1873), 23-4
20 Mair, 'The New Canada [Part 2],' 162
21 *Globe*, 14 April 1873
22 D.R. Owram, 'White Savagery: Some Canadian Reaction to American Indian Policy,' unpublished MA thesis, Queen's University, 1972
23 Grant, *Ocean to Ocean*, 33

243 Notes to pages 132-40

24 William Clint, *The Aborigines of Canada under the British Crown* (np 1878), 1; see also F.L. Hunt, 'Notes on the Qu'Appelle Treaty,' *Canadian Monthly and National Review*, IX, (March 1876), 178.
25 Grant, *Ocean to Ocean*, 34
26 Clint, *Aborigines of Canada*, 27
27 *Halifax British Colonist*, 9 Aug. 1870
28 Clint, *Aborigines of Canada*, 51 29 *Annual Report of the North West Mounted Police*, 1877, p. 46
30 Burrows, *North-Western Canada* (Winnipeg 1880), 34
31 M. McLeod, *Pacific Railway Canada* (Ottawa 1875), 9
32 'Current Topics and Events,' *Canadian Methodist Magazine*, XIV (Dec. 1881), 564
33 Grant Papers, vol. 4, Mair to Grant, 27 April 1881
34 G.B. Elliott, *Winnipeg as it is in 1874; And as it was in 1860* (Winnipeg 1874), 44-5
35 Grant, 'The North West: Manitoba,' in Grant, ed., *Picturesque Canada* (Toronto 1882), 293
36 *Ibid.*
37 [David Currie], *The Letters of Rusticus. Investigations in Manitoba and the North-West for the Benefit of Intending Emigrants* (Montreal 1880), 80
38 Russell, *The Red River Country, Hudson's Bay and the North-West Territories Considered in Relation to Canada* (Ottawa 1869), 97
39 Burrows, *North-Western Canada*, 7
40 William Brown, 'The Philosophy of Immigration,' *Rose-Belford's Canadian Monthly*, II, (June 1879), 699
41 Grant, *Ocean to Ocean*, 31. See also, on the British farmer, Charles Foy, *Emigration to Canada* (Belfast 1872), 3; Department of Agriculture, *Canada: A Handbook of Information for Intending Emigrants* (Ottawa 1877), 63.
42 *A Plea for the Early Development of Our Resources* (Winnipeg 1873), 5
43 Morris Zaslow, *The Opening of the Canadian North, 1870-1914* (Toronto 1971), 282
44 Cited in Lewis H. Thomas, *The Struggle for Responsible Government in the North-West Territories, 1870-97*, 2nd ed. (Toronto 1978), 110
45 Butler, *The Great Lone Land* (London 1872), app., 382
46 Grant, *Ocean to Ocean*, 201-2
47 PAC, Macdonald Papers, vol. 252, Morris to Macdonald, 16 Jan. 1873
48 Cecil Denny, *The Law Marches West* (Toronto 1939), 1
49 E.D. Clarke, 'In the North West with Sitting Bull,' *Rose-Belford's Canadian Monthly*, IV, (July 1880), 67-8

50 *Ibid.*, 66
51 Ralph Connor, *Corporal Cameron* (1912), 308; cited in Dick Harrison, 'The Mounted Police in Fiction,' Hugh Dempsey, ed., *Men in Scarlet* (Calgary 1974), 163-74, 165
52 *Ibid.*, 166
53 *Annual Report of the Department of the Interior*, 1879, p. x
54 Cross, 'Canada and the Empire,' 301
55 William Leggo, 'Canada and Her Indian Tribes,' *Rose-Belford's Canadian Monthly*, V (Aug. 1880), 147
56 Norman Shrive, *Charles Mair: Literary Nationalist* (Toronto 1965), 177
57 Queen's University Library, Mair Papers, Sproat to Mair, 17 Nov. 1883
58 *Statutes of Canada*, 1873, chap. 35, clause 17
59 Macdonald Papers, vol. 260, Russell to Macdonald, 13 June 1883
60 *Canada: A Handbook of Information*, 17
61 *Annual Report of the Department of Agriculture*, 1879, 'Report of the Tenant Farmer Delegates,' iv
62 Dick Harrison, *Unnamed Country: The Struggle for a Canadian Prairie Fiction* (Edmonton 1977), 59
63 Davin, 'The Future of Canada,' *Rose-Belford's Canadian Monthly*, VI, (May 1881), 491
64 *Canada: A Handbook of Information*, 17
65 'Our Mission Work,' *Canadian Methodist Magazine*, IV (Oct. 1876), 369-70
66 George Grant, 'Churches and Schools in the North-West,' in John Macoun, ed., *Manitoba and the Great North-West* (Guelph 1882), 533
67 W.L. Morton, *One University: A History of the University of Manitoba* (Toronto 1957), 25
68 George Bryce, *Early Reminiscences of Manitoba College* (Winnipeg 1891), 7
69 Presbyterian Church of Canada, *Acts and Proceedings*, 1876, p. 38
70 PAC, Fleming Papers, vol. 18, Grant to Fleming, 23 June 1875
71 Presbyterian Church, *Acts and Proceedings*, 1876, p. 38
72 Morton, *One University*, 19
73 Bryce, *Early Reminiscences*, 2
74 'Current Topics and Events,' *Canadian Methodist Magazine*, XVI (Sept. 1882), 280
75 *Ibid.*, 280
76 Grant, 'Organic Union of the Churches: How Far Should It Go?' *Canadian Methodist Magazine*, XX (Sept. 1884), 244-55, 245
77 S.D. Clark, 'Religious Organization and the Rise of the Canadian Nation,' *Canadian Historical Association Annual Report*, 1944, pp. 86-96

Notes to pages 148-57

78 W.H. Brooks, 'Methodism in the Canadian West in the Nineteenth Century,' unpublished PHD thesis, University of Manitoba, 1972, p. 206
79 Grant, *Ocean to Ocean*, 358

CHAPTER 7: John Macoun's Eden

1 William Brown, 'The Philosophy of Immigration,' *Rose-Belford's Canadian Monthly*, II (June 1879), 700
2 Spence, *The Saskatchewan Country* (Montreal 1877), 7
3 E.C. Hope, 'Weather and Crop History in Western Canada,' *Canadian Society of Technical Agriculture Review*, no 16 (March 1938), 347-58
4 Orders-in-council, 28 Feb. 1874, #173
5 J.S. Dennis, 'A Short History of the Surveys Performed under the Dominion Lands System,' Canada, *Sessional Papers*, 1892, no 13, p. 9
6 Don W. Thomson, *Men and Meridians* (Ottawa 1967), II, 38-41. As one example of the attitudes of this staff, see PAC, 'The Diaries of Otto Klotz,' vol. 1.
7 *Annual Report of the Department of the Interior*, 1879, part II, 'Report of the Surveyor General,' 6
8 *Ibid.*, 1878, part II, 6, 7
9 *Ibid.*, 1879, p. 6
10 Dawson, *Report on the Geology and Resources of the Region in the Vicinity of the Forty-Ninth Parallel* (Montreal 1875), 287-300, 299
11 *Manitoba Free Press*, 21 Nov. 1879
12 *Annual Report of the Department of the Interior*, 1880, part I, 13
13 PAC, Fleming Papers, vol. 33, Macoun to Fleming, 14 Aug. 1880
14 *Annual Report of the Department of the Interior*, 1880, part I, 18
15 Macoun, *The Autobiography of John Macoun* (Ottawa 1922), 11-43
16 Grant, *Ocean to Ocean: Sandford Fleming's Expedition through Canada in 1872* (Toronto 1873), 21-2, 62
17 Macoun, *Autobiography*, 55, 99
18 PAC, Macoun Papers, diary entry, 19 Oct. 1875
19 Macoun, ed., *Manitoba and the Great North-West* (Guelph 1882), 219, 66
20 Macoun Papers, diary entry, 30 Aug. 1875
21 Fleming Papers, vol. 18, Grant to Fleming, undated
22 *Ibid.*, vol. 33, Macoun to Fleming, 20 May 1878
23 Macoun, *Autobiography*, 163
24 *Ibid.*, 182
25 PAC, Macdonald Papers, vol. 260, Russell to Macdonald, 13 April 1883

26 Macoun, *Autobiography*, 132
27 Morris Zaslow, *Reading the Rocks* (Toronto 1975), 131-40
28 Hurlbert, *The Climates, Productions and Resources of Canada* (Montreal 1872), 3, 19, 23
29 *Ibid.*, attached map
30 Hurlbert, *Physical Atlas of the Dominion of Canada* (np 1880), map 3, 'Forest, Prairie and Desert'
31 Hurlbert, *Climate, Productions and Resources*, front cover
32 Department of Agriculture, *Canada: A Handbook of Information for Intending Emigrants* (Ottawa 1877), 17
33 Macdonald Papers, vol. 209, Dennis to Macdonald, 11 March 1880
34 Coffin, *The Winds of the Globe: Or, the Laws of Atmospheric Circulation over the Surface of the Earth* (Washington 1875)
35 Macoun, *Manitoba*, 148; see also Macoun, 'Notes on the Distribution of Northern, Southern and Saline Plants in Canada,' *Proceedings and Transactions of the Royal Society of Canada*, series I, vol. 1 (1882), section IV, 45-7.
36 Macoun, *Manitoba*, 146-7
37 *Ibid.*, 149; see also J.B. Hurlbert, 'Currents of Air and Ocean,' *Proceedings of the American Association for the Advancement of Science*, Aug. 1882, pp. 367-72, for Hurlbert's version of this theory.
38 Macoun, *ibid.*, 148
39 Charles Dana Wilber, *The Great Valleys and Prairies of Nebraska and the Northwest* (Omaha 1881)
40 See, for instance, D. McEachren, *Notes of a Trip to Bow River* (Montreal 1881), 5
41 *Annual Report of the Department of the Interior*, 1880, p. viii
42 Marquis of Lorne, *The Canadian North West* (Ottawa 1882), 13
43 Spence, *The Great North-West Prairie Lands* (Ottawa 1886), 6; Fleming, *England and Canada: A Summer Tour between Old and New Westminster* (London 1884), 213; Grant, 'The C.P.R. by the Kicking Horse Pass and the Selkirks,' *The Week*, I (13 Dec. 1883), 21; Gordon, *Mountain and Prairie* (Montreal 1880), 276
44 Dawson and Alexander Sutherland, *Geography of the British Colonies* (London 1892), 28
45 Macoun, *Autobiography*, 184-5
46 See, on this, F.G. Roe, 'An Unsolved Problem of Canadian History,' *Canadian Historical Association Annual Report*, 1936, 65-77; Pierre Berton, *The Last Spike* (Toronto 1971), 13-18
47 Macdonald Papers, vol. 315, Dewdney to Macdonald, 27 Aug. 1882

247 Notes to pages 162-8

48 John H. Warkentin, 'Western Canada in 1886,' in Michiel Horn and Ronald Sabourin, *Studies in Canadian Social History* (Toronto 1974), 27-63; fig. 1 shows population distribution in 1886.
49 *Annual Report of the Department of the Interior*, 1883, p. xxi
50 *Ibid.*, 1882, p. 40
51 Canadian Pacific Railway, *Manitoba and the Canadian North-West* (np 1883), 25
52 Hind, *A Sketch of an Overland Route to British Columbia* (Toronto 1862), v
53 Macoun, 'Sketch of that Portion of Canada between Lake Superior and the Rocky Mountains, with especial Reference to its Agricultural Possibilities,' in Sandford Fleming, *Report on the Surveys and Preliminary Operation of the Canadian Pacific Railway to January, 1877* (Ottawa 1877), app. x, 313-36; Macoun, *Manitoba*, 199
54 Begg, *Seventeen Years in the Canadian North-West* (London 1884), 16
55 Macoun, *Manitoba*, 119
56 Mair to G.A. Simpson, 10 Dec. 1881; cited in *Annual Report of the Department of the Interior*, 1881, p. 100
57 Laurie, *The Battle River Valley* (Battleford 1883), 8
58 Hind, *Manitoba and the North West Frauds* (Windsor 1883), 13
59 Hind, *The Corruption of the Geological Survey in the North West Territories* (np 1883), Hind to Selwyn, 13 April 1883
60 Hind, *Manitoba*, 4
61 Hind, *Corruption*, Macoun to Selwyn, 13 April 1883
62 Newton H. Chittenden, *Settlers, Miners and Tourists Guide from Ocean by the C.P.R.* (np 1885), 44; Peter Mitchell, *The West and North-West* (Montreal 1880)
63 CPR, *Manitoba and the Canadian North-West*, 17-18
64 W.B. Macdougall, *Guide to Manitoba and the North West* (np 1883), 7
65 J.P. Sheldon, *To Canada and Through it. With the British Association* (Ottawa 1886), 16
66 Macoun, *Manitoba*, 263-4
67 Hind, *Corruption*, Hind to Macdonald, 16 April 1883
68 Hind, *Manitoba*, 36

CHAPTER 8: Disillusionment

1 *Annual Report of the Department of the Interior*, 1887, p. xii
2 A.F.J. Artibise, *Winnipeg: A Social History of Urban Growth, 1874-1914* (Montreal 1975), 130

248 Notes to pages 168-76

3 PAC, Macdonald Papers, vol. 209, Dennis to D.L. Macpherson, 17 Aug. 1881
4 PAC, Grant Papers, vol. 4, McLaren to Grant, 9 June 1881
5 *Grip*, 18 March 1882
6 J.C. McLagan, 'Description and History of Winnipeg,' in John Macoun, ed., *Manitoba and the Great North-West* (Guelph 1882), 492
7 Macdonald Papers, vol. 209, Dennis to Macpherson, 17 Aug. 1881; W.H. Williams, *Manitoba and the North-West: Journal of a Trip from Toronto to the Rocky Mountains* (Toronto 1882), 40
8 PAC, Fleming Papers, vol. 83, 'Journals of Trips,' entries for 2, 4, 8, 16 Feb. 1882
9 Queen's University Library, Mair Papers, McLean to Mair, 3 Feb. 1882
10 Public Archives of Manitoba, James Gemmel Papers, Schultz to Gemmel, 27 Dec. 1884
11 'W.F.C.,' 'Manitoba Farming,' *The Week*, I (6 Dec. 1883), 4
12 *Annual Report of the Department of the Interior*, 1887, p. xii
13 PAC, Denison papers, Mair to Denison, 21 March 1885
14 *Ibid.*, 20 June 1884
15 *The Week*, III, 6 May 1886; letter to the editor from George Patterson
16 *Globe*, Toronto, 5 Sept. 1895; letter from Grant
17 Mair Papers, vol. 7, 'Speech of Mair at Banquet to Lieutenant Governor,' undated
18 Denison Papers, Schultz to Denison, 7 Oct. 1895
19 Charles Tuttle, *Our North Land: Being a Full Account of the Canadian North-West and Hudson's Bay Route* (Toronto 1885), 391
20 PAC, Alexander Mackenzie Papers, Microfilm Reel #M-199, Laird to Mackenzie, 1 July 1879; see also on the extermination of the buffalo, F.G. Roe, *The North American Buffalo* (Toronto 1951), 467-88.
21 G.F.G. Stanley, *The Birth of Western Canada* (Toronto 1960), 266-8
22 *The Week*, II (9 April 1885), 296; letter to the editor from 'C'
23 Cited in *ibid.*, 4 June 1885, p. 426
24 Cited in Charles P. Mulvaney, *The History of the North-West Rebellion of 1885* (Toronto 1885), 88
25 Denison Papers, Mair to Denison, 28 March 1885
26 28 April 1885
27 *Herald*, Halifax, 18 May 1885
28 *Witness*, Montreal, 10 June 1885
29 Grant papers, vol. 6, Gordon to Grant, 1 Feb. 1886
30 John C. Donkin, *Trooper and Redskin in the Far Northwest* (London 1888), 142

Notes to pages 176-85

31 PAC, Church Missionary Society Archives, 2/0, McLean to Fenn, 15 June 1885
32 Stanley, *Birth of Western Canada*, vii
33 Mason Wade, *The French Canadians, 1760-1967* (Toronto 1968), I, 393-446
34 Denison Papers, Mair to Denison, 8 May 1888, 13 Aug. 1889
35 See speech by Grant cited in Halifax *Herald*, 20 May 1885.
36 Although it might be argued that one seemingly meaningful course was to encourage a greater concentration of political power in the local government. It is interesting that concern over the powers of the Northwest Territories government began to develop simultaneously with the growing problems of the region around 1883-84. See Lewis H. Thomas, *The Struggle for Responsible Government in the North-West Territories, 1870-97*, 2nd ed. (Toronto 1978), 117-45.
37 P.H. Atwood, *Jubilee Essays on Imperial Confederation as Affecting Manitoba and the North-West* (Winnipeg 1887), 7
38 Denison Papers, Mair to Denison, 6 Nov. 1888
39 Smith in *The Week*, I (28 Feb. 1884); *Grip*, 8 March 1884
40 *The Week*, II (26 March 1885), 257
41 *Ibid.*, (9 April 1885), 257; 3 and 17 Dec., 1885, 21 Jan. and 25 March 1886
42 PAC, Colonial Office Records, 880: North America, print 113, 'Canada. Rising in the North-West Territory: Correspondence,' #25 Landsdowne to the Earl of Derby, 21 April 1885; enclosure #1
43 Howard A. Fleming, *Canada's Arctic Outlet: A History of the Hudson's Bay Railway* (Los Angeles 1957), 9
44 *Navigation of Hudson's Bay* (Ottawa 1878), Dennis to Macdonald, 11 Nov. 1878, 1-2; 5
45 Fleming, *Canada's Arctic Outlet*, 11-14. For Sutherland's aims, see Sutherland, *The Hudson Bay Railway; an open letter from the President of the Hudson's Bay Railway to members of the Parliament of Canada* (Ottawa 1890).
46 Fleming Papers, vol. 18, Grant to Fleming, 14 Dec. 1880
47 Macdonald Papers, vol. 127, Hurlbert to Macdonald, 17 Dec. 1880
48 Fleming Papers, vol. 18, Grant to Fleming, 21 June 1880
49 Macdonald Papers, vol. 373, Peter Imrie to John Lowe, undated [1880]
50 *Ibid.*, vol. 105, 'Resolution of the North West Council,' 1883
51 Denison Papers, Mair to Denison, 15 Aug. 1891
52 'A Bystander,' *The Week*, I (20 March 1884), 243
53 Murdoch, *Report on the Winnipeg and Hudson's Bay Railway* (Winnipeg 1884), 27-8
54 J.K. Johnson, ed., *The Canadian Directory of Parliament* (Ottawa 1968), 523
55 *Winnipeg Free Press*, 6 March 1971

250 Notes to pages 185-90

56 Nelson, *Proposed Hudson's Bay and Pacific Railway and New Steamship Route* (np 1893)
57 *New Route to the Interior of North America* (Montreal 1881), 13
58 Scoble, 'Our Crop Markets,' *Historical and Scientific Society of Manitoba*, Transaction no 15, 8 Jan. 1885, p. 9
59 Murdoch, *Report on the Winnipeg and Hudson's Bay Railway*, 26
60 Tuttle, *Our North Land*, 17
61 Bell, *Our Northern Waters* (Winnipeg 1884), 5
62 Tuttle, *Our North Land*, 241
63 Leacock, *Hudson's Bay Route* (np 1888), 3-4
64 Robert Bell, 'On the Commercial Importance of Hudson's Bay, with Remarks on Recent Surveys and Investigations,' *Proceedings of the Royal Geographical Society* (London), III, 10 (Oct. 1881), 577-86, 578, 581
56 Province of Manitoba, *Report of the Select Committee of the Legislative Assembly of the Province of Manitoba Appointed to Procure Evidence on the Practicability of a System of Communication with this Province via Hudson's Bay* (Winnipeg 1884), 12
66 Bell, *Our Northern Waters*, 48; Ballantyne, *Hudson's Bay* (Edinburgh 1848), 137
67 Canada, Journals of the House of Commons, 1884, Report of the Select Committee on Hudson's Bay, 5
68 For the official report on the expedition, see Canada, Department of Marine and Fisheries, *Report of the Hudson's Bay Expedition of 1884 under the Command of Lieutenant A.R. Gordon* (Ottawa 1884).
69 Tuttle, *Our North Land*, 103-4; 554-8
70 Bell, *Our Northern Waters*, 28
71 *New Route to the Interior of North America*, 3-4
72 Leacock, *Hudson's Bay Route*, 4; Tuttle to John Norquay, 22 Dec. 1884, cited in Tuttle, *Our North Land*, 464
73 PAM, Schultz Papers, Mair to Schultz, 26 April 1891
74 Denison Papers, Mair to Denison, 6 Nov. 1888
75 Tuttle, *Our North Land*, 396
76 'Garry,' 'The Hudson's Bay Railway,' *The Week*, III (25 Nov. 1886), 831
77 Tuttle, *Our North Land*, 470
78 Mair, 'Open the Bay!' in *Dreamland and Other Poems, Tecumseh: A Drama* (Toronto 1974), 169-70
79 Macdonald Papers, vol. 262, Scarth to Macdonald, 3 Feb. 1884; Stephens to Macdonald, 6 Feb. 1887; Scarth to Macdonald, 18 Feb., 25 June, 13 Sept. 1887; Macdonald to Scarth, 15 Sept. 1887

251 Notes to pages 192-8

CHAPTER 9: The West as past

1 Hargrave, *Red River* (Montreal 1871)
2 'Review of Hargrave's Red River,' *Canadian Monthly and National Review*, I (May 1872), 479. Most other periodicals did not bother to review the work or even to note its publication.
3 Morris, *The Hudson's Bay and Pacific Territories* (Montreal 1859), 7
4 PAC, Macdonald Papers, vol. 252, Morris to Macdonald, 14 July 1869
5 William Henderson, 'Reminiscences of the Early Fur Trade of Montreal,' *New Dominion Monthly*, Oct. 1867, p. 269
6 McLean, *Twenty-Five Years Service in the Hudson's Bay Territory*, (London 1849), 322
7 Denison, *Reminiscences of the Red River Rebellion of 1869* (Toronto 1873), 1-2
8 Macoun, ed., *Manitoba and the Great North-West* (Guelph 1882), 448
9 *Nor'Wester*, 24 Dec. 1862
10 Denison, *Reminiscences of the Red River Rebellion*, 2
11 W.L. Morton, *Manitoba: A History* (Toronto 1957), 53-4
12 Fitzgerald, *An Examination of the Charter and Proceedings of the Hudson's Bay Company* (London 1849), 55
13 McLean, *Twenty-Five Years Service in the Hudson's Bay Territory*, 321
14 Province of Canada, *Sessional Papers*, 1857, no 17
15 Great Britain, House of Commons, *Report from the Select Committee on the Hudson's Bay Company*, app. 8, 394
16 Henderson, 'Reminiscences of the Early Fur Trade,' 272
17 Canada, *Sessional Papers*, 1857, no 17
18 Province of Canada, *Parliamentary Debates on the Subject of the Confederation of the British North American Provinces* (Quebec 1865), 103
19 Charles Mair, 'Insurrection in Red River,' in Denison, *Reminiscences of the Red River Rebellion*, 2
20 Macoun, *Manitoba and the Great North-West*, 448
21 Denison, *Reminiscences of the Red River Rebellion*, 1; see also, Religious Tract Society, *British North America* (London, n.d.), 196
22 Fitzgerald, *Examination of the Charter and Proceedings of the Hudson's Bay Company*, 173
23 Aeneas Macdonnel Dawson, *Our Strength and Their Strength* (Ottawa 1870), 41
24 Withrow, *History of Canada* (Toronto 1886), 528. Andrew Archer, *A History of Canada. For the Use of Schools* (London 1876), uses almost the same words as Withrow in introducing the West, except that he uses the beginning of

expansionism as the starting point. See also, for organization, J.A. Sadlier, *Outlines of Canadian History* (Montreal 1888); Henry H. Miles, *A School History of Canada* (Montreal 1890); J. Frith Jeffers, *History of Canada* (Toronto 1878); Charles Tuttle, *History of the Dominion of Canada* (Montreal 1879), II.

25 Archer, *ibid.*, 413; Jeffers, *ibid.*, 100; Tuttle, *ibid.*, 56
26 Dent, *The Last Forty Years* (Toronto 1881)
27 Bryce, 'A Fragment of Canadian History,' *Canadian Monthly and National Review*, V (April 1874), 273-80, 280
28 Bell, 'Inaugural Address,' *Historical and Scientific Society of Manitoba*, Transaction no 34 (28 Feb. 1889), 1
29 Donald Gunn and Tuttle, *History of Manitoba* (Ottawa 1880)
30 George Bryce, *Manitoba: Its Infancy, Growth and Present Position* (London 1882); Bryce, *The New Canadianism* (Winnipeg 1898). The inside back cover has a partial list of Bryce's publications to that time.
31 Bryce, 'The Five Forts of Winnipeg,' *Proceedings and Transactions of the Royal Society of Canada*, series I, vol. 3 (1885), section II, 145
32 Public Archives of Manitoba, James Garrioch Papers, Schultz to Gemmel, 17 Sept. 1887
33 Bell, 'Inaugural Address,' 1
34 Such works as John McDougall, *In the Days of the Red River Rebellion* (Toronto 1903); John G. Donkin, *Trooper and Redskin in the Far Northwest* (London 1880); Charles P. Dwight, *Life in the North-West Mounted Police and Other Sketches* (Toronto 1892); George Young, *Manitoba Memories* (Toronto 1897), are typical of this genre.
35 John McDougall, *George Millward McDougall* (Toronto 1888), and *Forest, Lake and Prairie* (Toronto 1898); John McLean, *James Evans* (Toronto 1890); Egerton Ryerson Young, *The Apostle of the North: Rev. James Evans* (Toronto 1899)
36 Dennis, 'The Sources of North-Western History,' *Historical and Scientific Society of Manitoba*, Transaction no 6 (26 April 1883), 4
37 Gunn and Tuttle, *History of Manitoba*, 79, 296-7, 310, 328
38 Bryce, *A Short History of the Canadian People* (Toronto 1887), iii-iv, 181-94, 327-45, 438-9
39 Gunn and Tuttle, *History of Manitoba*, xii
40 Public Archives of Manitoba, George Bryce papers, Selkirk to Bryce, 21 Oct., 2 May 1881
41 Bryce, *Manitoba*, 10-11
42 *Canadian Methodist Magazine*, XVI (July 1882), 94
43 Begg, *History of the North-West* (Toronto 1894), I, 162
44 MacBeth, *The Selkirk Settlers in Real Life* (Toronto 1897), 16

253 Notes to pages 205-13

45 Bryce, *Manitoba*, 139
46 *Ibid.*, 23-4, 99, 95
47 *Ibid.*, 299
48 Bryce, 'The Mound Builders,' *Historical and Scientific Society of Manitoba*, Transaction no 18 (28 May 1885), 1
49 Bryce, *Manitoba*, 297-8
50 Edward Ermatinger, *The Hudson's Bay Territories* (Toronto 1858), 26
51 Bryce, 'Brief Outlines of the Most Famous Journeys in and about Rupert's Land,' *Proceedings and Transactions of the Royal Society of Canada*, series I, vol. IV, (1886), section II, 91-104, 93
52 Begg, *History of the North-West*, I, 81
53 Bryce, *Remarkable History of the Hudson's Bay Company* (Toronto 1900), 19
54 Laut, *The Conquest of the Great Northwest* (Toronto 1908), 395-6
55 Bryce, *Remarkable History of the Hudson's Bay Company*, 18
56 Begg, *Seventeen Years in the Canadian North-West* (London 1884), 4
57 John MacBeth, 'The Social Customs and Amusements in the Early Days in the Red River Settlement,' *Historical and Scientific Society of Manitoba*, Transaction no 44 (24 Jan. 1893), 4, 7
58 R.G. MacBeth, 'Farm Life in the Selkirk Society,' *Historical and Scientific Society of Manitoba*, Transaction no 50 (22 April 1897), 4
59 Begg, *History of the North-West*, I, 370
60 Hunt, 'Britain's One Utopia,' *Historical and Scientific Society of Manitoba*, Transaction no 61 (13 Feb. 1902), 3, 2
61 Bryce, 'Early Red River Culture,' *Historical and Scientific Society of Manitoba*, Transaction no 57 (Feb. 1901), 16
62 MacBeth, *The Making of the Canadian West* (Toronto 1905), 14
63 Bryce, 'Early Days in Winnipeg,' *Historical and Scientific Society of Manitoba*, Transaction no 46 (13 Feb. 1894); 'Worthies of Old Red River,' no 48 (11 Feb. 1896); 'Sketch of the Life and Discoveries of Robert Campbell,' no 52 (14 April 1898)
64 Bryce, *The Romantic Settlement of Lord Selkirk's Colonists* (Toronto 1909), 185, 240-55, 276
65 Bryce, 'Old Settlers of Red River,' *Historical and Scientific Society of Manitoba*, Transaction no 19 (16 Nov. 1885), 8
66 Bryce, *Romantic Settlement*, 277
67 Leo Marx, *The Machine in the Garden* (New York 1964)
68 Bryce, *Romantic Settlement*, 79
69 Carl Berger, *The Sense of Power* (Toronto 1970), 78-108
70 'Seven Oaks,' *Historical and Scientific Society of Manitoba*, Transaction no 43 (19 June 1891), 35-6, 30

71 Bryce, *Romantic Settlement*, 105
72 'Seven Oaks,' 36
73 MacBeth, *The Selkirk Settlers in Real Life*, 30
74 Bryce, *Remarkable History of the Hudson's Bay Company*, 425
75 Bryce, *Romantic Settlement*, 314
76 Bryce, 'Early Red River Culture,' 16
77 Bryce, *Early Reminiscences of Manitoba College* (Winnipeg 1891), 3-5
78 Bryce, *Romantic Settlement*, 318-19
79 PAC, George Denison Papers, Mair to Denison, 12 Feb. 1889; enclosure
80 Bryce, *Romantic Settlement*, 317

CONCLUSION

1 Smith, *Canada and the Canadian Question* (1891; Toronto 1971), 152
2 Shortt, 'Some Observations on the Great North-West,' *Queen's Quarterly*, II, (Jan. 1895), 183-7
3 L.G. Thomas, 'Associations and Communications,' *Canadian Historical Association, Historical Papers*, 1973, pp. 1-12, 8
4 'Review of the Times,' *New Dominion Monthly*, Feb. 1874, p. 128
5 *Globe*, Toronto, 11 Nov. 1893
6 *Mail*, Toronto, 4 April 1886
7 P.B. Waite, *Canada, 1874-1896: Arduous Destiny* (Toronto 1971), 214-15; see also, W.L. Morton, 'Manitoba Schools and Canadian Nationality, 1890-1923,' in Craig Brown, ed., *Minorities, Schools, and Politics* (Toronto 1969), 10-18.
8 George Bryce, for all his talk of a new interdenominational spirit in the West, opposed a continuation of the old educational system. See PAC, Wilfrid Laurier Papers, vol. 12, Bryce to Laurier, 27 June 1896.
9 Shortt, 'Some Observations on the Great North-West,' 188
10 *Globe*, 11 Nov. 1893
11 PAC, George Denison Papers, Mair to Denison, 6 Nov. 1888 (emphasis added)
12 Morton, 'The Bias of Prairie Politics,' Donald Swainson, ed., *Historical Essays on the Prairie Provinces* (Toronto 1970), 289-300, 290-1
13 Canada, Department of the Interior, *Canada West. The Last Best West* (Ottawa 1911), 3, 16
14 W.L. Morton, *The Progressive Party in Canada* (Toronto 1950), 3-26; Lewis Aubrey Wood, *A History of Farmers' Movements in Canada* (1924; Toronto 1975), 159-261
15 *Industrial Canada*, March 1910; cited in Robert Craig Brown and Ramsay Cook, *Canada, 1896-1921: A Nation Transformed* (Toronto 1974), 72

A note on sources

The Canadian West was the subject of a great deal of attention in the last half of the nineteenth century and the available materials reflect that fact. Many of the most important sources for this work are given in the notes and to list all of them again here would take up space unnecessarily.

Central to this study were the numerous published works dealing with the North West before 1900. The material varied greatly, from the voluminous works of Henry Youle Hind on the scientific expeditions of 1857-58 to slim pamphlets put out by the Canadian government. All proved useful, however, in understanding the ideas involved in what was very much a public movement. Particular works, however, stand out as classics in the area: George Grant's *Ocean to Ocean* (Toronto 1873), Alexander Morris's *Nova Britannia* (Montreal 1858), John Macoun's *Manitoba and the Great North-West* (Guelph 1882), and George Bryce's, *Manitoba: Its Infancy, Growth and Present Position* (London 1882). Jesse Beaufort Hurlbert's *The Climates, Productions and Resources of Canada* (Montreal 1872) also deserves special mention for its sheer audacity. In the case of published material the researcher interested in the West is fortunate in having available Bruce Peel's *Bibliography of the Prairie Provinces to 1953*, 2nd ed. (Toronto 1973); it provides a massive and easily used listing of books and pamphlets directly related to the West. The sources listed in Peel's work were supplemented by government reports, parliamentary debates, and various works which, though not directly concerned with the West, provided useful insights.

Periodical literature supplemented these printed sources. Various Canadian journals, scientific and popular, contained articles of considerable importance. The West was, seemingly, a highly interesting topic to contemporaries and such periodicals as the *New Dominion Monthly*, *Canadian Monthly and National Review*, *Rose-Belford's Canadian Monthly and National Review*,

256 A note on sources

and *The Week* never seemed to tire of articles on the subject. Only that perennial Canadian obsession with national identity could even compete with the topic, and editors must have been especially pleased when one article dealt with both subjects.

Manuscript collections were also of considerable assistance in understanding the less public concerns of the men involved in expansion. Some collections, such as the George Munro Grant Papers and the Sandford Fleming Papers in the Public Archives of Canada, Ottawa, and the Charles Mair Papers in Queen's University Library, Kingston, provided extremely useful records of the ideas and lives of men directly connected with expansionism. Other collections proved just as useful even though the individual was not an expansionist. The John A. Macdonald Papers (PAC) were important because of the link they provide between expansionist enthusiasm and government policy. The George Taylor Denison Papers (PAC) were valuable because of Denison's close connections with expansionists and especially with Charles Mair. Other collections were much more limited but even here such collections as the John Macoun Diaries (PAC), and the George Bryce Papers and the John Christian Schultz Papers, both in the Public Archives of Manitoba, Winnipeg, provided essential information at particular points.

The secondary literature consulted is far too vast even to begin to list. Numerous books and theses provided background material, filled in details, and provided ideas for research. Thoughtful articles like J.M.S. Careless's 'Frontierism, Metropolitanism, and Canadian History,' *Canadian Historical Review*, XXXV, 1 (March 1954), and W.L. Morton's 'The Bias of Prairie Politics,' in Donald Swainson, ed., *Historical Essays on the Prairie Provinces* (Toronto 1970), presented hypotheses which proved important to the conclusions of this work.

Index

Aborigines Protection Society 51
'Accurate Map of the Territories of the Hudson's Bay Company' 12
Adams, Archibald 112
Agriculture, Department of 112, 129
Anderson, David 14-15, 25, 73
Arrowsmith, Aaron 12
Asia, route to, see North West Passage
Astor, John Jacob 18

Ballantyne, R.M. 17-18, 70, 187
Bannatyne, A.G.B. 106
Battleford 163
Begg, Alexander: and Canadian party 82, 83; on Métis 85; on North West 117, 163; historical views of 204, 208-9
Bell, Charles Napier 47; and Hudson's Bay Railway 184-5, 187, 188; and western history 199, 213
Bell, Robert: and Hudson's Bay Railway 180-1, 186, 187-8
Berkeley, Bishop George 57, 127
Black, Rev. John 23, 145
Blackfoot Indians 13, 17, 105
Blake, Edward 107, 124, 178
Blakiston, Thomas Wright 63
Blodgett, Lorin 65-7, 109, 116, 157

Borgeau, Eugene 63
Bown, J.Y. 90
Bown, W.R. 83
British Empire, see Great Britain
Brown, Alfred 181
Brown, George: early interest in West 29-30, 37, 49; and expansionist movement 40, 45; on North West 59-60, 73, 76, 77; criticism of Hudson's Bay Company 54; and North West Company 53-4; mentioned 82; see also *Globe*, Toronto
Brown, Gordon 40
Bruce, John 80
Bryce, George: background of 145; and Manitoba College 146-7, 215; on soil of North West 108; historical work of 199, 200, 202, 203-4, 205, 207-8, 211; and myth of Selkirk settlers 210, 213, 215
Bryce, Marion 210, 215
Buckingham, William 82, 83
Burrows, Acton 111, 133, 137
Butler, Capt. William 114, 139

Canada, Province of: lack of interest in North West 11-12, 38; mood of in

258 Index

1850s 42-3; economy of in 1850s 43-4; lacks knowledge of West 60-1; claims North West 39, 50
Canadian Pacific Railway 200, 218; route of 114-15, 161-2, 169; importance of 119, 122, 123-4; Ontario concerns over 178-9; criticism of 181-3, 189; *see also* Railways
Canadian party 81-2
Carmichael-Smyth, Robert 31, 32, 34
Cartier, George-Etienne 94
Catlin, George 17
Cauchon, Joseph: on land for settlement 43, 44, 48; and claim to North West 50, 53
Cheadle, Dr William 70, 73
Christie, Alexander 26
Churchill Harbour 185
Coffin, James 159
Colonial Office, *see* Great Britain
Coldwell, William 82, 83, 195
Connor, Ralph 140
Cooper, James Fenimore 16, 17
Cree Indians 13
Crimean War 42
Crown Lands, Department of 41
Cypress Hills 152-3

Davin, Nicholas Flood 131, 144, 175-6
Dawson, Aeneas Macdonell 39
Dawson, George Mercer: assessment of North West 114, 153, 161; and international boundary commission 151-2
Dawson route 118, 119, 122-3; *see also* Lake Superior route; Dawson, Simon J.
Dawson, Simon J. 66, 122; as expansionist 39; on North West 72, 75, 118; on transportation 120-1, 185; on Métis 85; background of 62; *see also* Dawson route
Dawson, William: as expansionist 39; influence of 41, 50; and Lake Superior route 55, 121; on Selkirk 196
Denison, George Taylor: and Red River resistance 93, 99; criticism of Hudson's Bay Company 194; and North West 77, 118; and North West rebellion 175, 177
Dennis, John Stoughton: support for expansionism 41, 119, 158, 159, 181; Surveyor General 150; in Red River 80; and fertile belt 114; and Winnipeg land boom 168, 169
Dennis, William 201
Denny, Sir Cecil 140
Dent, J.C. 198
Deville, Ernest 164
Devine, Thomas 60
Dewdney, Edgar 162, 175
Dickinson, James 72
Disraeli, Benjamin 130
Dobbs, Arthur 11
Dominion Lands Survey: activities of 114, 150, 162; and Palliser's triangle 152
Draper, William 48; and British Select Committee on the Hudson's Bay Company 41, 56, 61; claims North West for Canada 50; on Lake Superior route 121
Drummond, George 181
Dugast, Georges 91

Edmonton 9, 114
Elgin, Lord 29, 30, 36, 38
Ellice, Edward 53, 63
English half-breeds (Red River) 86

Equal Rights Association 221
Ermatinger, Edward 207
Evans, Rev. James 9, 23, 26; histories of 201
Expansionist movement: leadership of 39-41; regional nature of 98, 224; commercial orientation of 48, 50; nationalism of 77, 175-6, 224; sense of mission 50-1, 125-6, 134, 145, 147-8; and social order of North West 135-7, 142-3; utopianism of 166-7; attitude to frontier 138-9, 141-2, 144; view of western history 193-7; and Hudson's Bay Railway 184-5; and Métis 84-7, 196-7; and United States 89, 117-18, 130-3; collapse of 178-9, 219, 220, 224; legacy of 222-3

Farmer's Union of Manitoba 173
Fertile belt: defined 68-9; comments on 109, 114; influence of 113-14, 149; becomes meaningless 162-3; *see also* Hind, Henry Youle
Fitzgerald, James Edward 35, 195
Fleming, Sandford: and expansionist movement 41, 104, 161; and transcontinental railway 114-15, 120; and Winnipeg land boom 170; friendship with George Grant 182; mentioned 83, 117, 153
Fort Pelly 114
Fort Walsh 152
Foster, W.A. 77
Franklin, Sir John 13
French, Col. G.A. 114, 156
French Canada: expansionists on 96, 98, 99-100; and Métis 87; suspicions of expansionism 96, 99-100; and Manitoba schools 221

Frontier thesis: Turner on 129-30; and expansionism 130-1, 138

Gates, H.B. 108
Geological Survey of Canada 45, 62, 164
Gladman, George 61
Globe, Toronto 40, 53, 169; supports expansion 47, 56; on North West 59, 77; and Red River resistance 88-9, 91, 95; and *Nor'Wester* 83; on North West rebellion 175; criticism of Hudson's Bay Company 29, 51; *see also* Brown, George
Gordon, Lieut. Andrew 187
Gordon, Daniel: on climate of North West 117, 161; and Manitoba College 146; and North West rebellion 176
Goulet, Elzéar 99
Grant, Cuthbert 85, 92, 195
Grant, George: and material aspects of North West 103, 110, 111, 129, 222; and expansionist mission 126, 136, 139, 145, 147; and United States 115; and Red River 108; and Manitoba College 146; and pacific railway 121-2, 146; and John Macoun 154, 156, 161; and western discontent 177
Great American Desert: existence of 14, 67-8, 115, 149; implications of 115-16, 158, 159-60
Great Britain: Select Committee on Hudson's Bay Company 41, 50, 52, 56, 60, 61; expansionist criticisms of 55-6; and Isbister petition 30, 36-7, 38; as model and inspiration 125-8, 129, 134, 143; to benefit by North West 31, 32-3, 55-6; North West as heir of 57-8
Grey, Earl 56
Griffiths, Major John 10-11

260 Index

Grip 168-9, 175, 179
Gunn, Donald 199, 201

Haliburton, R.G. 77, 96, 99, 118
Haliburton, T.C. 31
Hargrave, Joseph 192
Hector, James 63
Hill, James 112
Hind, Henry Youle: background of 62; expeditions of 1857-58 65-9; influence of 114, 149; on Indians 71; reaction to wilderness 70-4; and settlement in West 69, 163; on transcontinental railway 115, 119-20; and Hudson's Bay Railway 181; and John Macoun 164-6; mentioned 172, 218
Historical and Scientific Society of Manitoba 199, 200-1
Hodgson, John 12
Horetzky, Charles 109
Howe, Joseph 92, 94
Hudson Bay railway: background of 180-1; as rival to Canadian Pacific 183-4; arguments for 185-7, 189-90
Hudson Bay route 10, 54, 120
Hudson's Bay Company: merger with North West Company 10; and free trade 26; relations with missionaries 25-6; and Vancouver Island 28, 38; criticism of 27-8, 35, 36-7, 50-2, 54-5, 188, 193; conspiracy theories of 35-6, 52, 90; praise for 207-8
Hudson's Bay territories, *see* North West
Hunt, Frank Larned 210-211
Hurlbert, Jesse Beaufort: climatological theories of 157-8; and Canadian Pacific Railway 182
'Huron,' *see* Macdonell, Allan
Huyshe, Capt. G.L. 97

Icelandic settlers 104
Immigration 118-19, 224; promotion of 104-6; desirable settlers 103-4, 128-9, 137; United States attitude to 128
Imrie, Peter 182
Indian population: missionary view of 24-5; and Hudson's Bay Company 27, 29, 30; expansionists on 50-1, 71, 131-2; romantic image of 16-17; and United States 131, 133; Alexander Ross on 18
Information for Intending Emigrants 105
Institute of Rupert's Land 75
Interior, Department of 151-2, 162; criticized by Hind 164
Isbister, Alexander Kennedy: background of 26; petition to Colonial Secretary 27-8; and settlement of North West 30, 34; and Indian population 51, 126; influence of 30

Kane, Paul 15, 17, 86
Keefer, Thomas C. 32, 42, 46
Kennedy, Charley 17-18
Kennedy, Frank 17
Kennedy, Roderick 40, 81
Kennedy, William: criticism of Hudson's Bay Company 30, 37; and expansionist movement 40, 47; and Hudson's Bay Railway 187
Kittson, Norman 26

Laird, David 173
Lake Superior route: and Hudson's Bay Company 10, 54; importance of 120-1; *see also* Dawson route
Laurie, William 163
Laurier, Wilfrid 223
Laut, Agnes C. 208

La Vérendrye 8
Leacock, E.P. 186, 189
Lefroy, J.H. 60, 63, 121
Logan, Sir William 62, 164
Lowe, Robert 130
Luxton, W.F. 174

MacBeth, John 209
MacBeth, Roderick G.: historical writings of 204, 214; and myth of Selkirk settlers 209-10
McCarthy, Dalton 220-1
McDermot, Andrew 26
Macdonald, Sir John A. 104, 123, 157; and expansionist movement 40; attitude towards North West 138; and Red River resistance 90, 92; and Hudson's Bay Railway 92
Macdonell, Allan: and expansionist movement 39, 40, 56, 59; and transcontinental railway 37, 39, 47, 49; criticism of Hudson's Bay Company 51, 52; and myth of North West Company 53; influence of 50
McDougall, George 201
McDougall, William: as expansionist 40; named Lieut.-Gov. of North West 79; and Red River resistance 79-80, 84, 88, 89-90, 94; and French Canada 96; and Roman Catholic church 91, 92; and Manitoba Act 97; mentioned 104
McGee, Thomas D'Arcy 77, 217
Mackenzie, Alexander (fur trader) 7, 11
Mackenzie, Alexander (prime minister) 123, 124, 156
McLaren, J.B. 168
McLean, John (Bishop of Saskatchewan) 170, 176
McLean, John (fur trader): criticism of Hudson's Bay Company 30; and Canadian claim to North West 37, 50; historical views of 194, 195-6
McLeod, Alexander 142
Macleod, Col. J.F. 133
McTavish, William 90
Macoun, John: background of 153-6; explorations in West 152-3, 154, 156; and Palliser's triangle 153, 159, 163, 166; climatological theories of 159-60; influence of 160, 161-2, 165-6; criticism of 156-7, 164-5; on expansionist movement 195; on Métis 197; mentioned 219
Mair, Charles: as expansionist 64, 77; on promise of North West 72, 73, 78, 102, 109, 113, 128, 136, 163; and Red River 74, 84; and Red River resistance 93, 94; and Métis 87; life in West 142; on United States West 115, 117, 131; and western discontent 123, 171, 172-3, 178, 216; criticism of Canadian Pacific 183, 189, 223; and Hudson's Bay Railway 184, 189, 190; and North West rebellion 175, 177; mentioned 47, 170
Malmros, Oscar 89
Manitoba: racial tensions in 98-100; land in 108; disagreement with Dominion government 183
Manitoba Act 97, 221
Manitoba Club 142
Manitoba College 145-6
Manitoba: Its Infancy, Growth and Present Position 199
Manitoba Schools Question 221
Manitoba and South Western Railway 169
Manitoba University 146
Martin, Robert Montgomery 35
Matheson, Canon J.P. 213

Mennonite settlers 104, 117, 119
Methodism: and North West 148
Métis: Alexander Ross on 22: expansionist views of 81, 84-7, 93, 97, 98, 196-7; discontent of 80, 100, 173; sympathy for 174-5; and rights of 221
Milton, Lord 72, 86
Minnesota: compared to Red River 51; expansionism of 89
Missionaries: view of wilderness 23-5; relations with Hudson's Bay Company 25-6; histories of 201
Morgan, H.J. 77
Morris, Alexander: as expansionist 41, 55: and idea of new Britannic Empire 57-8, 126; and Métis 100; optimism of 43, 79; and University of Manitoba 146; criticism of Hudson's Bay Company 193; mentioned 47, 142
Morton, W.L. 223
Mountain, Bishop George J. 24
Murdoch, William 184, 185
Myth of the North 118, 185-6

Nelson, Joseph 185
Nelson Valley Railway and Transportation Company 181
New France 50, 53
North Saskatchewan Valley 114, 163
North West: negative image of 8, 11, 12-15, 29, 30, 34, 60-1; Canadian claim to 37, 50; positive assessment of 69, 74, 107-8; changing image of 64-5; climate of 109, 115-16, 149-50, 158, 160-1, 166; and agriculture 59, 65-6, 76-7, 107, 111-12, 151-2, 163; importance of 57-8, 76-7, 101-2; social order of 135-6, 139-42, 145-6; and Great Britain 32-3, 55, 56, 103-4, 125-6, 144; compared to United States West 116-18, 126, 128-9, 130-4, 141; settlement patterns in 113-14, 119, 161-2; promotion of 104-6, 165-6; prosperity of 168-9, 223-4; economic depression in 170-1; disillusionment 174-7, 179-80, 217-19; utopian image of 165-6, 218
North West Company: and Hudson's Bay Company 8, 10; myth of 53-5, 120-1, 194, 196; criticism of 205
North West Mounted Police 139-41, 143
North West Passage 13, 31-3, 46
North West rebellion 174-7, 179
Northern Railway 45
North-West Transportation and Navigation Company 39, 40, 48
Norway House 12
Nor'Wester: establishment of 82; and expansionism 79, 82-3; and Red River resistance 80; and importance of North West 102; praise of 202

Oliver, Frank 174, 184
One Big Union 224
Oregon boundary dispute 28
Ottawa Valley: as centre of expansionism 45-6

Palliser, Capt. John: background of 62-3; western expedition 64-8; influence of 86; on Métis 86; on Lake Superior route 121; *see also* Palliser's triangle
Palliser's triangle: definition of 67-8; influence of 109, 115, 149; dismissal of 152, 153, 159-62
Patterson, William J. 103
Peel, Robert 130
Perth, Canada West 46-7
Pitblado, Charles 146, 176

Polk, James 28
Portage la Prairie 97
Prairie: negative reaction to 13-14, 68; positive image of 110-11
Prince Albert 114
Progressive party 224

Railways: faith in 31-2, 34; growth of in Canada 42; idea of a Pacific railway 33-4, 48, 49, 120; necessity for Pacific railway 121-3, 124; *see also* Canadian Pacific Railway, Hudson's Bay Railway
Red River resistance: beginning of 79-80; expansionist reaction to 88-92, 95-8; and military expedition 93; and Canadian government 80, 92; legacy of 98-100
Red River settlement: establishment of 7-8; assessment of 8-9, 15-16, 74-6, 108; Alexander Ross on 20-3; and expansionists 51, 84; myth of Selkirk settlement 208-11
Reform party 40
Regina 162
Richards, A.B. 31, 33-4
Richardson, Sir John 13, 60
Riel, Louis: and Red River resistance 80, 88; and amnesty question 99-100; John A. Macdonald on 92; and North West rebellion 174, 177
Ritchot, Father J.N. 91
Roche, Alfred 41, 54, 58
Ross, Alexander: career of 18, 20; on Red River 20-3, 76; on the wilderness 18-20, 25, 144, 212; and English half-breeds 86; and Indian population 15, 18; mentioned 72
Ross, Donald 38
Ross, James 23, 83

Ross, John 49
Royal, Joseph 185
Royal Geographical Society 62
Russell, Alexander J. 41, 137, 151
Russell, Alexander L. 151
Russell, Lindsey 143, 151, 157, 164
Ryan, Thomas 181

St Lawrence empire 12
Sault Ste Marie 12
Saskatchewan Club 142
Saskatchewan River, *see* North Saskatchewan Valley
Schultz, John Christian: moves to Red River 64; and *Nor'Wester* 81, 82; and Red River resistance 93, 94, 95, 98; appointed to North West Council 100; on Hudson's Bay Company 90; on North West 119, 170, 173, 200; and Hudson's Bay Railway 181
Shanly, Walter 46
Shantz, J.Y. 117
Shortt, Adam 218, 222
Sifton, Clifford 224
Simpson, Sir George 15, 20, 38; views of North West 15, 16, 60; on Lake Superior route 121; criticism of 52; praise of 211
Simpson, Thomas 16, 35, 86
Sinclair, James 26
Sitting Bull 140
Smith, Goldwin 179, 183, 217
Smithurst, Rev. John 23
Snow, John 80
Southesk, Earl of 70
Spence, Thomas: career of 104-5; on North West 103, 106, 112; on Palliser's triangle 150, 161; on the United States 116, 122
Sproat, Gilbert 102

Strachan, John 7-8, 11, 37
Strange, T.B. 143
Stutsman, Enos 89
Sutherland, Hugh 181, 185
Synge, Henry Millington 31, 33

Taché, Bishop Alexandre 91, 96
Taylor, James Wickes 89
Thompson, David 11, 12
Toronto: and expansionist movement 44-5, 46, 47, 48
Toronto Board of Trade 50
Trow, James: and Committee on Immigration 106; on North West 108, 111, 117
Tucker, Sarah 16, 24
Turner, Frederick Jackson 129-30
Tuttle, Charles: and Hudson's Bay Railway 184, 186, 188, 189; historical writings of 199, 202-3
Tytler, P.F. 15

Umfreville, Edward 11
United Empire Loyalists 213-14
United States of America: rivalry with 48, 57, 102-3, 107, 115-16, 219-20; criticism of US West 115-16, 117, 130-3, 141, 157-8; as hinterland for Canada 12; reciprocity treaty with 42; and Red River resistance 89; attitude to frontier 128; *see also* Great American Desert

Vancouver Island 28, 36, 38
Vankoughnet, Philip M. 40, 46

Waddington, Alfred 105, 122
Walsh, Major James 175
Warre, Henry 14
Watkin, Edward 107, 120
West, Rev. John 23, 25
Wheat: as main crop of North West 111-13; Hurlbert on 158
White, Thomas 103, 185
Whitney, Asa 32
Wilderness: negative reaction to 23-6; romantic view of 16-17, 63, 70; and morality 18-20; expansionist attitude towards 70-3
Wilson, Daniel 70, 75, 87, 100
Wilson, F.A. 31, 33-4
Winnipeg: land boom in 168-70; attitudes towards 136-7
Withrow, W.H. 198
Wolseley, Col. G.J. 97

York Factory 12
The Young Fur Trader 17-18
Young Men's Literary and Athletic Club (Prince Albert) 142